Organizational Learning and the Learning Organization

Developments in Theory and Practice

Edited by
MARK EASTERBY-SMITH, LUIS ARAUJO
and JOHN BURGOYNE

SAGE Publications
London • Thousand Oaks • New Delhi

First published 1999

SAGE Publications Ltd
6 Bonhill Street
London EC2A 4PU

SAGE Publications Inc.
2455 Teller Road
Thousand Oaks, California 91320

SAGE Publications India Pvt Ltd
32 M-Block Market
Greater Kailash – I
New Delhi 110 048

British Library Cataloguing in Publication data

A catalogue record for this book is available from the British Library

ISBN 0 7619 5915 7
ISBN 0 7619 5916 5 (pbk)

Library of Congress catalog record available

Typeset by Mayhew Typesetting, Rhayader, Powys
Printed in Great Britain by Athenaeum Press, Gateshead

Contents

Contributors

Elena Antonacopoulou has recently moved to Manchester Business School at the University of Manchester. Previously she was a Lecturer at Warwick Business School, and Subject Leader on Managing Organizational and Individual Change and Critical Thinking of the School's MBA programmes. She is active in a number of international activities and currently serves on the Executive Board of the Management Education and Development Division of the American Academy of Management. She is currently the Book Reviews Editor of *Management Learning*. The main thrust of her research to date has been concerned with understanding the interaction between the individual and the organization, and the resulting association between change, learning, training and development processes. In the field of individual and organizational learning she is known for advancing new concepts in relation to attitudes towards learning.

Luis Araujo is a Senior Lecturer in Marketing at Lancaster University. He has worked on the topic of interorganizational relationships for more than a decade and published a number of papers and book chapters on the subject. His interest in the topic of organizational learning is relatively recent and very strongly tied to his research on interorganizational relationships in industrial markets.

Karen Ayas is a professor at Erasmus University Rotterdam in the Netherlands. Since 1992 she has been consulting, teaching and conducting research in the field of organizational learning, specifically its application in managing technological innovation projects and large-scale organizational change. She has a number of articles in scholarly journals, and her dissertation is published as a book entitled *Design for Learning for Innovation*. A world wanderer, formerly an engineer and human resource director now in the organizational behaviour field, her interests lie in merging cultures, and her efforts are directed towards bridging technology and people through learning.

Frank Blackler is Professor of Organizational Behaviour at Lancaster University Management School. His research has included studies of job design, organizational change and the introduction of new technologies. In recent years he has taken a particular interest in knowledge and organizations and in the management of organizations that depend upon esoteric experts. Most recently, with Norman Crump and Seonaidh McDonald, he has undertaken a major study of innovation in high technology organizations funded by the ESRC under their 'Innovation Programme'.

Silvia Bürgin Brand is in charge of organizational learning at the Swiss Post. She has been involved since the beginning in the efforts of the Swiss Post to become a learning organization and is currently managing a large organizational development programme. Previously, she was a scientific collaborator at the Graduate Institute of Public Administration in Lausanne. In her publications, she analyses the transformation of organizations in terms of organizational learning processes in two settings: the reform of the public sector and the greening of industry. Silvia holds an MA in Public Administration from the University of Lausanne, Switzerland.

John Burgoyne is Professor of Management Learning at Lancaster University, Adjunct Professor, University of Calgary, Canada, and recently Visiting Professor of Organization Behaviour at London Business School. He is a member of the Learning Company Project with Mike Pedler and Tom Boydell, and a Fellow of the British Academy of Management. He is concerned with applying the latest ideas from research in management and behavioural studies to the practical development of organizations, and is currently working with companies such as Volvo AB, Hewlett-Packard and the BBC. He has written, co-authored and edited a number of books including: *The Learning Company* (2nd edn, 1996, McGraw-Hill) and *A Manager's Guide to Self-Development* (3rd edn, 1994, McGraw-Hill).

Norman Crump is a lecturer in the department of Behaviour and Organizations at Lancaster University Management School. He has a degree in Organization Studies from Lancaster University, following a former career in the public sector. More recently he was involved in a major research project looking at the innovative management of innovation in high technology industries. His research interests include knowledge work, knowledge management and organizational learning.

Nancy Dixon is Associate Professor of Administrative Sciences at The George Washington University, Washington, DC. Her research interests centre around how organizations use learning to change and develop, both at the individual level and at the whole system level. Her writing reflects that perspective in *The Organizational Learning Cycle: How We Can Learn Collectively* (McGraw-Hill, 1994), which deals with learning at the system level. *Perspectives on Dialogue: Making Talk Developmental for Individuals and Organizations*, published by the Center for Creative Leadership (1996) continues that focus. Dr Dixon is currently working on a book with The Harvard Business School Press about how knowledge gained from experience is collected, shared and implemented within an organizational setting. She serves as an Editorial Reviewer for the *Human Resource Development Quarterly* and as a Member of the Editorial Board for *Management Learning*.

Mark Easterby-Smith is Professor of Management Learning at Lancaster University, and is currently Director of the School's PhD in Management. He is well known for his work on management research methodology where he is lead author of *Management Research: an Introduction* (Sage, 1991). He has been teaching about organizational learning on postgraduate courses since the mid-1980s, and has published a number of papers on this topic, including the recent 'Disciplines of organizational learning: contributions and critiques' in *Human Relations*.

Amy Edmondson is an Assistant Professor at Harvard Business School. Her research focuses on organizational and team learning in a variety of industries. Recent empirical research has investigated effects of teamwork on rates of medication errors in hospitals and supported a theoretical model of team learning behaviour in a manufacturing organization. She has published several journal articles on organizational and team learning and, with Bertrand Moingeon, she is co-editor of *Organizational Learning and Competitive Advantage* (Sage, 1996). Previously, Amy has worked as Director of Research for Pecos River Learning Centers, Inc., in the USA, where she developed organizational change programmes in Fortune 100 companies and as Chief Engineer for Buckminster Fuller. She is also the author of a book about the late architect/inventor's mathematical work, *A Fuller Explanation: the Synergetic Geometry of R. Buckminster Fuller* (Birkhauser, 1987).

Bente Elkjaer is an Associate Professor in the Department of Informatics at the Copenhagen Business School. She has been doing theoretical as well as empirical research on organizational learning for a number of years. Her special interest within this area is to contribute to an understanding of the organizational learning processes as situated in social practice. To do so she has been studying the works of American Pragmatism, especially the works of John Dewey. She has just finished a book (in Danish) called *Through the Eyes of the Learning Process: a Study of Consulting Projects in Small Firms.*

Matthias Finger holds PhDs in both Political Science and in Adult Education. He is currently professor and director of the 'Management of Public Enterprises' unit at the Graduate Institute of Public Administration in Lausanne Switzerland. Previously he taught at Teachers College, Columbia University, and at the Maxwell School of Citizenship and Public Affairs, Syracuse University. He is well known for his work in the area of social and organizational change. More precisely, his research interest pertains to the linkage between individual and structural transformations and learning, mainly within a public context.

Marleen Huysman studied Sociology at the Erasmus Universiteit, Rotterdam and received her PhD in Economics at the Vrije Universiteit, Amsterdam. She is currently senior researcher and lecturer in Organizational Behaviour at the University of Delft. She has been teaching about information systems and organizational learning and has published articles on this topic. Her research interests include theoretical aspects of organizational learning and processes of organizational learning in practice. She is currently researching on combinations between learning and information/communication technologies (ICT) such as learning with the use of ICT applications.

Seonaidh McDonald is a Lecturer at Sheffield University Management School. As an undergraduate she studied Management Science at Stirling University, where she later undertook a PhD in the waste management field. Following a period at the Department of Management Science at the University of Strathclyde, evaluating Group Decision Support methods with Professor Colin Eden, she joined a multidisciplinary research team at Lancaster looking at the management of innovation. Seonaidh is interested in how boundaries between different specialists and interest groups can be successfully managed, and in teaching the realities of research.

Bertrand Moingeon is Associate Professor of Strategic Management and Associate Dean for Executive Education at HEC-Paris. His work has been primarily in the area of socioeconomics, strategic management and organizational learning. In 1994, he was a Visiting Research Scholar at the Harvard Business School. He has published articles in international journals such as the *European Journal of Marketing*, *European Management Journal and Management Learning*. He is the co-author of a book on strategic management entitled *Stratégie, structure, décision, identité: Politique générale d'entreprise* (Masson, 1997) and, with Amy Edmondson, the co-editor of *Organizational Learning and Competitive Advantage* (Sage, 1996).

Hallie Preskill is Associate Professor and Program Coordinator of the Organizational Learning and Instructional Technologies graduate programme at the University of New Mexico, USA. She primarily teaches courses in Programme Evaluation, Organizational Learning and Instructional Design. Her research interests focus on programme evaluation theory and methods, evaluation use, organizational learning and the transfer of learning. She is co-author of the book *Evaluation Strategies for Communication and Reporting: Enhancing Learning in Organizations* (Sage, 1996) and is co-author of the book *Evaluative Enquiry for Learning in Organizations* (Sage, 1999). She has provided evaluation consulting services to business, education, non-profit and human services organizations for the past 18 years.

Christiane Prange is a former Research Assistant at HEC-Geneva University of Switzerland, where she obtained her PhD. Currently she consults companies on interorganizational cooperation and learning. Her particular interest is the telecommunications and multimedia industry where she has also conducted empirical research. She has published several articles on interorganizational learning, joint venture management and multimedia alliances.

David Sims is Professor of Management Studies at Brunel University, and Head of the School of Business and Management and of the Graduate Business School. David has an academic background in operational research and organizational behaviour, and has been a consultant to organizations in the oil, power, computer, publishing, airline, hotel and engineering industries, as well as in the public sector. His research interests are in management thinking and learning, particularly in agenda shaping, problem construction and managerial story telling. He is editor of the journal *Management Learning*, and is author or co-author of some 60 books and articles (including the textbook *Organizing and Organizations*) as well as being a regular contributor to international conferences.

Rosalie Torres is Director of Research at Developmental Studies Center (DSC) in Oakland, California where she implements a participatory, organizational learning approach to the evaluation of DSC's programs. Over the past 20 years she has conducted more than 30 evaluations in education, business, health care and non-profit organizations. She has worked as an internal evaluator for the Dallas Independent School District, the Chicago Public Schools and the Colorado Springs School District. Dr Torres is a co-author of *Evaluation Strategies for Communicating and Reporting: Enhancing Learning in Organizations* (Sage, 1996), and is co-author of a second Sage book, *Evaluative Enquiry for Learning in Organizations*.

1 Organizational Learning: Current Debates and Opportunities

Mark Easterby-Smith and Luis Araujo

The idea of organizational learning has been present in the management studies literature for decades, but it has only become widely recognized in the past ten years. For example, Crossan and Guatto's (1996) survey of the literature shows that as many academic contributions in this area were published in 1993 than in the whole of the 1980s. Landmark publications such as the special issue of *Organization Science* (Vol. 2, No. 1, 1991) and its updated version published in Cohen and Sproull (1996) have significantly contributed to raising the profile and generating interest in the topic of organizational learning.

Two developments have been highly significant in the growth of the field. First it has attracted the attention of scholars from disparate disciplines who had hitherto shown little interest in learning processes. For example, business strategists have realized that the ability of one organization to learn faster, or 'better', than its competitors may indeed be the key to long-term business success (Collis, 1994; Grant, 1996). Some economists have taken a similar path, arguing that firms learn by doing, as well as through formal learning processes. Thus Stiglitz (1987: 130) comments that: 'Just as experience in production increases one's productivity in producing, so experience in learning may increase one's productivity in learning. One learns to learn at least partly, in the process of learning itself.' Sociologists, too, have become aware of the central role that learning and organizational knowledge can play in the internal dynamics and politics of organizational life (Coopey, 1995). A consequence of this is that the field has become conceptually fragmented, and representatives of different disciplines now vie over who has the correct model of organizational learning. One debate which has therefore featured in the literature is around whether theorists should try to move toward a single integrated framework, or whether they should simply recognize that each discipline operates from distinct views of reality, and hence that a plurality of perspectives should be seen as a strength (Easterby-Smith, 1997).

The second development is that many consultants and companies have caught onto the commercial significance of organizational learning. Their work has been generally underpinned by a number of theorists such as Senge (1990) in the USA, Pedler et al. (1989) in the UK, and Field and Ford

(1995) in Australia who have focused on making practical interventions in organizations in order to help them become 'learning organizations'. Much of the effort of these theorists has been devoted to identifying templates, or ideal forms, which real organizations could attempt to emulate. Some models of the learning organization have been based on observations of organizations that appear to be good at learning, from which elements of good practice have been extracted and synthesized. Others have relied more on theoretical principles, such as systems dynamics or psychological learning theory, from which implications for design and implementation have been derived.

Consultants and practising managers have added to the theoretical literature on the learning organization with accounts of how their own interventions have worked out in practice. Although these accounts are often very insightful (see for example Ciborra et al., 1995), some may lack the critical objectivity of traditional academic work. Authors of this ilk usually have an eye to the further consultancy opportunities that will flow from a public demonstration of their successes, and hence they tend to be economical in their discussion of unsolved problems. This 'positive spin' is a feature of some of the most influential accounts of learning organizations and it also points to one of the limitations in the state of knowledge about organizational learning.

Although theorists of learning organizations have often drawn on ideas from organizational learning, there has been little traffic in the reverse direction. Moreover, since the central concerns have been somewhat different, the two literatures have developed along divergent tracks. The literature on *organizational learning* has concentrated on the detached observation and analysis of the processes involved in individual and collective learning inside organizations; whereas the *learning organization* literature has an action orientation, and is geared toward using specific diagnostic and evaluative methodological tools which can help to identify, promote and evaluate the quality of learning processes inside organizations (Tsang, 1997).

This divergence of interest was apparent in the papers presented at a Symposium on Organizational Learning held at Lancaster University in September 1996. The chapters of this book are based substantively on papers presented at the Symposium and inevitably follow the same divide: thus the two main parts of the book examine respectively *organizational learning* and *the learning organization*. Inevitably the distinction is not as clear-cut as might appear at first sight. Thus, some of the chapters in the second part consider the implementation of theoretical perspectives within organizational settings, and hence provide an opportunity in some cases to add to, or challenge, the precepts of the theories adopted. Indeed, since there is a major shortage of empirical (and potentially critical) research into the learning organization, the chapters in Part Two constitute one of the main contributions of this book. And we also hope that the juxtaposition of the two foci in the same book will enable some of the insights from the empirical studies in Part Two to throw light on the more abstract debates in Part One.

In this initial chapter we provide a general background for the chapters which follow. This is done first through providing an overview of the main debates and trends in the two fields of organizational learning and the learning organization. Second, we consider the main problems and opportunities for research and understanding in the field as a whole. Finally, we review the contributory chapters in the rest of the book according to how they illustrate or develop each of the debates and trends.

Debates and trends

We will start this section by looking at the current state of literature on organizational learning, before turning to the learning organization.

Organizational learning

The most significant distinction between authors who write about organizational learning can be summarized according to whether they emphasize it as a technical or a social process. The *technical* view assumes that organizational learning is about the effective processing, interpretation of, and response to, information both inside and outside the organization. This information may be quantitative or qualitative, but is generally explicit and in the public domain. One of the most elegant expositions of this view comes from Huber (1991: 89), who states that: 'An entity learns if, through its processing of information, the range of its potential behaviours is changed . . . an organization learns if any of its units acquires knowledge that it recognizes as potentially useful to the organization.'

Two of the major contributors to this school of thought are Argyris and Schön (1978), who have developed a number of important concepts including the distinction between single- and double-loop learning.[1] The former of these involves the detection and correction of error within a given set of governing variables; the latter involves changing the governing variables themselves. This distinction has become popular with managers and theorists alike, largely because it maps easily onto modes of organizational change (Argyris, 1996). Thus single-loop learning is linked to incremental change, where an organization tries out new methods and tactics and attempts to get rapid feedback on their consequences in order to be able to make continuous adjustments and adaptations. Double-loop learning is associated with radical changes, which might involve a major change in strategic direction, possibly linked to replacement of senior personnel, and wholesale revision of systems.

In managerial discourse, double-loop learning is often portrayed as superior to single-loop learning, particularly by proponents of radical change (Argyris, 1996; Miner and Mezias, 1996). What is often lost in such discourse is exactly what forms of change are associated with learning; and there is also the criterion problem of being able to determine when single- or double-loop learning is appropriate. For example, DiBella et al. (1996) point out that the Chernobyl disaster was caused by engineers experimenting with a new form of on-line refuelling which involved them departing radically from existing operational parameters. If they had been successful their work might have been hailed as a major scientific breakthrough carried out by people with the courage to engage in double-loop learning. But they were not successful, and we all know the rest of the story.

There are a number of dilemmas and problems identified by authors of this persuasion. For example, Levinthal and March (1993) examine the dilemma between *exploration* and *exploitation* in the use of technology. The former may lead to the development of new strategies and knowledge in the long term; the latter may lead to high profitability in the short term, but will not lay down the foundation for long-term prosperity. Organizations have to find the appropriate balance between these two, and there are no obvious criteria against which to choose. The main problems from this perspective emerge when people and organizations do not behave according to rational calculation and where political agendas take precedence. Managers do not necessarily follow the logical consequences of the information before them: they may distort and suppress information in order to support their preferred agendas; and they may use information selectively in order to 'validate' decisions taken on other grounds. These political processes may affect both access to, and ownership of, information as well as the process of establishing meaning to data and information (Coopey, 1995).

The emphasis on learning through the processing of information is also linked to the work of Zuboff (1988) on 'informating'. This is the idea that information technology can be put to different purposes: it can be used either to liberate all employees by making more information available to all (informating), or it can be used and accessed selectively in order to monitor and control the behaviour of individuals. While Zuboff argues strongly for the superiority of the former, it is evident that the latter is being used increasingly as a form of surveillance in standardized technological environments such as call centres or customer service departments (Orlikowski, 1996; Pentland, 1992). This distinction provides a neat bridge to the alternative perspective on organizational learning, as a social process.

The *social perspective* on organizational learning focuses on the way people make sense of their experiences at work. These experiences may derive from explicit sources such as financial information, or they may be derived from tacit sources, such as the 'feel' that a skilled craftsperson has, or the intuition possessed by a skilled strategist. From this view, learning is something that emerges from social interactions, normally in the natural work setting. In the case of explicit information it involves a joint process of making sense of data; for example, when looking at financial data there are always debates about whether figures are good or bad, and what kind of action is required. The more tacit and 'embodied' forms of learning involve situated practices, observation and emulation of skilled practitioners and socialization into a community of practice (Blackler, 1993; Lave, 1993).

Three of the key contributions of this school of thought are to see organizational learning as socially constructed, as a political process and as implicated in the culture of an organization. The idea of learning as *social construction* can be seen as remedying directly some of the limitations of the technical perspective, by recognizing that data have no significance in their own right until people determine what they mean. Brown and Duguid (1991) are strong proponents of the constructionist view. They believe that formal instructions about how to do jobs are always inadequate, and therefore look at the way new entrants into organizations learn the unwritten information about how to perform effectively. This is achieved through informal exchanges between experienced and less experienced people, and through the use of anecdotes and war stories (Orr, 1990). A central idea from this perspective is that much crucial organizational knowledge exists not on paper, nor in the heads of individuals, but within the 'community' as a whole. And hence learning takes place either through expansion of the community to incorporate new individuals, or through the adoption of new forms of behaviour and 'non-canonical' practices.

Nicolini and Meznar describe at a broader organizational level how knowledge gets reconstructed following perceived discontinuities in organizational functioning.

> Organizations, through the actions of those in charge, construe their identity by transforming change, past choices, past experiments, inventions and so on, into rational accounts of knowledge. In such a way, they symbolically shape the organization, transforming knowledge into the web of experiential constraints that members perceive as the objective aspect of the organization (that is, the constitutive order which transcends the individual power to act). (1995: 740–1)

The idea of organizational learning as a *political process* is touched upon by many of the authors of the 'technical' school, but from the perspective that this is a persistent problem which needs to be overcome and nullified if learning is to take place. Thus Argyris (1986) demonstrates how organizational defensive routines that reduce learning capacity arise because people need to protect themselves from political threat. Similarly, Senge (1990) sees political activity as a major constraint on the establishment of learning organizations and other authors prefer to focus on the need for dialogue amongst different occupational cultures rather than to acknowledge the political nature of organizational life (Schein, 1996).

From the social perspective, however, the goal of eliminating organizational politics is seen as naive and idealistic – because politics are a natural feature of any social process (Coopey, 1994, 1995). If knowledge is socially constructed by individuals and groups, it is inevitable that particular interpretations will suit the interests of some and harm the interests of others. In many cases the 'spin' given to the interpretation of information will be unconsciously produced according to the experiences and settings of individuals who wish to show themselves in a positive light to others. But increasingly within organizations the interpretive process is directly mediated by power relations. Departments, functional groups and project teams will organize consciously to present information internally and externally in a way that suits their purposes. One can argue that it is a *necessary* responsibility of unit managers to ensure that their groups are presented positively to external stakeholders – whether these are senior managers, shareholders, the media, or public auditors. It is unrealistic to hope that politics will somehow go away, when it is an integral part of organizational transactions and a direct consequence of interests that are differentiated both vertically and horizontally. What is needed, therefore, are conceptions of organizational learning which embrace political processes within them.

The third significant contribution from the social perspective is the notion of learning as a *cultural artifact*. Most normally, it is seen as part of an organizational culture, and most significantly 'learning' is something that takes place not within the heads of individuals, but in the interaction between people. It is manifest in the ways that people behave when working with others, and these patterns of behaviour are normally learnt by newcomers to the community through a process of socialization (Lave and Wenger, 1991). In most cases, the application of this principle is demonstrated by the evolution of tacit skills embodied in craftwork. For example, Orr (1990) looks at photocopy repair technicians, Cook and Yanow (1993) examine the learning process involved in producing flutes within craftshops, and Suchman and Trigg (1993) examine artificial intelligence as craftwork.

But a similar logic can also apply to managerial and professional domains. Diane Vaughan (1996), in her major documentary analysis of the Challenger space shuttle disaster, identifies the way a particular culture evolved within NASA and its suppliers which enabled potential technical problems to be interpreted as if they were not problems. This process, which she labels the 'normalization of deviance', involves regular formal redefinitions of acceptable and unacceptable risks in which all members of the engineering community participate. Thus the crucial decision to launch on the night of 28 January 1986 was fully within the technical guidelines laid down by NASA. The problem was that new circumstances had arisen which were not fully covered by the regulations and also that some of the engineers still had a feeling that the redefined operating criteria were too risky. The interest in high technology is continued in two chapters of the present book, where the examples studied will hopefully lead to more positive outcomes. Thus Ayas considers structural arrangements that can aid the transfer of ideas between and within groups of engineers engaged in aircraft design, and Blackler et al. consider the social process of learning among groups of scientists working in the defence industry.

The majority of studies adopting this perspective has tended to focus on culture as an attribute of organizations, or of groups within them. Some authors have described studies carried out across several different countries (Adler and Cole, 1993; Nevis et al., 1995), but which make virtually no reference to the possibility that cultural differences between countries may also have an impact on learning processes within organizations. A few researchers have, however, explicitly linked learning processes to cultural traits. Thus Shibata et al. (1991) demonstrated that senior Japanese managers in a sample of more than 300 companies provided strong support for innovation, risk-taking, wide dissemination of information and broad involvement in decision-taking. An earlier study by Sullivan and Nonaka (1986) which compared 75 US and 75 Japanese managers showed that senior Japanese managers espouse greater commitment to 'variety amplification' than their US counterparts. Hedlund and Nonaka (1993) and Hedlund (1994) contrast modes of knowledge in Western and Japanese firms and relate them to organizational characteristics of the two business cultures. These findings raise the possibility that different national business cultures and traditions may lead to different learning processes, and perhaps also that the product, or outcomes, of learning may be different in one culture compared to another. This area has received limited attention over recent years despite the increasing globalization of business, apart from a few recent studies of learning in transnational joint ventures (see for example, Barkema et al., 1996; Glaister and Buckley, 1996; Inkpen, 1996; Pilkington, 1996).

In summary, the distinction between the technical and social views of organizational learning can be linked to one current debate and one trend. The debate is about whether the field is becoming too fragmented and needs more effort devoted to integration of theory and practice, or whether distinct schools of thought are complementary and are necessary to the development of the field as a whole. Authors such as Huber (1991) and Miner and Mezias (1996) have argued strongly for the former position, and the debate around the project of integration is well summarized by Prange in the second chapter of this book. On the other hand, it is argued by Easterby-Smith (1997) that approaches to organizational learning are based on distinct, and largely incompatible, views of the nature of learning itself. He summarizes six main 'disciplines', each with its own ontological assumptions, which have started to colonize the territory of organizational learning: psychology/OD, management science, organization theory, strategy, production management, and cultural anthropology. It follows that development might best be pursued within each of these areas, while merely taking note of any parallel progress in related areas.

The trend is the strengthening of the social perspective on organizational learning, and the evolution of methodologies that enable it to be investigated empirically. While much reliance is already placed on traditional qualitative and ethnographic methods (Gherardi et al., 1998; Snell & Chak, 1998), there is a growing interest in the use of linguistic and narrative methods for researching learning processes within organizations. The logic for this is that if meanings are constructed through dialogue and visions are communicated through storytelling, then a closer analysis of the actual words and communicative practices employed is likely to be valuable. Sims argues the case for this particular approach to investigation in chapter 3 of this book. This approach also fits well with recent calls to develop narrative perspectives in management studies (see for example Barry and Elmes, 1997; Czarniawska, 1997).

The learning organization

As explained above, the literature on the learning organization is becoming increasingly distinct from that which addresses organizational learning. The key reason for this is that the two communities of authors recognize distinct purposes for their work, the former concentrating on the development of normative models and methodologies for creating change in the direction of improved learning processes, the latter concentrating on understanding the nature and processes of learning (and unlearning) within organizations. Typically, the former group is represented by consultants (or academics in their roles as consultants), while the latter group is represented by academic researchers. That being said, the learning organization literature is not devoid of theory; it draws very heavily from ideas developed within organizational learning but it is selective on the grounds of utility. So it is not surprising that a similar divide exists here between the technical and social approaches to the creation of learning organizations. Since the basic distinction has already been discussed above in some detail, we will simply focus here on the way that it has been implemented in practice.

The *technical variant* of the learning organization has emphasized interventions based on measurement. One traditional measure has been the 'learning curve', which involves taking historical data on production costs, which are plotted against the cumulative output of a particular product. In theory there should be an inverse logarithmic relationship between cost and output; thus for every doubling in cumulative output there should be a reduction in costs of 10 per cent. It is assumed that the reduction in costs results from some kind of internal learning process, and that by making the rate of cost reductions explicit this will encourage further learning to take place (see, for example, Argote et al., 1990 and Epple et al., 1991). Garvin (1993) argues for an extension of this principle on the grounds that cost is only one indicator of learning outcome, and hence other (supplementary) measures should be employed including product quality indicators, and attitude/behavioural surveys of employees. The key point here is that the focus is on the outcomes, rather than the mechanisms and processes, of learning.

The emphasis on measurement as the focus of intervention leads naturally to the introduction of information systems to support collection of relevant data. This was illustrated in the study by Adler (1993) of the NUMMI plant in California, a joint manufacturing venture between General Motors and Toyota. A high degree of standardization was established across the plant, which enabled information on production performance, new ideas and problem solutions to be shared rapidly across all relevant work units. In a subsequent study, Adler and Cole (1993) compared the performance of the NUMMI plant with a Volvo factory at Uddevalla in Sweden. The Volvo plant was designed on humanistic principles around the individual and the work group. Thus individuals were encouraged to develop themselves, financial rewards were offered to those who were able to demonstrate increased expertise, and autonomous work groups were expected to share knowledge and work collectively to solve problems. This is a good representation of the social perspective on the learning organization, which focuses on individual and group learning processes as the foundation of organizational learning. Incidentally, Adler and Cole (1993) argue that the NUMMI model was superior to the Uddevalla plant in terms of increased levels of productivity because of the ability to generalize learning right across the factory; whereas at Uddevalla, although groups may have achieved deeper insights into how to solve problems, the existence of group boundaries meant that these insights were not likely to be shared between groups, and even if they were, the high variability of tasks and contexts in Uddevalla meant that many of the insights gained in one location would not be relevant anywhere else.

The debate about the relative superiority of the technical and social variants continued (Adler and Cole, 1994; Berggren, 1994), and remains inconclusive to this day. One of the limitations to the debate is that much of it has been framed around technocratic criteria, such as productivity rates, which inevitably favour those with a technical bent. So we will not try to come to a conclusion about relative superiority at this stage, and will instead develop further the *social view* of the learning organization. As mentioned above, the starting point from a social perspective is the ability of individuals to learn from their experiences and to learn from/with each other in work settings. Researchers at the MIT Center for Organizational Learning have developed the concept of 'dialogue' as a means of improving the quality of communication between people. This is a structured method for intervention into ongoing workgroups which requires members to allow space for each other to speak, to avoid evaluating the comments of each other, and to be willing to speak out on their own views (Isaacs, 1993; Senge, 1990). This method has its roots in the practice of organization development which was most fashionable in the late 1960s – which is one of the two main inspirations of Senge's work, the other being the systems dynamics approach developed by Jay Forrester at MIT. Further discussion of this topic is outside the scope of this introduction, but Edmondson

(1996) provides a useful overview of the antecedents and genesis of MIT's Center for Organizational Learning.

Another feature common to most of the writers on the learning organization is a belief that normative processes can be defined, which will lead to enhanced learning capability. Writers can however, be divided into those who propose linear models with a series of hierarchical stages which become progressively more desirable, and those who propose cyclical models. Argyris' notion of single- and double-loop learning is the inspiration of the former, and has led to many different formulations, including Swieringa and Weirdsma (1992), who propose a three-level model, and Torbert (1994), who extends it to eight levels. The precise formulation varies a little in each case, but there are three assumptions common to all such models: that each level is conceptually distinct from each of the others; that organizational processes can be classified with some confidence as belonging uniquely to one or other of these levels; and that successive levels are increasingly desirable for organizations wishing to increase their learning capacity.

Cyclical models, by contrast, do not posit any hierarchies of desirability; their main claim is that the enhancement of organizational learning is a continuous process which will be helped by working through a series of stages involving the generation of information, the interpretation of information and development of actions on the basis of these interpretations. Most of these models are based loosely on Kolb's learning cycle, and with some additional process to iterate between individual and collective meaning structures (Kolb et al., 1984). Dixon (1994), for example, uses a model which includes the following stages: (i) the generation of information about internal and external performance (much along the lines that Garvin (1993) advocates); (ii) a sustained effort to integrate this information into the organizational context through training and conferencing systems; (iii) a collective attempt to interpret this information through improved interaction and reduced hierarchy; and (iv) encouragement for individuals and groups to take appropriate action on the basis of the shared understanding of the problems to be addressed.

Irrespective of the position taken there is a consistent concern among writers on the learning organization to understand why the concept is so difficult to implement. This has led pragmatically to interest in a wide range of implementation techniques and strategies, and most consultants will specialize on a particular framework or method. The diversity of strategies is reflected in the chapters in the second part of the book, which concentrates on the consequences of different implementation approaches.

Main problems and opportunities in the field today

We have provided above a brief overview of the fields of organizational learning and the learning organization, and have also tried to indicate where some of the contributions in the present book may be seen to extend our knowledge of this field. We now propose to provide a more personal view of some of the central problems and issues relevant to the development of the field, before returning to a more systematic account, and justification, of the structure of the book. We see these issues falling into three main categories: empirical work, theory development and utilization.

Empirical work

For a long time, authors have bemoaned the shortage of empirical work in the field of organizational learning (Fiol and Lyles, 1985; Huber, 1991; Miner and Mezias, 1996). Even recently there are no signs of the pattern changing. For example, of 150 papers on the learning organization abstracted in ABI Inform during 1997, only 15 (10 per cent) were based on new empirical data collected by the authors, and of these, ten were based on interventions carried out by the authors themselves. While we have nothing against action research *per se*, the shortage of independent studies of organizational learning, which might take a critical and 'objective' stance, is worrying.[2]

A range of approaches has been adopted by those authors who have carried out original empirical work in this field. In Table 1.1 we have specified contrasting features of empirical studies and have also attempted to classify each of the studies presented in this book. Since the empirical studies included in this book do not cover the range of possibilities we identify, we also make reference to other published studies to illustrate our classification system. Furthermore, although the choices represented in each row are intended to be independent of each other, in practice one would usually expect some clustering of options dictated by the need for theoretical or practical consistency amongst a set of choices. For example, studies where the researcher is an active participant (A1) indicate, for practical reasons, an involvement with a limited number of cases (B1). Similarly, a focus on micro-practices within organizational or transitional settings (C2) would normally focus on the processes that concentrate to the learning outcomes (D2), rather than the outcomes themselves (D1).

It seems to us that the most common forms of empirical research focus on processes where the researcher is either an active participant (A1) or a distant observer (A2), favour surveys (B1) over detailed case studies (B2), and privilege outcomes as indicators of learning processes (D1) over the processes themselves (D2). In our view there Is a particular shortage of studies that attempt to induce theory from existing practice (E1), use a small sample of in-depth cases (B2), focus on micro-practices within organizational or trans-organizational settings (C2) and study processes (D2) leading to learning outcomes.

One of the aims of this book is to redress the balance found in the literature more in favour of empirical studies and hence we are pleased to have obtained 5 significant empirical studies for Part II. According to the

TABLE 1.1 *Contrasting features of studies of organizational learning*

Role of Researcher	
(A1) Studies where the researcher is also a major player in the processes being examined (Dixon)	(A2) Studies where the researcher is detached and distant from the processes being investigated (Blackler et al.)
Methodological Approach	
(B1) Survey-based comparisons across numbers of organizations (Antonacopoulou)	(B2) In depth cases of one, or a small number of, organizations (Dixon, Finger and Bürgin, Ayas)
Unit of Analysis	
(C1) Macro studies which look at total organizations, especially the strategic apex (Finger and Bürgin)	(C2) Detailed studies of micro practices within the organizational or trans-organizational settings (e.g. Gherardi et al., 1998)
Focus on Learning	
(D1) Studies that focus on outcomes as indicators of organizational learning (Finger and Bürgin, Ayas, Antonacopoulou)	(D2) Studies that focus on internal processes that might contribute to organizational learning outcomes (e.g. Pak and Snell, 1998)
Epistemological Stance	
(E1) Studies which aim to describe practice and then to conceptualize what takes place in a 'grounded' way (e.g. Nevis et al., 1995)	(E2) Studies which attempt to link, or to apply, specific theories to the phenomena observed (Blackler et al.)

above scheme, the chapter by Nancy Dixon falls into types A1 and B2; the chapter by Finger and Bürgin falls into types B2 and D1; the chapter by Preskill and Torres falls into types B1 and E2; the chapter by Ayas falls into types B1 and D1; the paper by Blackler et al. falls into types A2 and E2; and the chapter by Antonacopoulou falls into types B1, C1 and D1.

In addition to the overall nature/design of research studies of organizational learning, there is also the question of the specific methods and techniques that may be used to investigate organizational learning. If our above suggestion is accepted, that there need to be more studies focusing on the micro processes of learning within organizations, then it will be important that methodologies will be available to do this work. Learning is a notoriously difficult process to investigate empirically, which is why most researchers have taken the easy option by objectifying it and focusing on outputs. It is even more difficult to isolate learning processes within complex organizations because of the many potential levels of analysis and the wide range of actors involved. In search of methods that can tap into the more subtle processes of learning within organizations, Miner and Mezias (1996) emphasize the need to move beyond traditional positivist methods, and advocate greater use of qualitative methods in general, of applied research, and of modelling tools such as simulations. In this context we can add that the analysis of language and stories is likely to prove important (Elmes and Kasouf, 1995), as are methods involving co-researchers, the development of multifaceted case studies over time and cognitive mapping.

Theory development

In parallel to the complaints about the lack of good empirical work on organizational learning, there is concern that insufficient attention is being paid to the cumulative development of the field (Huber, 1991; Miner and Mezias, 1996). This is manifest by a tendency to take for granted a small number of existing nostrums without submitting them to critical examination. We offer two examples below to illustrate this point.

First, as we have noted in the previous part of the chapter, many authors regard organizational politics as one of the main barriers to the establishment of learning organizations, and hence focus on ways of reducing the incidence and impact of political behaviour. It is assumed that 'good' learning takes place in a climate of openness where political behaviour is minimized (Argyris, 1986; Senge, 1990). But this is one assumption which can easily be questioned, and if so, we need to start looking for theories of organizational learning which take the political nature of information and knowledge as a starting point. A good example of this is Coopey (1995), who adopts a critical perspective on the learning organization, and who then starts to examine ways of helping managers to make explicit, and work with, these political processes (Coopey, 1998). The aim is therefore to incorporate politics into organizational learning, rather than to eradicate it.

The second example relates to the current dominance of North American theories of management and organization, which is reinforced by US control of key resources such as top journals and information databases. In this climate it is difficult for 'international', non-US views to become recognized as valuable (Boyacigiller and Adler, 1991). Usdiken and Pasadeos (1995) conducted a bibliographic study of two organization studies journals in the US and Europe, and demonstrated a highly divergent set of citations used by American and European authors: Americans rarely cite Europeans, and vice versa. Yet there is an increasing amount of work taking place outside the USA, such as the philosophical, critical and multicultural perspectives in Europe which are hardly recognized by US academics. The same can be said for the field of organizational learning where US models and literature still dominate internationally, and which contain a hidden bias towards North American cultural and institutional features such as: abundant economic resources; individualism in cultural values and career patterns; an emphasis on rationality and the importance of explicit information; and the application of scientific methods.

The work of Nonaka provides a rare example of an international contribution becoming accepted in the US mainstream, and is, perhaps, the exception that proves the rule. The originality of Nonaka's work lies in his detailed case studies of innovation processes in Japanese organizations where he argues that features of Japanese culture operate which makes innovation easier than in the US. These cultural features include the willingness of employees to identify with their work groups, the critical role of middle management in generating and interpreting information, and the preference for thinking of problems holistically. As a consequence, Nonaka has come up with concepts such as 'middle-up-down-management' and the knowledge creation spiral, which involves continuous translations between explicit and tacit knowledge (Nonaka, 1994; Nonaka and Takeuchi, 1995). These ideas are distinct and do not fit easily with the US mainstream, but they have attracted attention due to the interest within US management academia about Japanese economic recipes, and because Nonaka has worked in US academia and communicates well in English.

Following the lead of Nonaka, it seems that we should be looking for theories of organizational learning which are based on cultural and institutional assumptions other than those that prevail in the USA. There are enough cultural differences even between the UK and the USA to have resulted already in a distinct approach to the learning organization, based loosely around principles of Action Learning (see Burgoyne et al., 1994), and this has been matched by distinct centres of interest elsewhere in Europe (e.g. Trento, Nijenrode). It seems that if the field is to develop over the next few years in parallel with the globalization of business and economic affairs, then substantial efforts should be made to 'ground' new theories of organizational learning on the contexts of different countries outside North America and Europe. In this respect recent work on organizational learning in India, Singapore and China (Kumar, 1997; Snell and Chak, 1998; Tsang, 1997) are very welcome, and one hopes that further studies of this ilk will both enrich local practice, and be seen as a challenge to mainstream theories within North America.

Utilization of ideas

The third issue we would like to discuss in this section is both a problem and an opportunity. It concerns the utilization of theories and techniques around organizational learning by companies and other organizations. The notions of organizational learning and the learning organization have sustained considerable popularity in academic and corporate circles throughout much of the 1990s. As Dodgson (1993) noted, the concept of learning provides considerable promise – to academics because it may revitalize tired disciplines, and for managers because it may be the key to corporate competitiveness. The danger is that it may become over-applied, and hence either exhausted or discredited, especially amongst practitioners who have traditionally given very short shelf lives to corporate panaceas.

Much of the existing literature on the implementation of organizational learning has been produced by people who were closely involved with the examples described, either as internal sponsors (Butler, 1994; DeGeus, 1988; Lank, 1998) or as external consultants (Pedler, 1994; Senge, 1990). But a trend which has established itself recently is the idea of combining insiders and outsiders when studying organizational learning (Bartunek et al., 1998; Bood et al., 1998). This has the distinct advantages of making access easy and of allowing an accommodation between the emic perspective (insider interpretations) and etic perspective (outsider interpretations). It also allows a differentiation of roles between the insiders who may be considerably committed to the success of the initiative, and the outsiders who may be much more likely to adopt a critical perspective. Several of the chapters in the present volume involve a degree of insider/outsider collaboration (Finger and Bürgin Brand; Preskill and Torres), and it is a style of research that we would wish to encourage in the future.

Structure and overview of this book

We have clustered the chapters in this book into two main sections. The first part looks at theoretical debates to do with organizational learning; and the second part looks at issues of implementation in a range of settings. Chapters in the second part are roughly, but not exclusively, consistent with the literature on the learning organization. We say that because one of the explicit aims of this book is to provide a meeting place between the two communities of academics and practitioners in a way which does not assume a one-way traffic in concepts and theories – from the former to the latter. Thus we believe that there are direct practical consequences of the ideas developed in Part One, and there are significant theoretical insights to be gained from the empirical studies in Part Two.

Part One looks at the theoretical aspects of organizational learning and the four chapters provide reviews and critiques of current thinking and debates in the field. Christiane Prange critiques the realist ontology and positivist epistemology bias within much of the literature on the grounds that it leads to partial conceptualizations of the subject matter. She advances the idea of using metaphors to understand organizational learning, as a way to avoid the rush to prescriptive theories while acknowledging the complex and multifaceted nature of organizational learning. Marleen Huysman extends this critique by identifying and deconstructing five further 'biases' largely within the literature of the learning organization: improvement, individual action, systems thinking, normative, purposeful and systematic learning. Bente Elkjaer puts the critical spotlight onto one fashionable area of 'non-positivist' literature: communities of practice (COPs). Her argument is that COPs prove to be inadequate for dealing with areas of application, and hence she looks at the potential of ideas drawn from related fields such as symbolic interactionism and experiential learning theory. In particular, she is interested in developing

Dewey's notions of language as the 'tool of tools' in order to overcome the disjunction between action and cognition. The search for alternative conceptualizations based on a 'linguistic turn' is taken up by David Sims, who explores the possibility that organizational learning can be seen from a narrative perspective, as part of a 'canon of stories'. He regards learning as a matter of changes in memory, and memory as retained in stories rather than propositional statements. Hence, canons of stories are suggested as being a fruitful hunting ground for understanding both the content and process of organizational learning.

Part Two contains seven chapters which look at the implementation of organizational learning within a range of organizational settings by using a number of different intervention methodologies. There are a number of overlaps between chapters within this part, and with chapters in the first part. Thus Nancy Dixon and Matthias Finger and Silvia Bürgin Brand use similar Action Learning methodologies, respectively within Canadian and Swiss public sector organizations. Dixon focuses on learning between museums, whereas Finger and Bürgin Brand consider the extent to which the intervention has succeeded and failed in turning the Swiss Post Office into a 'learning organization'. The chapters by Karen Ayas and Frank Blackler et al. focus on the process of innovation in manufacturing organizations. But again there are differences. Ayas looks at the consequences of establishing a network of Project Groups within Fokker to disseminate innovations between aircraft designers; whereas Blackler et al. look at the effect of organizational and cultural changes on the roles and behaviour of scientists within the defence industry. The latter's emphasis on the conceptual value of metaphors provides a good link back to the chapter by Sims in Part One.

The other chapters in Part Two all make use of empirical data to examine different intervention strategies aimed at increasing organizational learning. Elena Antonacopoulou provides a carefully researched study which looks at the effect of training interventions within three UK banks, and it demonstrates the impact of organizational culture on the efficacy of these interventions. Hallie Preskill and Rosalie Torres note that external interventions in the form of evaluation studies so often fail to achieve the required results and speculate that they will be more likely to succeed if seen within the broad framework of organizational learning. Bertrand Moingeon and Amy Edmondson provide, from interviews and personal communications, a comparison of the intervention styles of two leading intervention theorists: Michel Crozier and Chris Argyris.

Concluding comments

It is normal practice, at this stage, for the editors to express the hope that their volume will contribute to push the frontiers of the field, and to call for more comprehensive and less fragmented theories of their subject matter. We do indeed hope that chapters in this volume will stimulate and encourage further research in the field. The co-existence of two related, but hitherto separate, approaches to learning in the same volume is bound to create feelings of unease and hopefulness in equal measure. We make no apologies for attempting to start a dialogue between two camps that may share little in common other than an interest in collective learning phenomena. But our agenda is clearly to stimulate dialogue and collaborative competition rather than paradigmatic closure, or an idyllic meta-theory of organizational learning.

The recent surge of interest in learning in and around organizations cannot disguise the fact that few or any of the perspectives we have identified in this introduction have developed to any great extent the theoretical and methodological implications of their approaches to learning. Nor is it legitimate to expect that they will do so in the near future. The magic juxtaposition of the terms 'organization' and 'learning' stresses, rather than hides, the need for clear and elaborate conceptualizations of what is meant by both 'organizations' and 'learning'. It also raises the possibility that the two terms may be co-existing precariously, in many instances. The notion that all forms of collective learning will necessarily encompass or be constrained by formal organizational boundaries is a shaky assumption.

In conclusion, our call is for a measured and healthy pluralism in developing theories of learning in and around organizations. Hopefully, this volume will illustrate the richness of the different perspectives on organizational learning and learning organizations and help to convince sceptics of the dangers of premature paradigm closure. In essence, we argue for an ecological view of theory development where variety must always precede selection and retention. On the other hand, we hope this volume contributes to erode some of the more artificial distinctions between descriptive and prescriptive intentions in theory building. We have argued that all descriptive theories have, potentially, prescriptive implications whether their proponents acknowledge it or not. But, equally, all prescriptive propositions are based on substantive, theoretical models which, all too often, remain implicit and hidden from view. Many of the contributions in this volume will, no doubt, help to clarify the practical implications of theoretical statements as well the advantages of basing interventions on sound theoretical ground.

Notes

1. The distinction was first propounded in Argyris (1977).
2. These figures also hold reasonably well for UMI citation searches between 1994 and 1998.

References

Adler, P.S. (1993) Time-and-motion regained. *Harvard Business Review*, 71 (1): 97–108.

Adler, P.S. and Cole, R.E. (1993) Designed for learning: a tale of two auto-plants'. *Sloan Management Review*, 34 (3): 85–94.

Adler, P.S. and Cole, R.E. (1994) NUMMI vs. Uddevalla – Rejoinder. *Sloan Management Review*, 35 (2): 45–9.

Argote, L., Beckman, S.L. and Epple, D. (1990) The persistence and transfer of learning in industrial settings. *Management Science*, 36: 140–54.

Argyris, C. (1977) Double-loop learning in organizations. *Harvard Business Review*, 55 (5): 115–25.

Argyris, C. (1986) Reinforcing organizational defensive routines: an unintended human resources activity. *Human Resource Management*, 25 (4): 541–55.

Argyris, C. (1996) Unrecognized defenses of scholars – impact on theory and research. *Organization Science*, 7 (1): 79–87.

Argyris, C. and Schön, D.A. (1978) *Organizational Learning*. Reading, MA: Addison-Wesley.

Barkema, H.G., Bell, J.H.J. and Pennings, J.M. (1996) Foreign entry, cultural barriers, and learning. *Strategic Management Journal*, 17 (2): 151–66.

Barry, D. and Elmes, M. (1997) Strategy retold: toward a narrative view of strategic discourse. *Academy of Management Review*, 22 (2): 429–52.

Bartunek, J.M., Krim, R.M., Necochea, R. and Humphries, M. (1998) Sense-making, sensegiving and leadership in strategic organizational development. Paper for Conference on Organizational Learning, George Washington University, March 1998.

Berggren, C. (1994) NUMMI vs. Uddevalla. *Sloan Management Review*, 35 (2): 37–45.

Blackler, F. (1993) Knowledge and the theory of organizations – organizations as activity systems and the reframing of management. *Journal of Management Studies*, 30 (6): 863–84.

Bood, R.P., Homan, T.H., Rietdijk, M.M. and van Udden, J. (1998) Studying organizational learning resulting from large-scale interventions. Paper for Conference on Organizational Learning, George Washington University, March 1998.

Boyacigiller, N.A. and Adler, N.J. (1991) The parochial dinosaur – organizational science in a global context. *Academy of Management Review*, 16 (2): 262–90.

Brown, J.S. and Duguid, P. (1991) Organizational learning and communities-of-practice: toward a unified view of working, learning and innovating. *Organization Science*, 2 (1): 40–57.

Burgoyne, J.G., Pedler, M. and Boydell, T. (1994) *Towards the Learning Company: Concepts and Practices*. London: McGraw-Hill.

Butler, J. (1994) Engaging and confronting the personal responsibility of the learning company perspective – adding new skills to old. In: J. Burgoyne, M. Pedler and T. Boydell (eds), *Towards the Learning Company: Concepts and Practices*. Maidenhead: McGraw-Hill.

Ciborra, C.U., Patriotta, G. and Erlicher, L. (1995) Disassembling frames on the assembly line: the theory and practice of the new division of learning in advanced manufacturing. Paper presented at the Information Technology and Changes in Organizational Work. Proceedings of the IFIP WG8.2 Working Conference, Cambridge.

Cohen, M.D. and Sproull, L.S. (eds) (1996) *Organizational Learning*. London: Sage.

Collis, D.J. (1994) Research Note – How valuable are organizational capabilities? *Strategic Management Journal*, 15: 143–52.

Cook, S.D.N. and Yanow, D. (1993) Culture and organizational learning. *Journal of Management Inquiry*, 2 (4): 373–90.
Coopey, J. (1994) Power politics and ideology. In: J. Burgoyne, M. Pedler and T. Boydell (eds), *Toward the Learning Company: Concepts and Practices*. London: McGraw-Hill.
Coopey, J. (1995) The learning organization: power politics and ideology. *Management Learning*, 26 (2): 193–214.
Coopey. J. (1998) Learning to trust and trusting to learn: a role for radical theatre. *Management Learning*, 29(3): 365–82.
Crossan, M. and Guatto, T. (1996) Organizational learning research profile. *Journal of Organizational Change Management*, 9 (1): 107–12.
Czarniawska, B. (1997) A four times told tale: combining narrative and scientific knowledge in organization studies. *Organization*, 4 (1), 7–30.
DeGeus, A.P. (1988) Planning as learning. *Harvard Business Review*, 66 (2): 70–4.
DiBella, A.J., Nevis, E.C. and Gould, J.M. (1996) Understanding organizational learning capability. *Journal of Management Studies*, 33 (3): 361–79.
Dixon, N. (1994) *The Organizational Learning Cycle: How We Can Learn Collectively*. London: McGraw-Hill.
Dodgson, M. (1993) Organizational learning: a review of some literatures. *Organization Studies*, 14 (3): 375–94.
Easterby-Smith, M. (1997) Disciplines of organizational learning: contributions and critiques. *Human Relations*, 50 (9): 1085–113.
Edmondson, A.C. (1996) Three faces of Eden – the persistence of competing theories and multiple diagnoses in organizational intervention research. *Human Relations*, 49 (5): 571–95.
Elmes, M.B. and Kasouf, C.J. (1995) Knowledge workers and organizational learning: narratives from biotechnology. *Management Learning*, 26 (4): 403–22.
Epple, D., Argote, L. and Devadas, R. (1991) Organization learning curves: a method for investigating intra-plant transfer of knowledge acquired through learning by doing. *Organization Science*, 2: 58–70.
Field, L. and Ford, B. (1995) *Managing Organizational Learning: From Rhetoric to Reality*. Melbourne: Longman.
Fiol, C.M. and Lyles, M.A. (1985) Organizational learning. *Academy of Management Review*, 10 (4): 803–13.
Garvin, D.A. (1993) Building a learning organization. *Harvard Business Review*, 71 (4): 78–84.
Gherardi, S., Nicolini, D. and Odella, F. (1998) Toward a social understanding of how people learn in organizations: the notion of situated curriculum. *Management Learning*, 29 (3): 273–98.
Glaister, K.W. and Buckley, P.J. (1996) Strategic motives for international alliance formation. *Journal of Management Studies*, 33 (3): 301–32.
Grant, R.M. (1996) Prospering in dynamically-competitive environments – organizational capability as knowledge integration. *Organization Science*, 7 (4): 375–87.
Hedlund, G. (1994) A model of knowledge management and the N-form corporation. *Strategic Management Journal*, 15: 73–90.
Hedlund, G. and Nonaka, I. (1993) Models of knowledge management in the West and Japan. In: P. Lorange (ed.), *Implementing Strategic Processes*. Oxford: Blackwell.
Huber, G. (1991) Organizational learning: the contributing processes and the literature. *Organizational Science*, 2 (1): 88–115.
Inkpen, A.C. (1996) Creating knowledge through collaboration. *California Management Review*, 39 (1): 123–40.
Isaacs, W.N. (1993) Taking flight: dialogue, collective thinking and organizational learning. *Organizational Dynamics*, 22 (2): 24–39.

Kolb, D., Rubin, I.M. and MacIntyre, J.M. (1984) *Organizational Psychology: an Experiential Approach to Organizational Behavior*, 4th edn. Englewood Cliffs, NJ: Prentice-Hall.

Kumar, R. (1997) Confucian pragmatism vs. Brahmanical idealism: understanding the divergent roots of Indian and Chinese economic performance. Paper for European Organizational Studies Symposium, Budapest, July 1997.

Lank, E. (1998) Café society. *People Management*, 19 February, pp. 40–3.

Lave, J. (1993) The practice of learning. In: S. Chaiklin and J. Lave (eds), *Understanding Practice. Perspectives on Activity and Context*. Cambridge: Cambridge University Press.

Lave, J. and Wenger, E. (1991) *Situated Learning: Legitimate Peripheral Participation*. New York: Cambridge University Press.

Levinthal, D.A. and March, J.G. (1993) Exploration and exploitation in organizational learning. *Strategic Management Journal*, 14 (Winter): 95–112.

Miner, A.S. and Mezias, S.J. (1996) Ugly-duckling no more – pasts and futures of organizational learning research. *Organization Science*, 7 (1): 88–99.

Nevis, E.C., DiBella, A.J. and Gould, J.M. (1995) Understanding organizations as learning-systems. *Sloan Management Review*, 36 (2): 73–85.

Nicolini, D. and Meznar, M.B. (1995) The social construction of organizational learning: conceptual and practical issues. *Human Relations*, 48 (7): 727–46.

Nonaka, I. (1994) A dynamic theory of organizational knowledge creation. *Organization Science*, 5 (1): 14–37.

Nonaka, I. and Takeuchi, H. (1995) *The Knowledge Creating Company*. New York: Oxford University Press.

Orlikowski, W.J. (1996) Improvising organizational transformation over time – a situated change perspective. *Information Systems Research*, 7 (1): 63–92.

Orr, J.E. (1990) Sharing knowledge, celebrating identity: community memory in a service culture. In: D. Middleton and D. Edwards (eds), *Collective Remembering*. London: Sage.

Pak, P. and Snell, R.S. (1998) Organizational learning: quietly contesting meaning between groups. Paper for Conference on Organizational Learning, George Washington University, March 1998.

Pedler, M. (1994) Organizational biography and organizational learning: Weldreck: a case study and commentary. In: J. Burgoyne, M. Pedler and T. Boydell (eds), *Towards the Learning Company: Concepts and Practices*. Maidenhead: McGraw-Hill.

Pedler, M., Boydell, T. and Burgoyne, J. (1989) Towards the learning company. *Management Education and Development*, 20 (1): 1–8.

Pentland, B.T. (1992) Organizing moves in software-support hot lines. *Administrative Science Quarterly*, 37 (4): 527–48.

Pilkington, A. (1996) Learning from joint ventures – the Rover Honda relationship. *Business History*, 38 (1): 90–116.

Schein, E.H. (1996) Culture: the missing concept in organization studies. *Administrative Science Quarterly*, 41 (2): 229–40.

Senge, P.M. (1990) *The Fifth Discipline: the Art and Practice of the Learning Organization*. London: Century Books.

Shibata, G., Tse, D., Vertinsky, I. and Wehrung, D. (1991) Do norms of decision-making styles, organizational design and management affect performance of Japanese firms? An exploratory study of medium and large firms. *Managerial and Decision Economics*, 12 (2): 135–46.

Snell, R.S. and Chak, A.M-K. (1998) The learning organization: learning and empowerment for whom? *Management Learning*, 29 (3): 337–64.

Stiglitz, J.E. (1987) Learning to learn, localized learning and technological progress. In: P. Dasgupta and P. Stoneman (eds), *Economic Policy and Technological Performance*. Cambridge: Cambridge University Press.

Suchman, L.A. and Trigg, R.H. (1993) Artificial intelligence as craftwork. In: S. Chaiklin and J. Lave (eds), *Understanding Practice. Perspectives on Activity and Context*. Cambridge: Cambridge University Press.

Sullivan, J.J. and Nonaka, I. (1986) The application of organizational learning theory to Japanese and American management. *Journal of International Business Studies*, 17 (3): 127–47.

Swieringa, J. and Weirdsma, A. (1992) *Becoming a Learning Organization, Beyond the Learning Curve*. Wokingham: Addison-Wesley.

Torbert, W.R. (1994) Managerial learning, organizational learning: a potentially powerful redundancy. *Management Learning*, 25 (1): 57–70.

Tsang, E. (1997) Organizational learning and the learning organization: a dichotomy between descriptive and prescriptive research. *Human Relations*, 50 (1): 73–89.

Usdiken, B. and Pasadeos, Y. (1995) Organizational analysis in North-America and Europe – a comparison of co-citation networks. *Organization Studies*, 16 (3): 503–26.

Vaughan, D. (1996) *The Challenger Launch Decision: Risky Technology, Culture and Deviance at NASA*. Chicago: Chicago University Press.

Zuboff, S. (1988) *In the Age of the Smart Machine: the Future of Work and Power*. Oxford: Heinemann.

PART ONE
REVIEW AND CRITIQUES

2 Organizational Learning – Desperately Seeking Theory?

Christiane Prange

Organizations are reeling from discontinuities created by a growing level of globalization, heightened volatility, hypercompetition, demographic changes, and the explosion of knowledge. Ever faster means of communication alter today's business climate and it is becoming more evident every day that we cannot anticipate the environment of tomorrow. Recently, ideas such as 'organizational learning' (Garratt, 1987; Garvin, 1993; Probst and Büchel, 1994) and the 'learning organization' have been proposed to increase the 'knowledge intensity' of companies, a prerequisite for coping with the previously mentioned trends (Starbuck, 1992; Tenkasi and Boland, 1996). This, in turn, has led authors to think about the 'management of knowledge' (von Krogh and Venzin, 1995), which gives credence to the fact that any occupation with learning requires some substantiation of the essence of the learning process, that is, of knowledge.

To classify knowledge along different distinctions and functions, and then think about possible methods of intervention, is a valuable effort. However, this is not the objective of this chapter. Nor will I participate in the equally fruitful discussion about the 'learning organization' which takes a similar 'hands-on focus' on action perspectives, and whose major proponents have deliberately tried to distinguish it from the concept of 'organizational learning'. In this chapter I will focus on 'organizational learning', which, in contrast to the 'learning organization', refers to processes of individual and collective learning – both within and between organizations (Dodgson, 1993; Prange, 1996; Wiegand, 1996). Although we are not dealing with a completely new topic, the popularity of organizational learning has continuously increased, and recently its shift to the centre stage of organization theory has been suggested (Glynn et al., 1994; Miner and Mezias, 1996).

If we examine the history of organizational learning we note that the concept was mentioned in the early 1950s in reference to the birth and death of public administrations. Especially in the early 1960s, researchers became attracted by the idea of organizational learning (Argyris, 1964; Cangelosi and Dill, 1965; Cyert and March, 1963). But it was only in the late 1970s that a sparse, but regular stream of articles and books began to flow (Argyris and Schön, 1978; Duncan and Weiss, 1979; March and Olsen, 1975). During the 1980s some 50 articles were published in academic journals, which can be compared with over 184 papers (written by 149 different authors, or groups of authors), appearing thus far in the 1990s (cf. Crossan and Guatto, 1996).[1]

The multitude of ways in which organizational learning has been classified and used purports an 'organizational learning jungle' which is becoming progressively dense and impenetrable. As Mackenzie (1994: 251) notes, 'The main conclusion is that after 30 years of effort, the scientific community devoted to organizational learning has not produced discernible intellectual progress.'

On the other hand, if the various communities interested in organizational learning have not yet resolved the different definitions and conceptualizations of organizational learning, one may ask whether perhaps they cannot, or even do not intend to do so. This, at least, is what Thatchenkery (1996: 5) formulates sarcastically: 'In a world where action rather than reflection is valued, even the reflective learning organization apparently has to race at a pace that leaves little room for deliberation.' One might just as well ask for any visible progress in theory development in the field of organizational learning.

Starting from these introductory remarks I propose that in organizational learning research theory building is impeded by an excessive concern for 'usefulness' to the practising manager. I suppose that many theorists, implicitly or explicitly, adopt a meta-theoretical position that deals with an objective world about which they can make valid judgements; the researchers' task then is to develop knowledge that finally represents this external world. In terms of the philosophy-of-science literature this has been referred to as a realist ontology and a positivist epistemology. I should mention at this point that I do not assume that organizational learning theorists follow a 'naive' realism that evaluates knowledge development according to its complete correspondence with an objective reality. I will show later that there is a range of alternative positions that go well beyond this 'simple-minded' objectivism.

In order to compare organizational learning theories I will use several criteria that have been formulated as to what constitutes a 'good' theory. These will help in identifying omissions in current approaches (section 1). Subsequently, I will show that the formulation of theoretical criteria follows a particular underlying philosophy-of-science logic; but the criticism against organizational learning theories may not be as convincing if one broadens the range of ontological and epistemological assumptions.

I will deconstruct three, partly overlapping, criticisms of organizational learning theory in order to show that this could indeed present a valuable way to liberate current theorizing from the shackles of prescriptive theories that are supposed to inhibit theory development. In more detail, I will analyse the criticism that:

1. organizational learning lacks theoretical integration, and research is being done in a non-cumulative way;
2. organizational learning does not provide 'useful' knowledge for practitioners;
3. organizational learning is mostly used in a metaphorical and/or analogous sense.

I propose to revise or, at least, broaden the assumptions on which this criticism is based (section 2).

I will use the last criticism of organizational learning, namely its largely metaphorical character, and advocate that it *is* the use of metaphors which can be of practical value because the reader will be sensitized to varying possibilities of interpreting the world. In this sense, organizational learning theories provide 'lenses', and not 'tools'. Concurrently, this can be a promising approach to theory development, one which goes well beyond a prescriptive stance (section 3). Finally, a short summary will be followed by a critical outlook on the 'desperate' endeavour of organizational learning theory and some positive alternatives for the future (section 4).

1 Towards an organizational learning theory – some criteria for evaluation

What is the value of 'good' theories? Against which criteria should 'good' theories be evaluated? Most generally, theories shape the landscape of facts by guiding thinking. They tell people what to expect, where to look, what to ignore, what actions are feasible, what values to hold. These expectations and beliefs then influence actions and retrospective interpretations, perhaps unconsciously (Rosenthal, 1966).

If one looks at evaluation criteria in more detail one finds that different researchers have provided different answers. Webb (1961), for instance, said that good theories exhibit knowledge, scepticism and generalizability. Lave and March (1975) proposed that good theories are metaphors that embody truth, beauty and justice; whereas unattractive theories are inaccurate or unaesthetic. McGuire (1983) noted that people may appraise theories according to either internal criteria, such as their logical consistency, or external criteria, such as the status of their authors. Others have distinguished between a theory's prescriptive and its descriptive value, and again other researchers have provided more formal requirements for theory building, such as, the relevant factors that are part of the explanation of the phenomenon, and their possible interrelation, that is, 'the theoretical glue that welds the model together' (Whetten, 1989: 491).

Also, the criterion of consistency has been widely used, and I will adopt it for my purposes. Further, I will evaluate organizational learning theories according to their descriptive versus prescriptive contribution, that is, whether they depict how something *is* done without reference to how it should be done, or whether they exhibit prescriptive, or normative features which explicate how some problem in an applied setting *should* be solved. In this last category, the practitioner can be seen as the final judge of the degree to which a theory's prescribed course of action is authoritative.

After the decision on evaluation criteria has been taken, there remains the question of which approaches are representative such as to be included in my review. Everyone who tries to provide a review within a fragmented field of research faces this question. What are sensible criteria along which to select approaches? Which approaches are relevant and/or interesting? Crossan and Guatto (1996) provided a distinction that proves useful for my purposes. They distinguished between four formal categories of articles: analysis, synthesis, review and application. As my objective is theory development, those articles that focus on application are clearly outside the scope of this work. Also, I deliberately excluded pure review and synthesis articles, because they do not generally present a completely new approach within organizational learning research. Instead, I decided to look for articles which fall into the group of analysis, which provide a novel approach to the study of organizational learning, and which attempt to advance the field.

Further, I apply the selection criterion of 'completeness', that is, in how far theories of organizational learning cover all those questions that have been considered relevant by researchers (e.g. Reinhardt, 1993; Wiegand, 1996). The following questions are by far the most reasonable ones that can be conceived of within a theory of organizational learning:

- What does organizational learning mean? (definition)
- Who is learning? (learning subject)
- What is being learned? (content of learning)
- When does learning take place? (incentives and motives for learning)
- What results does learning yield? (efficiency and effectiveness of learning)
- How does learning take place? (processes of learning)

In order to decide on a basis for selection I used a citation search conducted by Crossan and Guatto (1996), and synthesized those articles that are analytical, *and* complete according to the previously formulated six essential questions, *and* also representative according to the number of citations (for exact numbers see Crossan and Guatto, 1996: 110).

Table 2.1 depicts a comparison of major approaches to organizational learning, and I will now apply my two evaluation criteria, that is, consistency and descriptive/prescriptive undertaking. The most general result is that there is a lack of consistency *between* (and sometimes even *within*) approaches. The lack of consistency can be convincingly demonstrated with the following examples. We encounter the following rather confusing contradictions: for instance, if we want to study organizational learning through organizational routines, as Levitt and March (1988) suggest, we don't seem to get much help in spotting the object of interest. Their description of routines is so inclusive that we are reduced to saying that organizational learning is what happens in organizations. If we remain in the What? column of Table 2.1 we are unsure whether it is insights, behaviour or both that constitute the *content* of organizational learning, and what precisely is supposed to change.

One of the greatest myths of organizational learning is probably the who question, that is, the way in which learning might be considered *organizational*. It remains fairly unclear whether we are talking about individual learning in organizations (Argyris and Schön, 1978; Cangelosi and Dill, 1965; Duncan and Weiss, 1979; Hedberg, 1981; March and Olsen, 1975), organizational learning that is like individual learning (see especially Hedberg, 1981), or some kind of aggregate or emergent learning (Cyert and March, 1963; again Hedberg, 1981; Levitt and March, 1988; Weick and Roberts, 1993). Perhaps the idea of *organizational* learning is an anthropomorphic fallacy, that leads to an inappropriate reification of the concept of organization (Jones, 1995).

If we look at the *processes* of organizational learning we encounter 'learning from experience' as a genuine component of almost all approaches (most prominently: Duncan and Weiss, 1979; Hedberg, 1981; March and Olsen, 1975). Also, 'history dependence' is emphasized in some approaches. However, the consequences of *different* histories and *different* experiences, leading to an examination of *different* learning needs are neglected (see for an exception Levitt and March, 1988). A further point of irritation is that some authors emphasize the sources of knowledge and neglect *processes* of knowledge generation, that is, learning, altogether (Huber, 1991). One more example of theoretical omission can be seen in the distinction between levels or intensities of learning, for example, lower- vs. higher-level learning (Fiol and Lyles, 1985); single-loop vs. double-loop learning (Argyris and Schön, 1978). Referring to these hierarchies of learning does not produce veridical knowledge about the processes *as such*. For example, the question of how individual higher-level learning leads to organizational higher-level learning remains unanswered.

To give a last example of the heterogeneity of approaches, I suggest looking at the interrelation between *content* and *processes* of organizational learning. It is generally agreed that organizational learning leads to some form of knowledge. These forms of knowledge are previously referred to as routines (Cyert and March, 1963; Levitt and March, 1988), knowledge base

TABLE 2.1 *Building blocks in organizational learning theory development*

Author(s) (Year)	Definition of OL	Who? (subject of OL)	What? (content of OL)	When? (incentives for OL)	With what results? (efficiency of OL)	How? (processes of OL)
Cyert and March (1963)	Organizational learning is adaptive behaviour of organizations over time	Aggregate level of organization	Standard operating procedures and organizational rules	Slack resources	Adaptation to changing environmental states; improved adaptation as prerequisite for survival	Adaptation of goals, attention, and search rules; learning from experience
Cangelosi and Dill (1965)	Organizational learning consists of a series of interactions betwen adaptation at the individual, or subgroup level and adaptation at the organizational level	Individuals and subgroups in organizations	Complex management decisions	Stress stimulates learning, both sub-system learning and total system learning, separately and together	Reduction of stress, and improved decision-making	Adaptation to conflicting patterns of behaviour caused by stress
Argyris and Schön (1978)	Organizational learning is the process by which organizational members detect errors or anomalies and correct them by restructuring organizational theory-in-use	Individual learning in organizations	Organizational theories-in-use or theories-of-action	Match or mismatch of expected outcomes which confirms or discredits organizational theories-in-use	Link between learning and improved action	Assumption sharing; individual and collective enquiry constructs and modifies theories-in-use; exact process remains unclear

Duncan and Weiss (1979)	Organizational learning is defined as the process within the organization by which knowledge about action-outcome relationships and the effect of the environment on these relationships is developed	The individual is the only entity who can learn. However, he/she must be seen as a part of a system of learning with exchanges of what is learned among individuals	Organizational knowledge base	Slack resources	Depends on available organizational knowledge for decision making; adaptation to changing environmental states	Development of action-outcome-relations via: (a) sharing (b) evaluation (c) integration
Fiol and Lyles (1985)	Organizational learning means the process of improving actions through better knowledge and understanding	Organizational learning is not simply the sum of individual learning	Patterns of cognitive associations and/or new responses or actions (cognitive vs. behavioural change)	Tension between constancy and change; crisis (especially for higher-level learning)	Environmental alignment; future performance improvement	Lower-level learning as repetition of past behaviour, higher-level learning as development of complex associations
Levitt and March (1988)	Organizations are seen as learning by encoding inferences from history into routine behaviour	Organizational learning is more than individual learning, that is there is an 'emergent' component	Routines (which include: rules, procedures, frameworks, cultures, belief structures, paradigms etc.)	Outcomes in response to aspiration level	Adaptation to changing environmental states; balance between 'exploration' and 'exploitation'	Learning from direct experience; learning from the experience of others; learning of paradigms for interpretation

continued overleaf

TABLE 2.1 *(continued)*

Author(s) (Year)	Definition of OL	Who? (subject of OL)	What? (content of OL)	When? (incentives for OL)	With what results? (efficiency of OL)	How? (processes of OL)
Huber (1991)	An entity learns if, through the processing of information, the range of its potential behaviours is changed . . . (L)et us assume that an organization learns if any of its units acquires knowledge that it recognizes as potentially useful to the organization	Concept of entity, which includes individuals, groups, organizations, industries, society	Information/ knowledge	Probably not intended as author aims at describing a whole range of learning subcategories	Range of potential behaviour change, not necessarily resulting in *observable* changes	Information processing: acquisition, distribution, interpretation, and storage of information; the related *processes* of organizational learning remain unspecified
Weick and Roberts (1993)	Organizational learning[a] consists of interrelating actions of individuals, that is their 'heedful interrelation' which results in a 'collective mind'	Connections between behaviours, rather than people	Behaviour/actions	Necessity for nearly error-free operations, e.g. aircraft carriers	Decrease of organizational errors	Heedful interrelating via (1) contribution (2) representation (3) subordination

[a] In fact, Weick has never used the label 'organizational learning' in his work. He *has* used concepts which may substitute for learning, such as: improvisation, interpretation, assimilation, variation, selection, heedful interrelation etc. Weick (1979, 1991) and Weick and Roberts (1993) take it for granted that some kind of memory for something is available, and they then try to understand what people do with it. Thereby, they seem to work farther downstream than do many scholars of learning.

(Duncan and Weiss, 1979), organizational theories-of-actions (Argyris and Schön, 1978), cognitive systems (Hedberg, 1981) or collective mind (Weick and Roberts, 1993). Still, none of these concepts relates processes and results, that is precisely which learning processes lead to which kind of knowledge remains unspecified. It seems as if the criterion of consistency is far from fulfilled.

Considering the second criterion, that of prescriptive vs. descriptive value, requires a closer look at the basic assumptions[2] theorists had in mind when formulating their theory of organizational learning. These can mostly be derived from their research tradition; sometimes they are even clearly explicated. For example, the meta-theoretical orientation of Argyris and Schön (1978) and March and Olsen (1975), as major representatives of organizational learning can be posited within the objectivist approach to social science, or more precisely, within the 'functionalist paradigm' as distinguished by Burrell and Morgan (1979).

It suffices to evoke the basics of meta-theory to remind us that this orientation is commonly associated with a positivist epistemology. Along these lines a normative/prescriptive approach to organizational learning is purported (for example, Argyris and Schön, 1978: 331). Other authors, such as, for instance, Weick and Roberts (1993), and Hedberg (1981), start from a completely different set of assumptions. Weick's approach can be best derived from his 1979 work on *The Social Psychology of Organizing* according to which he can be posited within the subjectivist approach to social science, or again in Burrell and Morgan's terms, the 'interpretive paradigm'. The major tenet of this approach is that reality is socially constructed, and that such constructions are not generalizable. Consequently, Weick (1987) argues later that, '[T]he search for one unifying theory that explains organized human behaviour is fruitless because there is no such theory' (Weick, 1987: 118). From this perspective, it follows that one should *describe* processes and results of organizational learning, rather than undertake a futile attempt at prescriptive generalization.

In a similar vein, Hedberg's approach incorporates some interpretive tendencies, though it also echoes ideas formulated by Cyert and March. But when Hedberg talks about stages where action takes place, it is the skilled accomplishment of human actors that 'constructs' the play. This is clearly in opposition to a meta-theoretical position based on objectivity. Not surprisingly, his action perspectives are formulated as guidelines rather than as tools for intervention (for a further explication, see the next section).

These few examples should suffice to show both the non-cumulativeness, and differentiated contributions of organizational learning theories as related to their underlying meta-theoretical orientation. However, it is not within the scope of this chapter to equalize these trends. In contrast, I propose that the search for an integrated theoretical approach to organizational learning may not be a 'good thing', and that it is more interesting to look at *criteria for judging* organizational learning theories. Referring to

Cameron and Whetten (1983), I thereby assume that 'judgements about [value] generally tell us more about judges' implicit theories than about a [theory] being judged' (Cameron and Whetten, 1983: 263). Perhaps, we should revisit our set of criteria, which has so far pretended the desirability of cumulativeness in organizational learning theory.

The main argument, which I want to explain in more detail in the following section is that those who criticize the non-cumulativeness in organizational learning implicitly take a modernist or positivist view on scientific research. A positivist view purports an objective approach to social sciences which rests upon the premise that society has a real, concrete existence outside of consciousness (Burrell and Morgan, 1979). Looking at the research programme in organizational learning, a modernist or positivist approach assumes the following (Addleson, 1996: 33):

- Problems are readily identifiable and there exist optimal solutions to all problems.
- Learning means discovering how things work, or finding the right way of doing something.
- Knowledge is finite and is capable of being itemized, even to the extent of determining when and how it is incomplete or deficient.
- The world operates according to definite principles.

In this sense, organizational learning should aim at identifying how the world works. The issue is how to find the right way to cope with a problem. Solving it requires using the right methodology, or discovering the appropriate connections, to reveal the true nature of the problem and its solution. This presumes that while organizational processes are hidden and may need to be revealed, they none the less pre-exist. Accordingly, a positivist view has implications for organizational learning theory which is required to represent this existing reality in a coherent, integrated and 'useful' manner.

The degree of 'usefulness' has also quite often been used as a criterion for the scientific value of theories, that is, a 'useful' theory is one which has 'clear implications for practice and application in some area of management or organizational functioning' (Miner, 1984: 297). Within the constraints of this last definition, researchers are often accused of producing 'useful' theories at the expense of scientific progress (Brief and Dukerich, 1991).

2 Theory building in organizational learning research – 'usefulness' versus 'practicality'?

In the preceding section I suggested that it is the quest for usefulness which impedes progress in theory development. To reiterate, 'usefulness' is defined as a theory's prescriptive value in terms of the degree to which it contains actionable solutions to 'real world' problems. But a theory's value, in terms of practical implications, can go well beyond the development and application of directly useful tools. For instance, research may be primarily explanatory so that the concern is to understand and explain managerial practice. The problem then is to understand and explain why particular events and actions occurred in the way they did with a view to identifing the underlying processes at work. Less significant is their impact on managerial activities and resultant improvement of present practices.

Following Brief and Dukerich (1991), I suggest extending this view of a theory's value, which shall be called 'practicality'. In contrast to mere usefulness, a theory's *practicality* lies in its ability to sensitize one to what *may be*, and not to predict firmly what *will be* (Gergen and Gergen, 1986). That is, theories can serve in applied settings as *lenses*, to help one to see things a little differently; they are not useful as prescribed courses of action to remedy applied problems.

These statements need some developing. Especially as research in organizational behaviour is often considered an 'applied' field, the term 'applied' seems to be synonymous with 'useful'. There seems to be a shared belief that science is essentially a method of producing and validating knowledge which can be applied to management in a straightforward way. But 'usefulness' as such may encounter some serious problems which stem from the uncritical and sometimes unconscious adoption of a particular position in the philosophy of science literature:

1 an epistemological and ontological stance incompatible with useful, or prescriptive theory;
2 the problem of objectivity in data generation and interpretation;
3 the impediment it implies for theory development because researchers focus on variables presumed to be manipulable by practitioners (Astley, 1984; Brief and Dukerich, 1991). In short, there may just be a problem with prescriptive theory and thus usefulness in organizational behaviour as well as in organizational learning.

Epistemological and ontological concerns with usefulness

The seemingly perennial concern with the limited practical relevance of most organization theories has more recently been joined by attacks on the epistemological pretentions of many writers. To follow, or contradict them requires some aquaintance with the philosophy-of-science literature. For instance, Burrel and Morgan (1979) dissect social science by means of the philosopher's tool-kit of ontology and epistemology. Epistemology refers to assumptions made about how managers accumulate knowledge and what the limits of that knowledge may be. Ontology refers to the assumptions being made about the primitive elements or components of reality that constitute the basic phenomenon of policy. It describes such matters as the choice of material objects, persons, organizations, minds, numbers and facts to be considered. As mentioned in section 1, criticisms concerning organizational learning derive from positivist epistemology which is often associated with the ontological premise of realism, though the relation between epistemology and ontology should not be easily convoluted.

A crude version of realism presumes that a proposition is true if and only if it corresponds with objective reality. There is an objective, independent world, which we experience directly; our theories are supposed to represent actually existing entities; they are true or false by virtue of corresponding to the real world. Then, of course, there can be but one coherent organizational learning theory. In this form, realism has rightly been subject to criticism. However, in recent years a more sophisticated version has developed (for example, Bhaskar, 1989). This new, or critical realism accepts the epistemological criticism that observations are theory-dependent and that we cannot have pure access to an independent world. Science can no longer be seen as creating true theories, but as proposing and identifying potential causal objects, the descriptions of which are at least approximately true. It follows that a realist perspective implies explanation but not necessarily prediction. This is important for the criterion of usefulness, since 'for a theory to be useful, its application must produce the intended results; if one were not able to predict the results of applying a theory in some finite, well-defined population at a given point in time and space, then it cannot be concluded that the theory is useful in that context' (Brief and Dukerich, 1991: 331).

A realist perspective suggests that prediction cannot be achieved, as scientific rules are socially constructed and fallible. Given the fallible nature of scientific enterprise, an extraction from theory of prescriptive statements that hold true across different settings is problematic. It follows that the criterion of usefulness in organizational learning research, which implies the idea of universal principles, strategies, or action perspectives, is debatable.

Concerns with data collection and generalizability

If a theoretical prescription has been observed to prevail in one or more situations, then questions arise regarding the generalizability of those findings. Generalizability is normally restricted due to reasons of divergence, for example, divergence of persons treated, different settings, or different historical circumstances. Although we may be alerted to the possibility of these potential interactions, the probability of these interaction effects is not certain when seeking to determine whether findings obtained in one situation cover other situations. Thus, the finding one seeks to generalize may be the product of unknown and unmeasured situational characteristics. This is also purported by open systems approaches, where the maintenance of dynamics rather than statics implies that relationships (between system and environment) are alterable (Katz and Kahn, 1978). What follows is that usefulness as a criterion for evaluating research would appear to be threatened by such failure to expect generalizability or by the inability to specify a priori that a prescription will suffice in any given context.

Obstructing theory development

Attempting to build a theory to serve the needs of managers has implications that may obstruct theory development. Such an obstruction may occur as a result of limiting the scientist's focus on the phenomenon to be explained. It is normally held that for useful theorizing, independent variables must be subject to control by the practitioner. However, this increases the likelihood of excluding potentially potent explanatory concepts which happen to lie beyond the control of managers. Dubin (1978) has observed that because managers are concerned with *what* needs to be changed to obtain a desired outcome, process knowledge is considered irrelevant. That is, *why* a variable as a given effect is rarely a managerial concern. Yet, this is exactly at the centre of scientific explanation. In catering to the needs of managers, theorists run the risk of constructing models which are sufficiently predictive of outcomes for managers, but supply precious little explanation.

It is for these three reasons that Brief and Dukerich (1991) suggested the concept of 'practicality' instead of 'usefulness'. This seems a promising avenue for organizational learning researchers. I will briefly outline the concept of practicality, and then move on to methodological devices such as metaphors and analogies that tend to support this 'new' way of theorizing.

Given the attack against prescriptive action perspectives, what does theory in organizational learning have to offer in terms of 'practicality'? In these terms organizational learning cannot, and does not need to provide 'useful' knowledge for practitioners. For managers, researchers fulfil a largely symbolic, rather than directly useful, function. At a mainly ideational level theorists offer managers ideas, which, though without direct instrumental or technical implications, crucially impact managerial practice indirectly, in their role as symbolic constructs. In a business setting managers need to interpret the significance of their own actions as well as those of others; they constantly attribute and derive meaning from their practical experience (Astley, 1984). It is even possible that 'non-problems may come to be seen as problems and vice versa; thereby the *agenda for what requires action* becomes redefined' (Weiss, 1977; emphasis added). Scientific research in organizational learning thus offers alternative realities for interpretations and outcomes as solutions to practitioner problems not yet defined.

Such a conception seems somewhat remote from daily experience, that is, organizational learning may be categorized as an 'experience-distant concept' (Geertz, 1973) that does not invite an understanding of everyday life. This is not necessarily the case, as the following example illustrates.

Hedberg (1981) presents several factors that influence organizational learning, for example, communication channels, level of confusion, resources, diversity of structure etc. Instead of deriving concrete action perspectives from the knowledge of these factors, he concentrates instead on the improvement of abstract (cognitive) skills such as experimenting, redesigning the environment, and regulating awareness. However, in emphasizing desired balances or 'organizational seesaws' he approaches the everyday thinking of managers (Hedberg, 1981: 22):

> Cooperation requires minimal consensus.
> Satisfaction rests upon minimal contentment.
> Wealth arises from minimal affluence.
> Goals merit minimal faith.
> Improvement depends upon minimal consistency.
> Wisdom demands minimal rationality.

This example (re-)emphasizes some alternative avenues by applying methodological (language) devices such as aphorisms, metaphors and analogies to scientific research. However, these same methodological devices have encountered some serious criticism. I propose that, especially in organizational learning research, metaphors and analogies can be quite helpful, if applied in a thoughtful and reflective way. The next section will concentrate on this aspect, thus referring to the last major point advanced by organizational learning critics (see again the introductory remarks to this chapter).

3 Towards 'practicality' in organizational learning research: promoting the use of metaphors and analogies

Broadly speaking, a metaphor is a statement that maintains that two phenomena have certain common properties. As Stern (1988) puts it, metaphorical language is a kind of connotative, figurative language, where each metaphor is 'literally impossible but imaginatively suggestive'. By using metaphors, knowledge from one discipline (usually referred to as the *source* or *base* domain) is transferred to the domain to be explained (referred to as the *target* domain) (Bunge, 1967; Vosniadou and Ortony, 1989). In scientific discourse, metaphors can provide significant insights about the mechanisms that produce observable phenomena. Morgan (1980) argued that the successful use of metaphor always involves a degree of creative invention because it is based on a selective comparison between the subjects involved; the metaphorical process emphasizes features of similarity while it suppresses features of dissimilarity between them. Others have argued that though metaphors are deemed as initially inevitable, eventually they are detrimental to theoretical development due to their imprecision and low conceptual content (Pinder and Bourgeois, 1982).

Metaphors have been dismissed as 'dispensable literary devices' (for example, Bunge, 1967; Pinder and Bourgeois, 1982) or even 'potential ideological distortions' (Tinker, 1986; Tinker and Lowe, 1982). However, in organizational learning research, metaphors play a significant role, and if applied in a critical way yield substantive potential for theory development.

Metaphors in organizational learning research

In looking at metaphors in organizational learning research, I follow the view of researchers like Weick (1979) and Morgan (1980, 1983) and consider metaphors as a 'way of thinking'. The underlying assumption is compatible with an anti-positivist approach, in that there is no independent reality waiting to be discovered by researchers; rather the social world is continually constituted by human beings through linguistic and symbolic means. Thus, the use of different metaphors does not simply imply literary illustrations, but moreover provides a basic structural form of experience through which human beings understand the world. In drawing attention to alternative conceptions of reality, metaphors liberate imagination and thereby encourage varied perspectives for understanding organizations. This is also helpful for practitioners if they can be persuaded to see the complexity of organizational life and the limits of traditional theorizing as regards organizational phenomena. The implication of such a view is that practitioners must be encouraged to develop the art of 'reading' social situations through the spectacles of a wide range of metaphors (Morgan, 1986; Tsoukas, 1993).

However, all perspectives on metaphors share a deficiency of adequate methodologies or tools to develop metaphorical insight into scientific knowledge. Not surprisingly, critics ask questions like: How are strengths and weaknesses of metaphors and analogies to be assessed? Are all metaphors equally useful? Do metaphors lend themselves to independent criticism, improvement, and refutation? *How* can metaphorical insights be transmuted into bodies of scientific knowledge? Drawing on cognitive science, and on Gentner's (1983) structure-mapping theory of analogy in particular, I will show that the development of metaphorical language has an enormous potential for scientific knowledge of organizational learning (see also Wiegand, 1996: 72–3). In this view, metaphors and analogies need not be implicit, arbitrarily subjective images, nor mere literary devices, 'but they can supply the raw material which, suitably processed, may yield scientific models and theories' (Tsoukas, 1991, 1993: 324). This implies a sound knowledge of different forms of metaphors and the transfer mechanisms of knowledge from one domain to another.

The structure-mapping theory of analogy

The structure-mapping theory, as developed by Gentner (1983, 1989), outlines the rules for mapping knowledge from a base discipline into a

Table 2.2 *Kinds of domain comparisons*

	Attributes	Relations	Examples
Analogy	Few	Many	Heat is like water
Abstraction	Few	Many	The atom is like our solar system
Anomaly	Few	Few	Coffee is like the solar system
Mere appearance	Many	Few	The glass table-top gleamed like water
Literal similarity	Many	Many	Milk is like water

Source: Gentner, 1983, 1989: 206

target discipline. Two mapping principles form the basic idea of this theory: (1) relational structures mapped to the target domain, and (2) object attributes transferred to the target domain. The occurrence of these principles determines whether we deal with an analogy or a literal similarity. These can be regarded as two extremes along the continuum of possible metaphors[3] (see Table 2.2; Tsoukas, 1993).

Analogical reasoning involves the transfer of an explanatory structure of relationships from a pre-existing domain to a target domain. Relations between objects rather than mere attributes are mapped. An *abstraction* is a 'comparison in which the base domain is an abstract relational structure' (Gentner, 1983: 159). The base domain contains only abstract principles and not concrete properties of the object. An abstraction shares with an analogy the transfer of a relational structure from the source to the target domain. It differs from an analogy and the other comparisons in possessing few object-attributes in the base domain as well as few object-attributes in the target domain. An *anomaly* is a comparison in which there is no overlap, of either object attributes or relationships. Mere appearance is a comparison in which only attributes are carried over from the source to the target domain. These matches are often limited in their explanatory potential because they go no further than physical appearances. A *literal similarity* is a comparison in which a large number of both object attributes and relations are transferred from the source to the target domain.

Summarizing the differences, an overlap in relations is necessary for any strong perception of similarity between two domains. Overlap in *both* attributes and relations is seen as literal similarity, while overlap in *relations* but not objects is seen as analogical relatedness. Overlap in attributes but not in relationships is seen as a mere appearance match. Finally, a comparison with neither attribute overlap nor relational overlap is simply an anomaly.

Most of the above-mentioned approaches of organizational learning focus on analogical domain comparisons (see Table 2.1). Examples that may sensitize the reader to this usage can be found in Cyert and March's (1963: 99ff.) description of organizational routines, in the later ideas of March and Olsen (1975) and Levitt and March (1988) that take the 'garbage can model' in behavioural decision-making as their starting point (cf. Cohen et al., 1972), and also in Hedberg's (1981: 6) description of similarities in information processing functions. Hedberg, for instance, supposes that knowledge about how human brains process and store information provides important insights into processes of organizational learning. In contrast to these analogical comparisons, we often find mere appearance comparisons or anomalies in the popular literature.

These few examples may sensitize the reader to the (seemingly unconscious) application of metaphors in organizational learning research. For further theory development it is useful to distinguish between different forms of metaphorical reasoning and keep in mind that especially anomaly and mere appearance comparisons provide only limited explanation, and would rightly face the criticism of pseudo-explanations of what organizational learning 'exactly' is.

4 Organizational learning theory – are we going anywhere?

In this chapter I have tried to meet three commonly expressed criticisms towards research in organizational learning:

1. Organizational learning lacks theoretical integration and research is being done in a non-cumulative way.
2. Organizational learning does not provide 'useful' knowledge for practitioners.
3. Organizational learning is mostly used in a metaphorical and/or analogous sense.

In presenting a couple of representative approaches to organizational learning it has become obvious that the concept is heterogeneously applied and researchers do not seem to agree on the basics. However, this criticism is subject to a certain meta-theoretical orientation, and I suggest that non-cumulativeness can also be interpreted as an indicator of theoretical progression. Judged from an anti-positivist view it is even 'normal' to have divergent perspectives, as there is no 'objective' world to be discovered. Rather, knowledge and truth are created by the researcher, not revealed by his mind. This emphasizes a pluralistic character of reality – *pluralistic* in the sense that reality is expressible in a variety of symbols and language systems. Contrary to common sense, there is no unique 'real world' that pre-exists, independent of human mental activity and human symbolic language.

It follows that a good theory can be judged to be more plausible and of higher quality if it is *interesting* rather than obvious, irrelevant or absurd, a source of unexpected connections, high in narrative rationality, and aesthetically pleasing (Weick, 1989) – criteria which differ from those applied to directly applicable approaches and results. The contribution of such constructions does not lie in the creation of validated knowledge, which could be the ultimate lever for managerial praxis. Focusing on 'practicality' instead of 'usefulness' conceives of language itself as the essential subject matter of scientific deliberation. The criterion of 'usefulness' may thus be unduly narrow because theorizing does not always yield a response to a problem, and the single criterion of a solution may fail to explain why a conjecture might be selectively retained in theorizing. The structure-mapping theory could provide a valuable method of meeting the third criticism of unreflected metaphorical use in organizational learning research. In this view, *even* 'language games' attain the status of desirable instruments of theory development (Astley and Zammuto, 1992). If research in organizational learning wants to maintain (or rather regain) a reflexive attitude, it may be helpful to look at organizational learning and organization practice as temporarily and sometimes necessarily 'decoupled realities' and consider theory development as a valuable effort in its own right (Astley, 1984).

Notes

1 Ample evidence for this continuing interest is also provided by the number of special issues devoted to organizational learning (e.g. *Organization Science*, 1991, 2 (1) and 2 (2); *Zeitschrift für Betriebswirtschaft*, 1995; *Accounting, Management & Information Technology*, 1995; *Journal of Organizational Change Management*, 1996; *Organization Studies*, 1996, with emphasis on managerial and organizational learning).

2 Most theories of organizational learning could probably be anchored within a meta-theoretic framework as, for instance, the well-known aproaches to organization studies as formulated by Burrell and Morgan (1979). In trying to anchor the selected approaches more precisely, a first statement concerning their expected contribution can be made.

3 I follow Gentner's (1989) suggestion and use 'metaphor' as the most general term under which analogies can be subsumed.

References

Addleson, M. (1996) Resolving the spirit and substance of organizational learning. *Journal of Organisational Change Management*, 9 (1): 32–41.

Argyris, C. (1964) *Integrating the Individual and the Organization*. New York: Wiley.

Argyris, C. and Schön, D.A. (1978) *Organizational Learning. a Theory of Action Perspective*. Reading, MA: Addison-Wesley.

Astley, W.G. (1984) Subjectivity, sophistry and symbolism in management science. *Journal of Management Studies*, 21 (3): 259–72.

Astley, W.G. and Zammuto, R.F. (1992) Organisation science, managers, and language games. *Organization Science*, 3: 443–61.

Bhaskar, R. (1989) *Recaliming Reality*. London.

Brief, A.P. and Dukerich, J.M. (1991) Theory in organisational behavior: can it be useful? In: B.M. Staw and L.L. Cummings (eds), *Research in Organizational Behavior*, Vol. 13. Greenwich, CT: JAI Press. pp. 327–52.

Bunge, M. (1967) *Scientific Research I+II*, Vol. 3. Heidelberg: Springer.

Burrell, G. and Morgan, G. (1979) *Sociological Paradigms and Organizational Analysis*. London: Heinemann.
Cameron, K.S. and Whetten, D.A. (eds) (1983) *Organizational Effectiveness: a Comparison of Multiple Methods*. New York: Academic Press.
Cangelosi, V. and Dill, W.R. (1965) Organizational learning. Observations toward a theory. *Administrative Science Quarterly*, 10 (2): 175–203.
Cohen, M.D., March, J.G. and Olsen, J.P. (1972) A garbage can model of organizational choice. *Administrative Science Quarterly*, 17 (1): 1–25.
Crossan, M. and Guatto, T. (1996) Organisational learning research profile. *Journal of Organisational Change Management*, 9 (1): 107–12.
Cyert, R. and March, J.G. (1963) *A Behavioral Theory of the Firm*. Englewood Cliffs, NJ: Prentice-Hall.
Dodgson, M. (1993) A review of some literatures. *Organization Studies*, 14 (3): 375–94.
Dubin, R. (1978) *Theory Development*. New York: The Free Press.
Duncan, R. and Weiss, A. (1979) Organisational learning: implications for organisational design. In: B.M. Staw and L.L. Cummings (eds), *Research in Organisational Behavior*, Vol. 1. Greenwich, CT: JAI Press. pp. 75–123.
Easterby-Smith, M. (1997) Disciplines of organizational learning: contributions and critiques. *Human Relations*, 50 (9): 1085–113.
Fiol, C.M. and Lyles, M.A. (1985) Organizational learning. *Academy of Management Review*, 10 (4): 803–13.
Garratt, B. (1987) *The Learning Organisation*. London: Fontana/Collins.
Garvin, D.A. (1993) Building a learning organisation. *Harvard Business Review*, 71 (4): 78–92.
Geertz, C. (1973) *The Interpretations of Cultures*. New York.
Gentner, D. (1983) Structure-mapping: a theoretical framework for analogy. *Cognitive Science*, 7: 155–70.
Gentner, D. (1989) The mechanisms of analogical reasoning. In: S. Vosniadou and A. Ortony (eds), *Similarity and Analogical Reasoning*. Cambridge: Cambridge University Press. pp. 199–241.
Gergen, K.J. and Gergen, M.M. (1986) *Social Psychology*, 2nd edn. New York.
Glynn, N.A., Lant, T.K. and Milliken, F.J. (1994) Mapping learning processes in organisations. In: C. Stubbard, J.R. Meindl and J.F. Porac (eds), *Advances in Managerial Cognition and Organisational Information Processing*. pp. 43–83.
Hedberg, B. (1981) How organizations learn and unlearn. In: W. Nyström and W. Starbuck (eds), *Handbook of Organizational Design*, Vol. 1. Oxford: Oxford University Press. pp. 3–37.
Huber, G.P. (1991) Organisational learning: the contributing processes and the literature. *Organization Science*, 2 (2): 88–115.
Jones, M. (1995) Organisational learning: collective mind or cognitivist metaphor? *Accounting, Management and Information Technology*, 5 (1): 61–77.
Katz, D. and Kahn, R.L. (1978) *The Social Psychology of Organisations*, 2nd edn. New York.
Lave, C. and March, J. (1975) *An Introduction to Models in the Social Sciences*. New York: Wiley.
Levitt, B. and March, J.G. (1988) Organisational learning. *Annual Review of Sociology*, 14: 319–40.
Mackenzie, K.D. (1994) The science of an organisation. Part I: A new model of organizational learning. *Human Systems Management*, 13: 249–58.
March, J.G. and Olsen, J.P. (1975) The uncertainty of the past: organisational learning under ambiguity. In: J.G. March (1988), *Decisions and Organisations*. Oxford: Blackwell. pp. 335–58.
McGuire, W.J. (1983) A contextualist theory of knowledge: its implications for

innovation and reform and psychological research. In: L. Berkowitz (ed.), *Advances in Experimental Social Psychology*. Orlando, FL: pp. 1–47.
Miller, D. (1996) A preliminary typology of organizational learning: synthesizing the literature. *Journal of Management*, 22 (3): 485–505.
Miner, A.S. and Mezias, S.J. (1996) Ugly ducking no more: past and futures of organisational learning research. *Organization Science*, 7 (1): 88–99.
Miner, J.B. (1984) The validity and usefulness of theories in an emerging organisational science. *Academy of Management Review*, 9: 296–306.
Mirvis, P.H. (1996) Historical foundation of organisational learning. *Journal of Organisational Change Management*, 9 (1): 13–31.
Morgan, G. (1980) Paradigms, metaphors, and puzzle solving in organization theory. *Administrative Science Quarterly*, 25: 605–22.
Morgan, G. (1983) More on metaphor: why we cannot control tropes in administrative science. *Administrative Science Quarterly*, 28: 601–7.
Morgan, G. (1986) *Images of Organisations*. Newbury Park, CA: Sage.
Pinder, C.C. and Bourgeois, W.V. (1982) Controlling tropes in administrative science. *Administrative Science Quarterly*, 27 (4): 641–53.
Prange, C. (1996) Interorganisationales Lernen: Lernen in, von und zwischen Organisationen. In: G. Schreyögg and P. Conrad (eds), *Managementforschung* 6. Berlin, New York: Springer-Verlag. pp. 163–89.
Probst, G. and Büchel, B. (1994) *Organisationales Lernen*. Wiesbaden: Gabler.
Reinhardt, R. (1993) *Das Modell organisationaler Lernfähigkeit und die Gestaltung lernfähiger Organisationen*. Frankfurt u.a.:.
Rosenthal, R. (1966) *Experimenter Effects in Behavioral Research*. New York: Appleton-Century-Crofts.
Starbuck, W.H. (1992) Learning by knowledge-intensive firms. *Journal of Management Studies*, 29 (6): 713–40.
Stern, B. (1988) Medieval allegory: roots of advertising strategy for the mass market. *Journal of Marketing*, 52: 84–94.
Tenkasi, R.V. and Boland, R.J. (1996) Exploring knowledge diversity in knowledge-intensive firms: a new role for information systems. *Journal of Organisational Change Management*, 9 (1): 79–91.
Thatchenkery, T.J. (1996) Editorial to the special issues on 'Organizational Learning: Past, Present, Future'. *Journal of Organisational Change Management*, 4–9.
Tinker, T. (1986) Metaphor or reification: are radical humanists really libertarian anarchists? *Journal of Management Studies*, 23 (4): 363–84.
Tinker, T. and Lowe, T. (1982) The management science of management sciences. *Human Relations*, 35 (4): 331–47.
Tsoukas, H. (1991) The missing link: a transformational view of metaphors in organizational science. *Academy of Management Review*, 16 (3): 566–85.
Tsoukas, H. (1993) Analogical reasoning and knowledge generation in organisation theory. *Organization Studies*, 14 (3): 323–46.
von Krogh, G. and Venzin, M. (1995) Anhaltende Wettbewerbsvorteile durch Wissensmanagement. *Die Unternehmung*, 6: 417–36.
Vosniadou, S. and Ortony, A. (1989) *Similarity and Analogical Reasoning*. Cambridge: Cambridge University Press.
Webb, W.B. (1961) The choice of the problem. *American Psychologist*, 16: 223–7.
Weick, K.E. (1979) *The Social Psychology of Organizing*, 2nd edn. Reading, MA: Random House.
Weick, K.E. (1987) Theorizing about organizational communication. In: F.M. Jablin et al. (eds), *Handbook of Organizational Communication*. Newbury Park, CA: Sage. pp. 97–122.
Weick, K.E. (1989) Theory construction as disciplined imagination. *Academy of Management Review*, 14: 516–31.

Weick, K.E. (1991) The non-traditional quality of organizational learning. *Organization Science*, 2 (1): 116–24.
Weick, K.E. and Roberts, K.H. (1993) Collective mind in organizations: heedful interrelating on flight decks. *Administrative Science Quarterly*, 38/3: 357–81.
Weiss, C.H. (ed.) (1977) *Using Social Research in Public Policy Making*. Lexington, MA
Whetten, D.A. (1989) What constitutes a theoretical contribution? *Academy of Management Review*, 14 (4): 490–5.
Wiegand, M. (1996) *Prozesse Organisationalen Lernens*. Wiesbaden: Gabler.

3 Organizational Learning as the Development of Stories: Canons, Apocrypha and Pious Myths

David Sims

This chapter offers a model of organizational learning from the perspective of narrative research. The term 'organization' has been regularly problematized from textbooks upwards over recent years (for example, Hatch, 1997; Sims et al., 1993). There has also been considerable discussion about the meaning of learning. In the narrative spirit, this chapter does not enter into propositional debate, but rather offers another way of telling the story of what happens in organizational learning which may be enlightening and engaging, rather than being presented as a superior story; compelling, I hope, but not compulsory.

Learning has been defined within the behaviourist tradition as a change in behaviour, whether or not memory was affected (Drever, 1952). However, for a meaning that makes sense in the post-behaviourist environment of endeavours in organizational learning it is better thought of as the creation of, or a change in, memory. This chapter considers what we mean by organizational memory, and what that might tell us about organizational learning. It then proposes a narrative approach to further investigation and categorization of organizational memory. It argues that organizational memory is best understood by examining the stories and myths of which it consists and by which it is created, developed and sustained.

In more detail, the chapter begins by exploring briefly the nature of organizational memory, and some of the disparate and occasionally desperate attempts that have been made to imbue the concept with meaning. It goes on to consider the place of stories in organizations, particularly as they relate to memory. It discusses the significance of stories not being static, but changing and developing, and the effect this has on the way that stories function in organizational memory. It then takes the notion of a canon of stories, such as the canon of stories that are given official acceptance in the scriptures of a religion, and juxtaposes this with the lived experience of organizational learning. Over time, faith communities have recognized certain books as canonical, part of an authentic and authoritative corpus, while ruling others out from inclusion in the main body of scriptures. Canon is defined (among other things) in the Collins Electronic Dictionary as 'a list of writings, esp. sacred writings, officially recognized as genuine'. As well as a canon, there is sometimes an apocrypha, which in the Jewish and Christian traditions means a collection of writings which are not regarded as fully within the canon but are also not completely ruled out. In addition, most bodies of writing also have a number of stories which are given no official recognition but are also not placed on any official 'index' of disapproved stories. Such examples of 'pious myths' often come to be incorporated in at least semi-official thought at a later stage.

The nature of organizational memory

Discussions of organizational memory have often been framed within thoroughly mechanistic views of memory and its changes, and even within those frameworks have not been very satisfactory. Thus Huber (1996) says, 'Organizational memory, as a determinant of organizational learning and decision making, was found to be much in need of systematic investigation' (p. 151).

Both Huber (1996) and Levitt and March (1996) mention some of the artifacts that carry organizational memory, including the accounting system. The notion that different people may remember things differently is so core to current views of organization that any view of memory which cannot handle this is unlikely to be in any way helpful. Levitt and March handle inconsistency in organizational memory as follows:

> Experiential knowledge, whether in tacit form or in formal rules, is recorded in an organizational memory. That memory is orderly, but it exhibits inconsistencies and ambiguities. Some of the contradictions are a consequence of inherent complications in maintaining consistency in inferences drawn sequentially from a changing experience. Some, however, reflect differences in experience, the confusions of history, and conflicting interpretations of that history. These latter inconsistencies are likely to be organized into deviant memories, maintained by subcultures, subgroups and subunits. (p. 527)

The word 'deviant' in this quotation seems to posit something to deviate from, where it might be better to think of organizations consisting only of different subcultures, with no culture being widespread or official enough for a departure to count as official deviance. However, Levitt and March describe well the kind of memory we are interested in here – the kind that exhibits inconsistencies and ambiguities – rather than memories with a clear and indisputable aura. Whether there are any memories with such indisputable clarity is of course questionable; few participants in interdepartmental budget meetings seem content to accept others' interpretations of financial accounts as consistent and unambiguous. However, most interesting to us in this quotation is the notion of orderly memory, which will correspond roughly with a memory that is founded on the canon of stories in the organization, while deviant memories are maintained by subcultures with apocryphal stories, or by smaller subgroups with pious myths.

Before I develop this further, we need to consider more fully the reasons for entertaining a narrative or storytelling view of organizations. Cook and Yanow (1993) point out that the knowledge to undertake a highly skilled operation in an organization 'resides not in any one individual, but in the organization as a whole. The organization was not "born" with that knowledge; it had to learn it' (p. 381). There is no reason to speak about organizational memory as a fixed quality. It has to be developed and sustained by some active principle. In the next section I will explain why I think that storytelling is the means by which such memories are conveyed, maintained and developed in organizations.

Stories in organizations

Harré and Secord (1972) proposed an 'anthropomorphic model' of persons – that we should consider people, purely for scientific purposes, as if they were human beings as we know them. Much of what Harré and Secord commended has now become part of the repertoire of the social sciences, but one of the features of human beings as we know them has only started receiving widespread attention in the last few years, and that is the aspect of human beings as *storytellers*, as weavers of narrative. The notion has been well summarized by Christie and Orton (1988), in casting human beings as '*homo narrans narratur*' – both storytellers and the objects of storytelling. In this chapter I am both claiming that people in organizations are habitual storytellers, and casting them as actors in a story that I am telling about them. Boland and Tenkasi (1995) say:

> The importance of narrative has not gone unnoticed in organizational research. . . . Myth and saga are important, but they can distract our attention from the way that human cognition operates almost continuously in a narrative, storytelling mode. (p. 357)

How wide is the scope of a narrative study of social life? Some authors have almost boundless ambition for it. For example, Hardy says:

> We dream in narrative, daydream in narrative, remember, anticipate, hope, despair, believe, doubt, plan, revise, criticise, construct, gossip, learn, hate and love by narrative. (1968: 5)

Similarly bold claims are made for narrative by Proust, as recounted by Widdershoven (1993). Proust

> describes a visit to the theater, where Berma performs *Phèdre* (Proust, 1919). The narrator tells us how he tries to retain each utterance and each expression of Berma, in order to be able to remember the experience fully. In this, however, he does not succeed. In fact, his ongoing efforts to capture the present cause him to see hardly anything. His first feeling of admiration is aroused by the applause of the public. It is only later, when he reads the report in the newspaper, that he becomes truly convinced of the qualities of the performance. The narrator describes how the story in the newspaper fuses with his own experience, and adds something to it, so that his admiration grows, resulting in the exclamation: 'What a fabulous artist!' He then notices that this may seem not very honest, because the experience in the theater was not nearly as positive as his judgment after reading the critics. He warns the reader, however, not to draw the conclusion of dishonesty too easily. Our stories about what we have experienced are always influenced by those of others, the narrator says, and we derive much of the strength of our most personal ideas from familiar ideas in other persons. (pp. 6–7)

This example is used by Widdershoven to argue that 'experiences have little value as long as they are not connected to, or as Proust says, fused with stories' (pp. 6–7).

While it may be unhelpful to insist that everything is narrative, it may be less problematic to say that everything that we can remember is cast in narrative form, that narrative *is* sense-making and vice versa. As Weick (1995) puts it:

> The requirements necessary to produce a good narrative provide a plausible frame for sensemaking. Stories posit a history for an outcome. They gather strands of experience into a plot that produces that outcome. The plot follows either the sequence beginning–middle–end or the sequence situation–transformation–situation. But sequence is the source of sense. (p. 128)

This may help us also to make sense of notions such as identity. As Funkenstein (1993) puts it: 'The identity of an individual and the identity of a group consists of the construction of a narrative, internal and external' (p. 23). Funkenstein's argument is that one of the legacies of the holocaust is the impossibility of constructing a narrative of the Jewish role in it, that the death camps dehumanized people even in their own eyes, as demonstrated by the very fragmented memories that survivors seem to have. These fragmented memories are seen by Funkenstein as the inevitable consequence of loss of narrative:

> The Nazis robbed them of their identity, of their capacity to construct a narrative, of investing the events of their lives with meaning and purpose. (p. 24)

So, not only is memory carried through stories and narrative, but also there is nothing to remember unless people have constructed a narrative and thus gained meaning and purpose. Boje (1994) says:

> Storytelling is a collective dynamic that scripts, sways and disciplines organizational learning. . . . People do not just freely and openly engage in storytelling; they temper their storytelling, to present only a few sides of a discussion or a few voices in the governance of the enterprise. . . . Organizational learning is constituted by storytelling. (p. 435)

Bruner (1986) recognizes a larger place for non-narrative statements. He says that 'a good story and a well-formed argument are different natural kinds' (p. 11); they have fundamentally different ways of convincing people: 'arguments convince one of their truth, stories of their lifelikeness' (p. 11). When he goes on to show some of the properties of narrative, however, he comes up with notions such as Rorty's concept of 'how we come to endow experience with meaning, which is the question that preoccupies the poet and the storyteller' (p. 12), or Joyce's view of the particularities of the story as 'epiphanies of the ordinary' (p. 13). It is interesting to note the similarity of these notions to Kelly's view of the activity of the scientist (Kelly, 1955), whose activity is very much to do with endowing experience with meaning. It therefore seems to me that Bruner may have conceded that argument and story are different in kind too easily. Perhaps argument may be conducted in a propositional fashion, but for the argument to become memorable it needs to be converted into narrative. As Cook and Yanow (1993) put it:

> No one says during the course of a typical working day, for example, 'Powell values its identity as producer of the flutes with a particular feel to the mechanism.' Rather, that part of Powell's culture is incorporated into the artifacts of daily life in the organization. It is reflected, for example, in the company's stories and myths . . . (p. 384)

It is essentially the activity of the textbook to tell memorable stories that encapsulate the propositions of the theorists (Ritti and Funkhouser, 1982; Sims et al., 1993, or for a classic example of meaning being conveyed by stories, Peters and Waterman, 1982; citations of the latter may also use their propositional labels, but usually quote the exemplifying story too). But it is also an essential part of how the scientist or other technical expert handles complexity; propositions can only be remembered a few at a time, but when they are built up into stories, far more propositions can be handled together. An accountant faced with a balance sheet can describe propositionally a few items to be seen there. They will often not stop at that, however, but will use the balance sheet as a script for a story of how a particular year has been for a company. Birts et al. (1997) show a similar thing happening with financial managers looking at data about different types of organization. Before long, they are away from dry propositions and into the constructing of narrative.

O'Connor (1997) summarizes this particularly well:

> To discover how anything happens in an organization, we ask people to tell us stories. To convince others that we know something about how things happen in

organizations, we construct and tell stories about those stories. As others react to our stories, they tell stories about the stories we have told – and so on. (p. 304)

Elmes and Kasouf (1995), in what they describe as a 'science narrative perspective', come to a similar view in summarizing how organizational learning is itself best seen as a narrative or story:

> In our analysis of how biotechnology workers characterized organizational learning, we discovered two contrasting and, we believe, competing narratives: (a) learning as a process of rational, scientific inquiry and action to identify and develop effective new products and (b) learning for the purpose of survival in a hostile economic and regulatory climate. (p. 418)

The development of stories

As O'Connor says above, stories are not simply told by one person to another. They are also one of the ways in which we talk to ourselves, in which we shape and retain events for ourselves. Indeed, the role that we give ourselves within the stories is one of the means by which we construct ourselves. As MacIntyre puts it: 'I can only answer the question "What am I to do?" if I can answer the prior question, "Of what story or stories do I find myself a part?"' (1981: 216).

In several different perspectives on the person, the role of internal dialogue (also known as talking to yourself) is important. Bruner (1990) talks about it with respect to young children:

> Why do any of us talk to ourselves? And why especially a young child . . .? John Dewey proposed that language provides a way of sorting out our thoughts about the world. . . . About a quarter of [Emily's] soliloquies were straightforward narrative accounts; autobiographical narratives about what she had been doing or what she thought she would be up to tomorrow. Listening to the tapes and reading the transcripts repeatedly, we were struck by the *constitutive* function of her monologic narrative. She was not simply reporting; she was trying to make sense of her everyday life. She seemed to be in search of an integral structure that could encompass what she had *done* with what she *felt* with what she *believed.* (pp. 88–9)

Here too the role of narrative in helping us to remember something complicated enough to be worth remembering is important. Boland and Tenkasi (1995) summarize Bruner's argument: 'We narrativize our experience almost continually as we recognize unusual or unexpected events (the noncanonical) and construct stories which make sense of them (restore canonicality) (p. 353). Bruner (1990) summarizes the argument of Pea and Kurland (1984) and Perkins (1990) thus:

> A 'person's' knowledge is not *just* in one's own head, in 'person solo,' but in the notes that one has put into accessible notebooks, in the books with underlined passages on one's shelves, in the handbooks one has learned how to consult, in the information sources one has hitched up to the computer, in the friends one can call up to get a reference or a 'steer,' and so on almost endlessly. All of these, as Perkins points out, are parts of the knowledge flow of which one has become a part. And that flow even includes those highly conventionalized forms of rhetoric that we use for justifying and explaining what we are doing, each tailored to and 'scaffolded' by the occasion of use. (p. 106)

Bruner's comment is of particular interest in our context because many of the features he is talking about take knowledge outside the individual, and give it characteristics much closer to organizational than to individual learning. The rhetoric to which he refers is not simply a remembering and piecing together activity. It has more creative content than that. As Boland and Tenkasi (1995) put it:

> Narrative, by making the implicit and the tacit inferable to the reader or the listener, is a critically important first step in achieving perspective taking within and among communities of knowing. (p. 367)

Gardner (1993) argues that this is one of the chief differences to be found in cognitive studies between the time of the first edition of his book (Gardner, 1984) and the second. Cognition was no longer seen as being predominantly within the skull. One of the ways in which people organize this distributed knowledge for themselves is in stories. Listen to Bruner (1990) again, this time summarizing Spence (1984):

> Spence addressed the question of whether a patient in analysis *recovered* the past from memory in the sense in which an archeologist digs up artifacts of a buried civilization, or whether, rather, analysis enabled one to *create* a new narrative that, though it might be only a screen memory or even a fiction, was still close enough to the real thing to start a reconstructive process going. The 'truth' that mattered, so went his argument, was not the historical truth but the *narrative* truth. (1990: 111)

Other views of the importance of what we say to ourselves stress the importance of narrative fragments. Ellis (1962), in his 'rational-emotional therapy', stresses the importance of internal sentences, and the efficacy of change and development by manipulating these sentences. He argues, for example, that it is virtually impossible to sustain an emotion without the use of some kind of internal sentence. Anger is transitory, unless it can be sustained by some sentence along the lines of 'she should not have said that to me', or 'that is totally unjust'. The power of Ellis' argument lies in the narrative in which such sentences are embedded; 'she should not have said that to me' because of the plot structure that I place on a particular situation, the character that I assign to myself and to her within that plot, and so on; 'that is totally unjust' requires a narrative framework in order for the injustice to be felt, and will only take on meaning within a narrative. When I tell anyone else about why 'she should not have said that to me', or why 'that is totally unjust', I will always do so in the context of a story, spoken or assumed, which I believe supports my view of the wrongdoings of others involved. I will explain who I take her and myself, or the parties to the injustice, to be within this story. Otherwise it would not make sense to say that she should not have said what she did or to complain of the injustice.

Nor are such stories told in isolation. The notion that Bruner and Gardner have both developed of the physical distribution of knowledge is matched by a social distribution in story telling. Boje (1991) has given a cogent account of this, exemplifying how stories in organizations often have multiple authors, as different members pick up the story, pass it on to another, embroider parts of it, and make assumptions about the extent to which others of their colleagues will already have heard parts of the story or of another related story.

The development of a canon

To develop the metaphor of a canon, let us take the case of the Old Testament, the Jewish Scriptures. Here we find that the notion of a canon is less fixed and agreed than might at first be supposed. Barr (1983) says that the usual view is that the three sections of the Old Testament were canonized in the same order as they were written; the Torah was settled first, about the fifth century BC, then the Prophets by about 200 BC, and finally the Writings, which may well not have been fixed until Christianity was on the scene. Barr also points out that the difference of sequence can be taken to correspond to a widely accepted difference in the perceived importance of the different sections, with the Torah very much preponderant among the scriptures; the longer something is believed to have had canonical status, the higher that status becomes.

Also of considerable interest is the process that Barr describes by which a list of books comes to be seen as the 'canon'. The way this happened was different for the three sections, and in all cases less formalized than the corresponding and much later process for the New Testament.

> The Old Testament materials were a national literature, much of it known and recognized throughout the nation from an early time. The existence of parallel-running books covering the same ground, which was central to the growth of the idea of a canonical group of four gospels, was probably of little importance. (Barr, 1983: 51)

Metzger and Coogan (1993) discuss how books came into the biblical canon:

> Many factors contributed to the recognition of certain books as canonical; among them are the following; the tradition that many of the books came from Moses or one of the other acknowledged prophets; the spiritual authority of the books themselves, as it was experienced in public or private reading, and in exposition; the fact that the books had come to be laid up in the Temple as sacred; the opinions of religious leaders and the common convictions of the people about the books. (p. 100)

The process is more complex and interesting than I am giving it credit for. Different Jewish communities may have had different canons; for example, the Septuagint (as adopted for the Old Testament of the Christian Church) may be based on the Alexandrian canon of the Egyptian Jewish community. But this is to take the metaphor too far. More fruitful would be to consider the way in which people treat their canons – from fundamentalist reverence to liberal critical questioning. So let us take the criteria that Metzger and Coogan use for why scriptures become canonical, and apply them to stories in organizations. In summary, they find the criteria for canonical status to be:

1 Authoritative source (in their case Moses).
2 Experiential authority (in their case spiritual).
3 The physical placing of the books (in their case, the Temple).
4 The view of leaders and other people.

The development of an apocrypha

Canons, as has been pointed out above, are not necessarily stable over the very long term – though they are often presented as if they were. However, while we might accept that some of the stories that constitute the memory of an organization can reasonably be seen as a canon, this is clearly not true for all. In some cases the fluidity and the number of different tellers and authority figures involved in an organization mean that stories may receive a considerable degree of telling and retelling without canon being an appropriate metaphor for the multiplicity of different views and voices involved in storytelling and thus memory preservation in organizations.

Canons can be enriched (or undermined, depending on your point of view) by apocrypha, other writings that are regarded as valuable by some while not receiving the full weight of canonical support. This may be seen as extending the process described by Barr (1983) and outlined above, whereby different scriptures are given different canonical weight, so that apocryphal scriptures are simply given a little less weight again than the lightest layer of canonical scripture. Alternatively, they are given equal weight but by a subgroup or subculture within the organization. Thus, while we might see an organizational story about how the founder started the business in a garage, or the managing director took no salary during a recession, as meeting all the requirements above for a canonical story, the story about how the human resources director turned up drunk to a board meeting, or the finance director was refused a credit card, are more likely to have good currency in some parts of the organization and not others. They thus become apocryphal.

Such apocryphal stories face us up to a problem with the term 'organizational learning'; the learning which such stories represent is not held in the same way as it is for the stories that are fully in the organizational canon, and nor are these stories as widely shared in the organization. They enter the memory of a part of the organization, and with a different kind of authority. Like gossip (Sims, 1993, Dalton, 1993) they may not be seen as completely trustworthy, but may none the less be told with great zest and may have an impact on how people behave towards each other.

Pious myths

The third type of metaphor we are considering in this chapter is that of 'pious myths'. As well as stories that form into a solid canon of organizational storytelling, and others that do not have that canonical status but none the less take a position of some status in an apocrypha, there are also other stories that are told, retold, developed and forgotten in organizations that do not fit either of these categories. These stories seem to come and go, and not to become a long-term part of the way that members understand the organization. It is possible to conceive, for example, of fashions in stories, so that a particular kind of story becomes more or less fashionable at some historical juncture (the popularity of cock-up stories has been noted in the UK of the 1990s by Fineman and Gabriel, 1996). The kind of stories that British children were told in Victorian times to teach them what was good thought and behaviour are now regarded as hilarious collectors items (on the lines of 'masturbation makes you go blind'). Is such a change in fashion easier to understand if we take it that there is no canon of stories, but simply a lively interacting cacophony of pious myths? Is the continuous interplay more importantly fluid than continuous?

The metaphor that we are using here recognizes that most religious systems develop a number of stories that may never receive official sanction but also attract little disapproval, being regarded as healthy myths, whether or not they have any historical basis. Sometimes these myths can survive for very long times and appear to have official approval, while never being encoded in a canonical scripture. Almost all the traditions surrounding the Christian Christmas would fit this category, and it is an instructive parallel because while some of the stories have remained fixed over time, other stories can be traced to pre-Christian traditions (for example, Yuletide), or have moved from one culture to another with adaptation (Santa Claus/St Nicholas). Other such myths receive official sanction without ever being fully accepted into the canon (for example, for Catholics the Immaculate Conception of the Blessed Virgin Mary).

In organizations, these stories are told for the wide mixture of reasons that characterizes other arenas too – for entertainment, for instruction, for inculturation, for managing the impression of the storyteller and the relationship with the listener. Their messages can range from the frankly manipulative (staying late to finish off your work for me will be noticed by higher management), through the cautionary (no one ever got on here by seeming cleverer than their boss), to the canonical-in-waiting (they always look after you in trouble).

Canons, apocrypha and myths in organizational learning

Now that we have considered the place of stories in organizational learning and memory, and the nature of those stories as canonical, apocryphal or mythological, does this help us understand more about organizational learning? To answer this, let us go back to Metzger and Coogan's list of characteristics of canonical writings, and consider in a little more detail whether the lived experience of organizations fits them.

Authoritative source Do the stories that circulate in organizations show signs of being affected by authoritative sources? There can be little question that they do. Often these will be in the form of founder myths (Randall and Southgate, 1980), whereby stories about the beliefs and principles of the founder going on having a powerful effect on their successors well after the founder's death. There are companies, for example, whose central training facilities are governed by the anti-alcohol views of their long dead founders. In most cases no legal covenant is involved, but a number of stories are to be found in circulation about the views of the founder, and these are honoured in regulations that affect current behaviour.

There is also undeniable power in being told that a story came from a powerful source. For example, a story about what happened at the trade show which is attributed to the marketing director is likely to carry more weight than if it is attributed to a little known subordinate. The story about the forthcoming office move is going to be treated quite differently according to the believed source. An authoritative source is often helpful to a story in gaining currency in an organization. Stories get attributed to senior or charismatic figures. This is often thought of as name dropping, but may have the function not only of demonstrating a link between the speaker and some powerful figure, but also of giving authority to the story.

But does this apply to the elements of organizational memory? Let us take, for example, the story that seems to exist in most organizations in some variant, about the week when the company made 100 people redundant 'because of the need to save money' and the new office furniture turned up. Such stories are persistent enough that they may be seen as an important part of organizational memory. But do they come from an authoritative source? In most cases I would suggest that if they do this is not reported as part of the story, and that therefore the aspect of stories that carries memory and thus constitutes the content of organizational learning does not behave in a canonical way so much as in an apocryphal one. That kind of story may also be seen as the property of a disaffected group in the organization. For example, it is sometimes found among the longer serving members of an organization that has been taken over, to illustrate the foolishness of their new masters – a classic apocryphal situation.

By contrast, myths are very rarely attributed to an authoritative source, and are beginning to be converted to apocryphal or canonical status if they are.

Experiential authority Do stories persist because they are experienced as authoritative, as good sense-making devices, because they ring true? They make good sense, and this gives them experiential authority. This surely is precisely why many stories persist so well. There is a range of stories that are told to new recruits to an organization to help them understand what is going on, and to give them the background they are thought to need to lead their organizational lives, or to give them the perspective that the storyteller would like them to have. The mixture of motives is slightly more complex here than in the scriptural example; as we said above, stories are told for the purpose of putting the teller in the role of wise expert, entertainer, or well-informed insider, as well as simply because of experiential authority. They are not necessarily believed by the listeners, but they are remembered – all the more, the more bizarre features the teller includes – and in turn duly passed on to another generation of recruits. The qualities that make a story memorable and fit for retelling include experiential authority, but not necessarily as one of the more dominant qualities. A story may persist just as strongly on the basis of certain bizarre features, or even because it does not seem to fit very well with canonical stories. Perhaps this is more like the apocryphal than the canonical model.

This may understate the role of the story in organizational learning, however. Experiential authority is the key quality for successful and long-lasting myths. Thus in organizational learning, experiential authority may function mostly to keep a story current long enough for it to develop apocryphal or even canonical status.

The physical placing of the books Physical placing as a means of giving canonical status may best be seen in stories that reach the company newsletter, although at an organizational level there is the ironic counter-finding that people are more likely to believe communications that they think they have accidentally overheard than ones that have been deliberately made to them. Perhaps the physical placing of a conversation in a lift might give it more credibility, though less canonical status, than the newsletter. Items from the newsletter may also lack the crucial quality of memorability. Try to think of a few stories from the newsletter of your own organization that you can remember and that you think of as influencing the organizational learning. If you cannot think of any, that makes the point that physical placing may give canonical status to organizational stories, but those that become canonical by this means do not get remembered.

The view of leaders and other people Each of the above qualities of a canon is mediated by the views of leaders and other people, which are inseparable from the first three sources of canonicity. The acceptance of stories as canonical is a social and distributed process, and not merely a matter of individual definition. The question is, which leaders? If a story is given credence by the most senior leaders in the formal structure, and in public fora (for example, it is published in the annual report, or in an official company history) it is canonical.

Many of the more interesting stories, however, circulate on the basis of a lower level of official support. They may be the account that one senior individual gives of an event – the slightly disaffected marketing director's story of what happened in the board meeting, for example. This would be organizational learning at the apocryphal level.

Stories do not survive without the support of some people other than the teller. So this aspect of being canonical is always present. But it is quite possible for a story to have considerable impact on the organizational memory without official sanction from the top, as an apocryphal story, or without any weight of acknowledged support from highly placed figures, in which case we are in the realm of myths.

Conclusion

This chapter has argued that learning, by individuals or organizations, is a matter of change in memory. Memory is retained not so much in propositions as in stories. The more complicated the memory, the more essential is a story to the retention of the memory. Stories are a main currency of organizational life. Stories develop and change over time, as does the canon of stories which are told and retold in an organization. We will find this change in the stories that are told a particularly fruitful area for hearing and understanding both the content and the process of organizational learning.

We have used a typology of canon, apocrypha and pious myth to describe different kinds of stories in organizations, and to understand their relationship to organizational learning. Stories carry organizational memory, and the development of stories constitutes organizational learning. Canons, apocrypha and pious myths all have some value as models of the way that stories operate in organizational learning. To understand the likely organizational learning to be gained from a story, we might wish to consider which of those three types it fits. We might also want to consider those organizations that appear to learn the wrong lesson from stories (Locke, 1996), and ask what might be done to help organizations consider the process of attributing or denying canonical status.

References

Barr, J. (1983) *Holy Scripture: Canon, Authority, Criticism.* Oxford: Oxford University Press.

Birts, A., McAulay, L., Pitt, M., Saren, M and Sims, D. (1997) The expertise of finance and accountancy: an interdisciplinary study. *British Journal of Management*, 8: 75–83.

Boje, D. (1991) The storytelling organization: a study of story performance in an office-supply firm. *Administrative Science Quarterly*, 36: 106–26.

Boje, D. (1994) Organizational storytelling: the struggles of pre-modern, modern and postmodern organizational learning discourses. *Management Learning*, 25 (3): 433–61.

Boland, R.J. and Tenkasi, R.V. (1995) Perspective making and perspective taking in communities of knowing. *Organization Science*, 6 (4): 351–72.

Bruner, J. (1986) *Actual Minds, Possible Worlds.* Cambridge, MA: Harvard University Press.

Bruner, J. (1990) *Acts of Meaning.* Cambridge, MA: Harvard University Press.

Christie, J.R.R. and Orton, F. (1988) Writing a text on the life. *Art History*, 11 (4): 543–63.

Cook, S.D.D. and Yanow, D. (1993) Culture and organizational learning. *Journal of Management Inquiry*, 2 (4): 373–90.

Dalton, K. (1993) The performance of narrative and self in conversational storytelling. Unpublished PhD Thesis, University of Bath.

Drever, J. (1952) *A Dictionary of Psychology.* Harmondsworth: Penguin.

Ellis, A. (1962) *Reason and Emotion in Psychotherapy.* New York: Lyle Stuart.

Elmes, M.B. and Kasouf, C.J. (1995) Knowledge workers and organizational learning: narratives from biotechnology. *Management Learning*, 26 (4): 403–22.

Fineman, S. and Gabriel, Y. (1996) *Experiencing Organizations.* London: Sage.

Funkenstein, A. (1993) The incomprehensible catastrophe: memory and narrative. In: R. Josselson and A. Lieblich (eds), *The Narrative Study of Lives.* London: Sage. pp. 21–9.

Gardner, H. (1984) *Frames of Mind.* London: Heinemann.

Gardner, H. (1993) *Frames of Mind: the Theory of Multiple Intelligences*, 2nd edn. London: Fontana.

Hardy, B. (1968) Towards a poetics of fiction: an approach through narrative. *Novel*, 2: 5–14.

Harré, R. and Secord, P.F. (1972) *The Explanation of Social Behaviour.* Oxford: Blackwell.

Hatch, M.J. (1997) *Organization Theory: Modern, Symbolic and Postmodern Perspectives.* Oxford: Oxford University Press.

Huber, G.P. (1996) Organizational learning: the contributing processes and the literatures. In: M.D. Cohen and L.S. Sproull (eds), *Organizational Learning.* Thousand Oaks, CA: Sage. pp. 124–62.

Kelly, G. (1955) *A Theory of Personality*, Vols 1 and 2. New York: Norton.

Levitt, B. and March, J. (1996) Organizational learning. In: M.D. Cohen and L.S. Sproull (eds), *Organizational Learning.* Thousand Oaks, CA: Sage. pp. 516–40.

Locke, R. (1996) *The Collapse of the American Management Mystique.* Oxford: Oxford University Press

MacIntyre, A. (1981) *After Virtue.* Notre Dame, IN: University of Notre Dame Press.

Metzger, B. and Coogan, M. (1993) *The Oxford Companion to the Bible.* New York: Oxford University Press.

O'Connor, E. (1997) Telling decisions: the role of narrative in organizational decision making. In: Z. Shapira (ed.), *Organizational Decision Making.* New York: Cambridge University Press. pp. 304–23.

Pea, R. and Kurland, D. (1984) On the cognitive effects of learning computer programming. *New Ideas in Psychology.* pp. 137–68.

Perkins, D. (1990) Person plus: a distributed view of thinking and learning. Paper delivered at the Symposium on Distributed Learning at the annual meeting of AERA, Boston, MA.

Peters, T. and Waterman, R. (1982) *In Search of Excellence: Lessons from America's Best-Run Companies.* New York: Harper and Row.

Proust, M. (1919) *A la recherche du temps perdu. A l'ombre des jeunes filles en fleur. Premiere Partie: Autour de Mme Swann.* Paris: Gallimard.

Randall, R. and Southgate, J. (1980) *Cooperative and Community Group Dynamics.* London: Barefoot.

Ritti, R. and Funkhouser, G. (1982) *The Ropes to Skip and the Ropes to Know: Studies in Organizational Behavior.* Columbus: Grid.

Sims, D. (1993) Coping with misinformation. *Management Decision,* 31 (5): 18–21.

Sims, D., Fineman, S. and Gabriel, Y. (1993) *Organizing and Organizations: an Introduction.* London: Sage.

Spence, D. (1984) *Narrative Truth and Historical Truth: Meaning and Interpretation in Psychoanalysis.* New York: Norton.

Weick, K. (1995) *Sensemaking in Organizations.* Thousand Oaks, CA: Sage.

Widdershoven, G. (1993) The story of life: hermeneutic perspectives on the relationship between narrative and life history. In: R. Josselson and A. Lieblich (eds), *The Narrative Study of Lives.* Newbury Park, CA: Sage. pp. 1–20.

4 Balancing Biases: a Critical Review of the Literature on Organizational Learning

Marleen Huysman

In this chapter, several shortcomings which I believe to be present in the literature on organizational learning (OL) will be reviewed by means of four identified biases. These biases concern hidden ideas and assumptions behind the literature that have not been made explicit and which ensure that the received theories on organizational learning lean unnecessarily in certain directions while overlooking others. I shall attempt here to indicate how these biases could be balanced.

The biases are identified as follows: a bias towards improvement, an individual action bias, an environmental adaptation bias, and a planned learning bias.

The various questions through which Prange (Chapter 2) has characterized the literature on OL form the basic criteria for identifying the four biases. Posing these questions while reviewing the literature not only reveals that there exist many different perspectives on the phenomenon, it also shows that these contributions to the field of OL are biased in various respects.

• Who learns?	Individual action bias
• How do organizations learn?	Environmental adaptation bias
• When do organizations learn?	Planned learning bias
• With what results?	Improvement bias

The question 'Who learns?' while reviewing the literature reveals an 'individual actor bias'. Although most contributions perceive organizational learning as more than the sum of individual learning, they still emphasize the role of individuals as active agents. Posing the question 'What are the results of learning?' while reading the various contributions shows another bias. Most contributions to the field of OL perceive learning as an activity leading to improvement. As a result of this 'improvement bias', which is a direct result of an outcome perspective on learning, less attention has been given to the actual processes through which organizations learn. Posing the question 'How do organizations learn?', reveals an environmental adaptation bias. Although the literature on OL is still conspicuously silent about the way organizations really learn, most contributions assume that this learning takes place through aligning the organization with its environment. A fourth question posed by Prange which reveals another bias is 'How do organizations learn?'. This planned learning bias refers the tendency within the field of OL to perceive learning as an organizational activity that can be planned for. As a result, spontaneous unsystematic learning has been given relatively less attention.

Prange poses yet another question, and that is 'What is the content of learning?' Addressing this question shows that the literature on OL can be said to be relatively equally distributed among the various learning contents, in other words, the literature seems not to be significantly biased in this respect. Some studies refer to organizational routines or standard operating procedures (Cyert and March, 1963; Levitt and March, 1988; March and Olsen, 1976), to assumptions, theories in use, or cognitive systems (Argyris and Schön, 1978; Hedberg, 1981), to organizational knowledge or information (Duncan and Weiss, 1979; Huber, 1991), or to changes in behaviour or information (Fiol and Lyles, 1985; Weick and Roberts, 1993). In fact, Shrivastava (1983), argued that the literature can be classified into four related perspectives dealing with four different contents of learning: adaptive learning, dealing with rules and standard operating procedures; assumption sharing, dealing with cognitions and theories in use; development of the knowledge base, dealing with knowledge and information; and institutionalized experience effects, dealing with changes in behaviour.

It is not our intention to provide mutually exclusive biases. In fact, all biases seem to correlate in various extents with each other. For example, because much of the literature on OL assumes that learning leads to improvements – improvement bias – a lot has been written about strategies to enhance learning – planned learning bias. However, the presumptions on which the biases are based are believed to be distinct enough to treat them separately.

In order to make explicit what theories are being considered in the identification of the biases, I refer the reader to the work of Prange (Chapter 2) or to the many reviews of the literature on OL that have been published elsewhere (Dodgson, 1993; Easterby-Smith, 1997; Fiol and Lyles, 1985; Huber, 1991; Huysman, 1996; Levitt and March, 1988; Shrivastava, 1983).

Improvement bias

Most of the literature on OL perceives improvement, intelligence and wisdom etc. as the main results of learning. In that case, learning is not so much defined in terms of a process of which its result depend on that process, but more in terms of its outcomes. OL is often approached as an *achievement* verb (Sandelands and Drazin, 1989). As a result, it conceals rather than reveals the dynamics of the process of learning (Weick and Westley, 1996). If OL is treated as a *process* verb, more attention can be given to these dynamics, leaving the issue of whether learning results in positively valued outcomes for further investigation.

The learning curve theory, as one of the first contributions to OL, already assumed that learning results in improvement. Observations done by the US Airforce showed that for a given activity, the hours per unit were found to decrease by a constant percentage each time total repetitions of the activity doubled (Ascher, 1965). This drop in costs was attributed to the learning that takes place every time the worker repeats the task. Organizations are believed to have learned when their performances have improved.

Proponents of the 'Learning Organization', such as Garratt (1987), Garvin (1993), Pedler et al. (1991) and Senge (1990), also positively value learning. A learning organization is seen as a form of organization that enables the learning of its members in such a way that it creates positively valued outcomes, such as innovation, efficiency, better alignment with the environment and competitive advantage. Again, the focus is not so much on the process of learning but more on conditions that may allow successful outcomes to flourish.

Organizational change, too, is often perceived as an improved outcome of organizational learning. What is more, many contributions to the theory of organizational learning perceive radical change as superior to incremental change (e.g. Argyris and Schön, 1978; Senge, 1990; Swieringa and Wierdsma, 1990).

Another group of contributors to the field of OL do indeed agree that there is a lot of problematic learning going on in organizations. The main outcome of this problematic learning is conservatism, due, for example, to incomplete learning cycles (Kim, 1993), to the inability to think in wholes instead of (individual) pieces (Senge, 1990) or to a defensive tendency among organizational members to protect themselves from open confrontation and critique (Argyris and Schön, 1978).

What these and other authors share is that they still assume that learning is a good thing that should be strived for but that there are various (structural, cultural and personal) conditions that may hamper OL. This encourages them to introduce models or methods designed to improve conditions in such a way that OL can occur free from any hindrances.

One reason why most of these proponents link learning with improvement might be their optimistic and humane stance. Contributions to 'the learning organization' are based on a coalition model of organizations (Lammers, 1983), where shared participation, team building and collective learning are the building blocks of the organizations and ascertain a feeling of individual – and especially group – responsibility. Aspects of an arena model of organizations (Strauss, 1978) in which organizations are made up of individuals striving for their personal goals, are hard to find. The driving force behind organizational learning is solidarity instead of coercion. In terms of McGregor (1960), these perspectives are based on a theory *Y*: a positive image of the organizational member who is putting a lot of effort into keeping the organization a learning organization. The notion of a learning organization consisting of a theory *X*: an image of organizational members in which the idea that individuals are perceived as egoistic, lazy and not willing to learn is hardly conceivable.

Another related assumption that feeds the 'improvement bias' is the modernistic belief in prosperity and truth (Addleson, 1996; Thatchenkery, 1996). As Prange argued in Chapter 2, much of the literature on OL is directed towards creating 'useful' knowledge. From this modernistic standpoint it directly follows that learning is something to strive for since organizations become more knowledgeable whenever they learn.

A third related reason is that OL is often approached from a managerial perspective (Elkjaer, Chapter 5). As such, contributions are made in order to inform others how to 'create' conditions that foster learning.

The improvement bias refers to the tendency to perceive learning as resulting in positively valued outcomes, while treating other outcomes of the same process as less or even not relevant. However, learning does not necessarily result in positive outcomes. This becomes clear when we perceive organizational learning as a process instead of as an outcome. When organizational learning is studied as a process, the outcome of learning remains one of investigation. To quote James March, organizational learning should not be seen as:

> following a path of greater and greater elaboration, beauty, civility or fit with the environment. The essential element is not that development leads to higher and higher states but that it inexorably leads somewhere. (March, 1990: 40)

There are various reasons why learning does not always lead to improvement. Organizational behaviour is often far from being efficient and effective. Unexpected events, myopic forces, and the confusion of history for example may complicate learning processes (Levinthal and March, 1993; March et al., 1991). Conservatism as a result of learning can also be explained by a self-referential use of information. It is organizational identity which largely determines what information will be searched for and how it will be interpreted in order to learn (Huysman et al., 1995).

Furthermore, too many changes produces chaos and instability; the organization is not able to stand still and reflect on its past. In other words, changes that are too frequent inhibit learning (Lounamaa and March, 1987). Next to theoretical considerations, the practice of learning also shows that most changes happen incrementally (Genschell 1997; Nelson and Winter, 1982; Rosenberg and Frischtak, 1985; Sahal, 1981). The idiosyncratic organizational nature, its identity, or the existing organizational knowledge strongly influence what will be learned in the future.

Of course, the outcome of learning also heavily depends on the content of what is learned. Just as learning from watching soap operas will probably not produce perfect wisdom, so too should we be careful in equating organizational learning with improvement. For example, it is hard to acknowledge that learning within the Mafia necessarily improves society, but it certainly involves a development. What is considered improvement by one group, for instance by top management, does not necessarily apply to another group, say a group of employees. And what is improvement for a garbage disposal company is not always improvement for its neighbourhood.

In order to balance the improvement bias, contributors to the field of OL should, to a greater extent than at present, treat the phenomenon as a process of which the outcomes are reserved for further investigation. Although there are a few people who indeed treat learning as a process, and as a consequence allow for the possible occurrence of 'negative outcomes' equally with the occurrence of 'positive outcomes' (for example, Dodgson, 1993; Levinthal and March, 1993; Levitt and March, 1988; March, 1994), they are still under-represented.

Individual action bias

Addressing the question 'Who learns?' while reviewing the literature encourages us to identify yet another bias towards individuals as learning agents. Although organizational learning has been studied both from a micro as well as a macro approach, many organization theorists treat organizational learning at the level of individuals and groups. They stress the individual action part of learning, neglecting more structural considerations. In fact, only some theorists (for example, Cyert and March, 1963; Saha, 1981) emphasize these structural considerations. These efforts, in turn, tend to neglect the action part of the story.

Perhaps the most cited controversy within the field of OL is the difference between individual learning and organizational learning (e.g. Fiol and Lyles, 1985; Hedberg, 1981; Jones, 1995; Kim 1993). According to Fiol and Lyles, a consensus has been reached within the field concerning an implicit confirmation that *organizational* learning is distinct from individual learning. However, there still seems to be a lot of confusion about the nature of the relationship between the two forms of learning (Nicolini and Meznar, 1995).

Some authors support the idea that it is the individual who acts and learns within the organizational framework (e.g. Dodgson, 1993; March and Olsen, 1976). 'Individuals are the primary learning entity in firms and it is individuals which create organizational forms that enable learning in ways which facilitate organizational transformation' (Dodgson, 1993: 377).

Many contributions to the learning organization perspective take 'organizational' as referring to the site of learning, as in the term 'rural' or 'environmental' (Jones 1995). A learning organizations is one that creates structures and strategies which facilitate the learning of all its members (e.g. Garvin, 1993; Pedler et al., 1991; Senge, 1990).

Others consider OL as a metaphor (Argyris and Schön, 1978; Kim, 1993). Although OL occurs through individuals, it should not be seen as a cumulative result of the learning of its members (Hedberg, 1981). Argyris and Schön (1978) argue that organizations do not literally remember, think or learn. If the individual member's theories are not encoded in organizational theories, then the individual has learned but the organization has not. A similar assumption is taken by Kim (1993), who argues that 'organizations can learn independent of any specific individual but not independent of all individuals' (p. 37). Other writers, such as Duncan and Weiss (1979), Hedberg (1981), Huber (1991), Weick and Westley (1996), Fiol and Lyles (1985), take a similar point of view by accepting the organizational instead of individual aspect of learning while at the same time claiming that individuals are the principal agents of OL.

There is indeed a relatively small group of contributors who treat OL as independent of its individuals (Jones, 1995). However, these contributions cannot be seen as representative to the field of OL. Sandelands and Stablein (1987), for example, argue that organizations have a sort of collective mind. Some proponents from artificial intelligence argue that the capacity to learn can be embedded in expert systems (Huber, 1991). Another group that perceives OL as independent of its individuals stems from cybernetics, which conceives organizations as self-organizing systems (Morgan, 1986).

In general, OL is approached as an activity made up by individuals. Individual members are often considered as active agents of OL. The problem with this 'individual action bias' is that it tends to overlook the role played by structural conditions such as institutional forces, organizational histories, cultures, group structures and power structures. Institutional patterns such as organizational norms and values, but also environmental rules and beliefs impose prior constraints on the actions of agents. For example, it is conceivable that the learning of organizations within the industrial revolution manifested a different way of learning than for example organizations within the 'information revolution' (Beninger, 1986) or the 'knowledge society' (Drucker, 1988). In a similar vein, an increase in the number of organizations within an organizational field ensure a more 'aggressive' style of learning than is the case within an organization in a sparsely populated organizational field. Furthermore, organizations in Sweden with their tradition of work councils will be likely to portray a different style of learning than organizations in Belgium where the lines of authority are formally and informally maintained (Hofstede, 1980).

That OL is mainly approached from an individual actor perspective might be seen as a legacy of the theoretical pluralism within organization theory concerning the interplay between what Dawe (1970) refers to as 'the two sociologies'. One views individual action as the derivative of the social system (such as structural-functionalism) and the other views the social system as the derivative of individual action (such as the interpretative sociologies). The 'system argument' begins analysis with the organization as a whole and locates individual action according to its place and function within the system. The 'individual argument' on the other hand begins with the individual and proceeds to find the system only as the aggregated outcome of individual action.

The structure/action debate can also be perceived as a deterministic/voluntaristic debate. Seen from the voluntaristic orientation, individuals and their created institutions are autonomous, proactive, self-directing agents; individuals are seen as the basic unit of analysis and source of change in organizational life. The deterministic orientation focuses not on individuals, but on the structural properties of the context within which action unfolds, and individual behaviour is seen as determined by and reacting to structural constraints. These constraints provide organizational life with an overall stability and control (Astley and Van de Ven, 1983).

A major shortcoming of the structural-functionalist perspective when dealing with organizational learning is its neglect of the active behaviour of individual members, or 'agents' (Giddens, 1984). The organization learns but the link between this learning and the behaviour of the individuals 'within' the organization remains obscure. A major shortcoming of the interpretive perspective is the notion that structure is an emergent property of ongoing action. This idea suggests that action unfolds free of any preconceptions, and it underestimates the degree to which institutional patterns impose prior constraints on the action from which structures emerge (Weick, 1990).

There have been some attempts to perceive the two schools of thought as dualities rather than mutually exclusive pairs. In this way, organizational processes are not seen as voluntaristic bottom-up processes alone, nor as complete deterministic top down structural processes either (Berger and Luckmann, 1966; Boden, 1994; Giddens, 1984; Whittington, 1994). In a similar way, OL can be perceived as taking place through the action of individuals when these actions are simultaneously constrained by institutional forces. Although organizational learning is influenced by the activities of active agents, it is at the same time a top-down process. Organizational history, assimilated in organizational memory, structures the activities of these learning agents. Thus, individual learning is not free from any preconception.

Because of this dual character between on the one hand the voluntaristic actions of individuals – 'active agents' – and on the other hand the deterministic force of existing organizational structures – 'structural properties' – organizational learning can be seen as a process of structuration (Giddens, 1976, 1979, 1984) or institutionalization (Berger and Luckmann, 1966; Schutz, 1971). Although the 'structuration theory' of Giddens provides an interesting perspective on this reciprocal nature of social phenomena, the use of the concept of 'institutionalization' as approached by Berger and Luckmann in their *Social Construction of Reality* (1966) seems more relevant. Unlike Giddens, these authors focus explicitly on the (re)construction of knowledge and how this (re)constructed knowledge influences and is influenced by subsequent (re)constructions. Berger and Luckmann refer to three phases or 'moments' that can be distinguished in the process of institutionalization: 'externalization, objectivation, and internalization' (Berger and Luckmann, 1966). Externalization is the process in which personal knowledge is communicated to others. Through externalization, 'society becomes a human product'. Objectivation is the process during which 'society becomes an objective reality'. Durkheim (1964) considers these objectified behaviour patterns as 'things'. During the moment of internalization, 'the objectified social world is retrojected into consciousness in the course of socialization' of the individual. 'Through internalization man becomes a product of society' (Berger and Luckmann, 1966: 79). As such, the authors refer to a dialectical relation between action and structure:

> The relationship between man, the producer, and the social world, his product, is and remains a dialectical one. That is, man (not, of course, in isolation but in his collectivities) and his social world interact with each other. The product acts back upon the producer. (p. 78)

In terms of organizational learning, externalizing occurs when individual knowledge is shared among individuals. The process through which this externalization results in organizational knowledge, which is often influenced by power structures as well as by history, is the process of objectifiying knowledge. Internalizing occurs when individual actors integrate this organizational knowledge into their personal belief (Huysman, 1996).

Analysing organizational learning as a reciprocal process creates awareness that it cannot be considered as an entirely voluntaristic one in which (purposeful) individual (inter)action will lead to a change in the organizational memory or knowledge. Individual learning agents are also constrained by structural properties in their learning behaviour.

Environmental adaptation bias

As argued above, posing the question as to how organizations learn may frustrate the reviewer. After all, OL is mostly conceived of as an activity leading to improvement, while the actual process through which these outcomes have been reached remains most often unclear (Dodgson, 1993; March, 1994). This does not imply that contributors do not refer to the way organizations (should) learn, albeit this attempt is mostly of a normative nature. In general, organizations are said to learn by adapting to their environments. Most theories on learning are based on some translation of the open system approach to organizations (Thompson, 1967). The organization adapts to changes in the environment, to responses to organizational action, or to feedback information reporting organizational errors (e.g. Argyris and Schön, 1978; Cyert and March, 1963; Fiol and Lyles, 1985; Levitt and March, 1988; March and Olsen, 1976; Senge, 1990; Weick and Roberts, 1993).

In general, organizational learning is perceived as a way to correct errors and to adapt to environmental demands. Organizations need to learn in order to adapt successfully to environmental changes. The greater the uncertainty in the environment, the greater the need for learning. Feedback information and information from external environments are the keys to 'successful' outcomes of learning.

According to Fiol and Lyles (1985), a consensus area within the field of OL centres on the notion that organizations must align to their environment in order to remain competitive and innovative. Two related theoretical assumptions lie behind this reasoning: one is the premise of strategic management, the other is the premise of contingency theory, both deriving from open systems theory.

Strategic management focuses on the strategies that managers can implement which have the effect of reducing competition in an industry. Some writers such as Stata (1989), DeGeus (1988), Adler and Cole (1993), are explicit in linking OL to this premise of strategic management. However, as Nicolini and Meznar (1995) argue, 'accepting the environmental alignment argument depends on accepting the validity of the strategic management approach on which it rests' (p. 729). Referring to those who warn against an excessive confidence in strategic management such as Scott (1977), Morgan (1982, 1986), Pondy and Mitroff (1979) and Smirchich and Stubbart (1985), they dispute the ability of the organization to align with its environment. In a similar vein, Levinthal and March (1993) state that the literature on OL has become very much influenced by ideas taken from strategic management literature. They argue that because of several myopic forces, organizations are seldom able to learn meaningfully from aligning with the environment.

The other related assumption on which the idea of learning as alignment rests is contingency theory (Lawrence and Lorsch, 1967). Some writers, such as Duncan and Weiss (1979) and Shrivastava (1983), are very explicit in saying that organizations learn through alignment with the external environment. One of the problems of contingency theory is its environmental determinism which tends to make organizations and their members dependent upon forces operating in the external world. As with strategic management, it ignores the possibilities of individuals constructing their own environments. Social constructionist theories (Berger and Luckmann, 1966; Gergen, 1994; Schutz, 1971; Weick, 1979) as well as the theory of autopoiesis (Maturana and Varela, 1980; Van der Blonk et al., 1997; Veld et al., 1991), have taught us that we are able to shape the environment we desire. To be sure, adapting to enacted environments will result in outcomes which are different from those that the proponents of strategic management and contingency theory may envision.

Next to these problems, the 'environmental adaptation bias' is problematic in that it refers only to a single kind of incentive to learn, namely the wish to stay aligned with the environment. As a result of the predominance of the open systems approach, other triggers to learn are often neglected. For example, the incentive to learn may also be internally driven, in which case the open system paradigm becomes less relevant. Organizations learn, for example, from the stories organizational members tell each other (Brown and Duguid, 1991). Organizations also learn from plain chance events, to which we return in the next section. Or organizations may learn as a result of the need for managers to make a difference, or the almost inherent drive of innovation champions to seek adventure. In a broad review of 'some of the literature on organizational learning', Dodgson (1993), for example, observes that:

> (o)rganizations, and the forms of collective and individual learning within them, importantly affect learning processes and outcomes. Indeed, the role of human agency and individual goals such as the drive for self-actualization are almost completely ignored in many accounts of organizational adaptability. Organizational learning is stimulated both by environmental changes and internal factors in a complex and iterative manner. (p. 387)

In order to balance the 'environmental adaptation bias' and to allow for a broader range of ways through which organizations learn, it is necessary to study learning from a process perspective. More importantly, perhaps, is the need for more empirical stories on how organizations really learn.

Planned learning bias

Finally, posing the question 'when organizations learn' shows a fourth bias in the literature on OL. Many theories refer to learning as an activity that deliberately takes place and thus can be planned for. For example, Argyris and Schön (1978) and Argyris (1990) argue that, in order radically to change basic assumptions, defensive routines can be brought to the surface when open communication sessions are organized. These organizational development tools can be designed beforehand and can be used in various situations. In line with Gregory Bateson (1973), the authors refer to so called 'deutero learning' (second order learning) when dealing with the institutionalization of these learning processes. Institutionalized processes of learning can be found, for example, in research and development departments and planning and marketing departments (McKee, 1992).

Another example of deutero learning which has become popular in today's writing on OL, is 'the Learning Organization' concept (Burgelman, 1990; DeGeus, 1988; Garvin, 1993; Senge, 1990; Stata, 1989). Learning Organizations are deliberately 'created' so as to facilitate the learning of their members. Various design criteria have been introduced which could foster OL. It is argued that whenever managers put these 'guidelines' into action, organizations will turn into more efficient learning centres. In other words, organizations can anticipate their future learning behaviour.

Planned learning has also been a theme for those writers who argue that organizations can learn through the use of information systems. In general, authors within this perspective assert that information systems can be built to support this deutero or institutionalized learning. For example, Jelinek (1979) and Shrivastava (1983) have analysed organizational learning systems that capture the information that is needed from the environment. Some proponents of the artificial intelligence discipline suggest that information systems like expert systems and neural networks can substitute for the learning of and within organizations (e.g. Johnson-Laird, 1988). Boland et al. (1994) show that information systems based on multimedia technologies may enhance the appreciation of diverse interpretations within organizations and as such support OL. Information systems that may serve as simulation tools have also been proposed as important means to support OL (Senge, 1990; Stata, 1989). The downside of all these contributions is that they tend to overlook the more accidental and path-dependent nature of organizational learning.

As mentioned earlier, structural conditions may cause conservative learning behaviour. As a result of such forces, individual members or, specifically managers, are not able to engineer the future fully (March, 1990). Next to this rule-following learning behaviour, organizations are often confronted with internal as well as external unanticipated events. These events limit the possibility of planned learning.

The stochastic nature of knowledge construction has become accepted within the literature of strategy formation (Mintzberg, 1988; Quinn, 1989; Vissers, 1994). Quinn (1989) for instance recommends 'logical incrementalism' thereby recognizing the cognitive and process limits that constrain formal strategic practices. Such a process of strategy formation allows for a continuous evolving process. Mintzberg and Waters (1985) propose a continuum ranging from 'pure deliberate' to 'pure emergent' strategies. Emergent strategy acknowledges the possibility of unplanned action; patterns develop in the absence of intentions. Thus action can take place without previous thinking, courses of action called 'strategy' – in retrospect – may not be based on previous plans. It is just a small step towards acknowledging this rather unplanned nature of knowledge construction in cases of organizational learning. March (1990) for example talks about a 'meandering' evolution, thereby referring to the unplanned unanticipated traces that learning process can leave behind. Organizations face various problems and unforeseen events when learning.

> There are irreversible branches, thus path-dependence and decisive minor moments. The branch-points, involving things like mutations, mating, communication contacts, and fortuitous opportunities often seem almost chance like in their resolution, yet decisive in their effects on subsequent history. Though the path of developments is explicable in terms of a comprehensible process, the realized course of natural evolution is difficult to predict. (March, 1990: 44)

Because the course of the evolution depends upon the sequence of particular branches that are realized along the way, organizational learning processes are not easily predicted – with obvious implications for planning processes (Huysman et al., 1994).

Although unsystematic and unintentional learning is a common way through which organizations learn (Huber, 1991), there appear to be few published studies where spontaneous learning was the focal topic of interest (exceptions are e.g. March, 1990; March and Olsen, 1976; Pennings, 1992; Pentland et al., 1994; Sahal, 1981). With the publication of the work of Lave and Wenger (1991) and that of Brown and Duguid (1991) it seems that a new perspective within the OL literature is emerging (Elkjaer, Chapter 5). This 'social constructivist perspective' (Huysman, 1996) is based on the idea of 'communities of practice' and focuses on non-canonical practices during which members create new ideas and insights about their work at hand. These learning processes take place during day-to-day activities, and seem to be 'successful' by virtue of being unplanned.

In short, the planned learning bias can be balanced when OL is considered as a process of organizational evolution. From such a perspective it follows that the attention is not only focused on planned learning practices but also on spontaneous learning that takes place during day-to-day organizational activities.

Concluding remarks

In this chapter, four general weaknesses of the existing OL literature have been addressed. As well as the uncovering of the hidden assumptions that lie behind each of the identified biases, ways to balance each bias were proposed. The improvement bias can be balanced when OL is approached from a process perspective. In order to balance the individual action bias, the use of the institutionalization theory is proposed where action and structure find each other in a reciprocal relationship. The environmental adaptation bias can be balanced when a wider scope of learning processes is adopted. The planned learning bias can be balanced when writers perceive learning as an evolutionary process made up of both stochastic as well as purposefully planned events.

In a way, this chapter could be considered as a first attempt to deconstruct writings on OL. Deconstruction is an activity that has become popular with the work of Jacques Derrida. Derrida's objective in deconstruction is to reveal the ambivalence and double binds that lie latent in any text (Cooper, 1989). Surely, however, Derrida's deconstruction of texts is in many aspects different from the present effort to identify biases. Most importantly, Derrida is not criticizing a text nor is he interpreting it. After all, criticizing and interpreting a text means that one uses an already existing framework which serves to analyse the texts. It was not my intention to follow a postmodernistic endeavour of deconstructing the field of OL. In other words, I cannot claim that a deconstruction of the present text will not reveal various hidden assumptions that have influenced the analysis and of which I was not aware. What I do wish to have reached with the present analysis, is a certain understanding of the hidden assumptions that lie behind most of the writings of OL and which may necessarily tend to slant the literature in certain directions thereby ignoring other possible views on organizational learning.

References

Addleson, M. (1996) Resolving the spirit and substance of organizational learning. *Journal of Organizational Change Management*, 9 (1): 32–41.

Adler, P.S. and Cole, R.E. (1993) Designed for learning: a tale of two auto plants. *Sloan Management Review*, Spring, pp. 85–94.

Argyris, C. (1990) *Overcoming Organizational Defenses: Facilitating Organizational Learning* Needham Heights, MA: Allyn and Bacon.

Argyris, C. and Schön, D. (1978) *Organizational Learning: a Theory of Action-Perspective*. Reading, MA: Addison-Wesley.

Ascher, H. (1965) *Cost Quality Relationships in the Air Frame Industry*. Santa Monica, CA: Rand Corporation.

Astley, W.G. and van de Ven, A.H. (1983) Central perspectives and debates in organization theory. *Administrative Science Quarterly*, 28: 245–73.

Bateson, G. (1973) *Steps to the Ecology of Mind*. Frogmore: Paladin.

Beninger, J.R. (1986) *The Control Revolution*. Cambridge, MA: Harvard University Press.

Berger, P. and Luckmann, T. (1966) *The Social Construction of Reality*. London: Penguin Books.

Boden, D. (1994) *The Business of Talk: Organizations in Action*. Cambridge: Polity Press.

Boland, R.J, Tenkasi, R.V. and Te'eni, D. (1994) Designing information technology to support distributed cognition. *Organization Science*, 5 (3): 456–75.

Brown J.S. and Duguid, P. (1991) Organizational learning and communities-of-practice: towards a unified view of working, learning, and innovation. *Organization Science*, 2 (1): 40–57.

Burgelman, R.A. (1990) Strategy-making and organizational ecology: a conceptual framework. In: J.V. Singh (ed.), *Organizational Evolution*. Newbury Park, CA: Sage. pp. 164–81.

Ciborra, C.U. and Lanzara, G.F. (1994) Formative contexts and information technology, understanding the dynamics of innovation in organizations. *Accounting, Management and Information Technology*, 4 (2): 61–86.

Cooper, R. (1989) Modernism, postmodernism and organizational analysis 3: The contribution of Jacques Derrida. *Organization Studies*, 10 (4): 479–502.

Cyert, R.M. and March, J.G. (1963) *A Behavioral Theory of the Firm*. Englewood Cliffs, NJ: Prentice-Hall.

Dawe, A. (1970) The two sociologies. *British Journal of Sociology*, 21: 207–18.

DeGeus, A.P. (1988) Planning as learning. *Harvard Business Review*, March–April: 70–4.

Dodgson, M. (1993) Organizational learning: a review of some literatures. *Organization Studies*, 14 (3): 375–94.

Drucker, P.F. (1988) The coming of the new organization. *Harvard Business Review*, January–February, pp. 45–53.

Duncan, R.B. and Weiss, A. (1979) Organizational learning: implications for organizational design. In: P.M. Staws and L.L. Cummings (eds), *Research in Organizational Behavior*. Greenwich, CT: JAI Press. pp. 75–123.

Durkheim, E. (1964) *Rules of Sociological Method*. New York: Free Press.

Easterby-Smith, M. (1997) Disciplines of organizational learning: contributions and critiques. *Human Relations*, 50 (9): 1085–113.

Fiol, C.M. and Lyles, M.A. (1985) Organizational learning. *Academy of Management Review*, 10 (4): 803–13.

Garratt, B. (1987) *The Learning Organization* Worcester: Billings.

Garvin, D.A. (1993) Building a learning organization. *Harvard Business Review*, 71 (4): 78–91.

Genschell, P. (1997) The dynamics of inertia: institutional persistence and change in telecommunications and health care. *Governance*, 10 (1): 43–66.

Gergen, K.J. (1994) *Realities and Relationships, Soundings in Social Construction*. Cambridge, MA: Harvard University Press.

Giddens, A. (1976) *New Rules of Sociological Method*. London: Hutchinson.

Giddens, A. (1979) *Central Problems in Social Theory*. Berkeley, CA: University of California Press.

Giddens, A. (1984) *The Constitution of Society*. Cambridge: Polity Press.

Hedberg, B.L.T. (1981) How organizations learn and unlearn. In P.C. Nystrom and W.H. Starbuck (eds), *Handbook of Organization Design*, Vol. 1. London: Cambridge University Press. pp. 3–27.

Hofstede, G. (1980) *Culture's Consequences: International Differences in Work Related Values*. Beverley Hills, CA: Sage.

Huber, G.P. (1991) Organizational learning: the contributing processes and the literatures. *Organization Science*, 2 (1): 88–115.

Huysman, M.H. (1996) *Dynamics of Organizational Learning*. Amsterdam: Thesis Publishers.

Huysman, M.H., Fischer, S.J. and Heng, M.S.H. (1994) An organizational learning perspective on information systems planning. *Journal of Strategic Information Systems*, 3 (3): 165–77.

Huysman, M.H., Frisart, R. and Heng, M.S.H. (1995) Autopoiesis and organizational learning, implications for information systems. Paper presented at the *SISnet Conference on strategic information systems*, Berne.

Jelinek, M. (1979) *Institutionalizing Innovations, a Study of Organizational Learning Systems*. New York: Praeger.

Johnson-Laird, P. (1988) *The Computer and the Mind*. Cambridge, MA: Harvard University Press.

Jones, M. (1995) 'Organizational learning: collective mind or cognitivist metaphor? *Accounting Management and Information Technology*, 5 (1): 61–77.

Kim, D.M. (1993) The link between individual and organizational learning. *Sloan Management Review*, Fall, pp. 37–50.

Lammers, C.J. (1983) *Organisaties Vergelijkenderwijs* (*Organizations in comparison*). Utrecht: Het Spectrum.

Lave J. and Wenger, E. (1991) *Situated Learning: Legitimate Peripheral Participation*. Cambridge: Cambridge University Press.

Lawrence, P.R. and Lorch, J.W. (1967) *Organization and Environment*. Cambridge, MA: Harvard Graduate School of Business Administration.
Levinthal, D. and March, J.G. (1993) The myopia of learning. *Strategic Management Journal*, 14: 95–112.
Levitt, B. and March, J.G. (1988) Organizational learning. *Annual Review of Sociology*, 14: 319–40.
Lounamaa, P.H. and March, J.G. (1987) Adaptive coordination of a learning team. *Management Science*, 33: 107–23.
March, J.G. (1990) The evolution of evolution. In: J.V. Singh (ed.), *Organizational Evolution*. Newbury Park, CA: Sage.
March, J.G. (1994) *A Primer on Decision Making*. New York: Free Press.
March, J.G. and Olsen, J.P. (1976) *Ambiguity and Choice in Organizations*. Bergen, Norway: Universitetsforlaget.
March, J.G., Sproull, L.S. and Tamuz, M. (1991) Learning from samples of one or fewer. *Organization Science*, 2 (1): 1–13.
Maturana, H.R. and Varela, F.J. (1980) *Autopoiesis and Cognition: the Realization of the Living*. Dordrecht, NL: Reidel.
McGregor, D. (1960) *The Human Side of Enterprise*. New York: McGraw-Hill.
McKee, D. (1992) An organizational learning approach to product innovation. *Journal of Product Innovation Management*, 9: 232–45.
Mintzberg, H. (1988) Opening up the definition of strategy. In: J.B. Quinn et al. (eds), *The Strategy Process; Concepts, Contexts and Cases*. Englewood Cliffs, NJ: Prentice-Hall. pp. 13–20.
Mintzberg, H. and Waters, J.A. (1985) Of strategies, deliberate and emergent. *Strategic Management Journal*, 6: 257–72.
Morgan, G. (1982) Cybernetics and organization theory: epistemology or technique? *Human Relations*, 35: 521–37.
Morgan, G. (1986) *Images of Organization*. Newbury Park, CA: Sage.
Nelson, R. and Winter, S.G. (1982) *An Evolutionary Theory of Economic Change*. Cambridge, MA: Addison-Wesley.
Nicolini, D. and Meznar, M.B. (1995) The social construction of organizational learning: conceptual and practical issues in the field. *Human Relations*, 48 (7): 727–46.
Pedler, M., Burgoyne, J. and Boydell, T. (1991) *The Learning Company*. New York: McGraw-Hill.
Pennings, J.M. (1992) Structural contingency theory: a reappraisal. In: P.M. Staws and L.L. Cummings (eds), *Research in Organizational Behavior*, Greenwhich, CT: JAI Press. pp. 267–309.
Pentland, B.T. (1995) Information systems and organizational learning: the social epistemology of organizational knowledge systems. *Accounting, Management and Information Technology*, 5: 1–21.
Pondy, L. and Mitroff, I. (1979) Beyond open system models of organization. In: B. Staw (ed.), *Research in Organizational Behavior*, Vol. 1. Greenwich: JAI Press. pp. 3–39.
Quinn, J.B. (1989) Strategic change: logical incrementalism. *Sloan Management Review*, 45: 45–60.
Rosenberg, N. and Frischtak, C. (eds) (1985) *International Technological Transfer*. New York: Praeger.
Sahal, D. (1981) *Patterns of Technological Innovations*. Reading, MA: Addison-Wesley.
Sandelands, L.E. and Drazin, R. (1989) On the language of organizational theory. *Organization Studies*, 10: 457–78.
Sandelands, L.E. and Stablein, R.E. (1987) The concept of organization mind. In: S. Bacharach and N. DiTomaso (eds), *Research in the Sociology of Organizations*, Vol. 5. Greenwich, CT: JAI Press. pp. 135–61.

Schutz, A. (1971) *Collected Papers*, Vols 1 and 2. The Hague: Nijhoff.
Scott, W. (1977) On the effectiveness of the studies of organization effectiveness. In: P. Goodman and J. Pennings (eds), *New Perspectives on Organization Effectiveness*. San Francisco: Jossey-Bass.
Senge, P. (1990) *The Fifth Discipline, the Art and Practice of the Learning Organization*. London: Randon House.
Shrivastava, P. (1983) A typology of organizational learning systems. *Journal of Management Studies*, 20 (2): 7–28.
Smirchich, L. and Stubbart, C. (1985) Strategic management in an enacted world. *Academy of Management Review*, 10: 724–36.
Stata, R. (1989) Organizational learning: the key to management innovation. *Sloan Management Review*, Spring, pp. 63–74.
Strauss, A. (1978) *Negotiations*. San Francisco: Jossey-Bass.
Swieringa, J. and Wierdsma, A.F.M. (1990) *Op weg naar een lerende organisatie. Over het leren en opleiden van organisaties* (Becoming a Learning Organization: On Learning and Teaching in Organizations). Groningen: Wolters Noordhoff.
Thatchenkery, T.J. (1996) Organizational learning, language games and knowledge creation, Editorial note. *Journal of Organizational Change Management*, 9 (1): 4–11.
Thompson, J. (1967) *Organizations in Action*. New York: McGraw-Hill.
Van der Blonk, H., Huysman, M.H. and Spoor, E. (1997) Autopoiesis and the evolution of information systems. Proceedings of SCI'97, World Multiconference on Systemics, Cybernetics and Informatics, July, Caracas.
Veld, in 't R.J., Schaap, L., Termeer, C.J.A.M. and Twist, M.J.W. (eds) (1991) *Autopoiesis and Configuration Theory: New Approaches to Societal Steering*. Dordrecht: Kluwer.
Vissers G. (1994) The Production of Strategy. PhD thesis, Erasmus University Rotterdam. Delft: Eberon.
Weick, K.E. (1979) *The Social Psychology of Organizing*. Reading, MA: Addison-Wesley.
Weick, K.E. (1990) Technology as equivogue: sensemaking in new technologies. In: P.S. Goodman and L. Sproull (eds), *Technology and Organizations*. San Francisco: Jossey-Bass.
Weick, K.E. and Roberts, K.H. (1993) Collective mind in organizations: heedful interrelating on flight decks. *Administrative Science Quarterly*, 38 (3): 357–81.
Weick, K.E. and Westley, F. (1996) Organizational learning: affirming an oxymoron. In: S.R. Clegg, C. Hardy and W.R. Nord (eds), *Handbook of Organization Studies*. London: Sage.
Whittington, R. (1994) Sociological pluralism, institutions and managerial agency. In: J. Hassard and M. Parker (eds), *Towards a New Theory of Organizations*. London: Routledge. pp. 53–74.

5 In Search of a Social Learning Theory

Bente Elkjaer

I have followed the development of organizational learning (OL) and its counterpart, the learning organization (LO), from the time where people gave me a blank look whenever I used the terms until today, where the concept almost has become *the* contemporary (but perhaps very temporary) buzzword. Therefore, I think it is appropriate to start with a few reflections on OL and the LO as conceptual constructs. It may not be 'authorized', but to me the term OL signifies an emphasis on the processual character of learning. Using the noun connotes a reification of OL into almost fixed procedures that must be followed in order to achieve an LO. It is as if writers who use the noun version regard the LO as 'just another' organizational design to choose among many others, that is, as a more or less unproblematic, organizational state created by the 'right' management and 'suitable' attitudes among employees. On the other hand, writers who tend to use the term OL often acknowledge the complexity of organizational life and the learning process itself.[1] In this chapter I use both terms at random, as my 'project' aims to develop a social learning theory, which can be applied *as* OL and *in* LOs.

However, it is possible to distinguish, albeit crudely, two different approaches within OL/LO.[2] The first approach views OL/LO as a management tool for developing (mostly) tacit, cognitive abilities, that is, the thinking abilities of individual members in organizations. The second approach, which does not use the term OL/LO very often, deals with how learning occurs in social settings, that is, in so-called *communities of practice*. From this perspective, learning is viewed as an inevitable part of participating in social life and practice. In addition to (individual) cognitive learning, this version involves both membership of a community and improving the skills of its members. The latter perspective can be subsumed into the term *situated* learning.[3]

In this chapter I will elaborate on these two approaches to OL/LO. I will place the first approach, learning as individual cognition, in an organizational perspective that views organizations as *systems*. In this perspective theory and practice on OL/LO focus upon working with individual members' mental models or maps. The second approach, the situated learning, is not developed as an OL/LO theory as such. However, I will try to place it in a domain, which we can call an *interactionist* perspective on organizations, and within a framework of a pragmatist theory of learning.

The purpose of this chapter is to show that a theory on OL/LO must take its point of departure in a *social* learning theory. In other words, it should acknowledge that learning in organizations also has a social aspect. It is not merely an individual affair, as it takes place within the realm of collective human actions and interactions. Furthermore, I believe it is important that the organizational perspective of the OL/LO theory tries to encompass the complexities of organizational life, which will illustrate how complex it is to develop OL/LO theories – and practices.

OL/LO as a management tool

In recent years, the market for theories on OL/LO has grown explosively,[4] and several overviews of the many books and articles on OL/LO have been published.[5] Much of the literature on OL/LO has a normative character, trying to tell managers how to design a learning organization (Schein, 1992; Senge, 1990). Within the realm of normative management theory we may even talk of a movement from Total Quality Management (TQM) over Business Process Re-engineering (BPR) to the design of LOs (Bjørn-Andersen and Chatfield, 1996). We may, therefore, view the design of an LO as yet another way of linking so-called customer satisfaction and development of personnel competency, where one of the abilities involved is continuous learning.[6]

The objective of one version is to develop the capacity for so-called *systems thinking* in members of organizations, that is, thinking of the organization in wholes instead of in parts (Roth and Senge, 1996; Senge, 1990). Another version is to develop systems to 'store' outcomes of organizational development, that is, a so-called organizational memory (for example, an information system, and/or organizational processes and routines). Individual members can draw upon such systems when they have to solve problems and make decisions. The purpose is to reduce dependency on individual members' performance of tasks in organizations (Huber, 1991; Levitt and March, 1988; Nevis et al., 1995; Shrivastava, 1983). One may say that where the former version focuses on developing the capacities of individual members by developing their cognitive (that is, thinking) abilities, the latter is grounded in a reification process of normally very fluid activities, namely the production and reproduction of information and knowledge.

I find that this approach to OL/LO implies a regulation of organizational members. Their way of thinking is developed with the express purpose of modifying and aligning their behaviour within the organization, that is, the vision of management. However, the emphasis on organizational structures and processes at the expense of individual members may also be viewed as an instrument to control organizational processes. In other words, OL/LO may be viewed as a *tool* for aligning the behaviour of organizational members and the organization as a whole.

The view of OL/LO as a tool to regulate and control organizational members and processes may entail developing a 'learning culture' (Schein, 1992) and so-called 'shared visions' (Senge, 1990) initiated and kept alive by management. Evidently, there is a strong belief that learning can be 'managed'.[7] If managers are to sustain this belief in organizations, they must have the tools to design LOs and create intrinsic motivation – or rather aspiration – in 'their' organizational members. The specific interventionist actions within this approach to OL/LO are more or less an attempt to change people's minds, thinking, attitudes and, in so doing, their actions.

Organizations as systems

What I have now termed the approach to OL/LO as a management tool to regulate and modify so-called inappropriate behaviour of organizational members entertains a systems perspective on organization. Senge (1990) admits to a systems perspective on OL/LO, or rather his studies on OL/LO are based on the need to develop systems thinking in members of organizations.[8] Here, the role of management is crucial, maybe the most crucial. The manager should act as a 'model' for the employees, a 'star learner' and developer of the organizational vision, expounding the *mental model* to be shared by all. According to Senge, a systems perspective on organizations offers a new way of seeing and thinking, a way in which it is possible to perceive underlying structures and wholes. And it offers a language in which to communicate.

> Systems thinking is a discipline for seeing wholes. It is a framework for seeing interrelationships rather than things, for seeing patterns of change rather than static 'snapshots'. . . . And systems thinking is a sensibility – for the subtle interconnectedness that gives living systems their unique character. . . . Systems thinking is a discipline for seeing the 'structures' that underlie complex situations, and for discerning high from low leverage change. (Senge, 1990: 68–9)

In a further development of his ideas, Senge places the organization in a 'four by four' model that explains organizational complexity. On the one hand, it comprises the dynamic complexity referring to how the relations 'between cause and resulting effects are distant in time and space' (Roth and Senge, 1996: 94), that is, the so-called *technical* issues of organizational life. On the other hand, there is *behavioural* complexity referring to the 'diversity in the organizations, mental models, and values of decision makers' (Senge, 1990: 93). The model is supposed to help detect the type of problems that have to be solved in organizations and to anticipate any potential difficulties in solving them.

The 'four-by-four' model is supposed to represent a 'holistic' view on the organization as a system. But in fact, it turns into a partial view as specific systems elements are pointed out, for example, the dynamic and behavioural complexities, to the effect that they become *the* structural and processual elements in focus. Consequently, it is these elements that members in organizations must learn to incorporate in their work, so to speak. What I find most distressing, however, is the recognition that any actual work with members in organizations is based on learning that focuses on *individual cognition.*

It may seem as a contradiction in terms that the systems thinking on OL/LO, which is based on the idea of seeing wholes and not parts, is based on a theory of learning that focuses on individual cognition. It is as if the systems perspective, through its reification of organizational structures and processes, has lost sight of the importance of collective human actions and interactions and, thus, of a social theory of learning. The organizational perspective in this approach becomes the perspective of individuals who – separately – encounter organizational structures and processes. In other words, the perspective implies that specific behavioural complexities (read: individuals separated by their skin) meet specific dynamic complexities (read: tasks of high or low complexity), and based on the character of this 'meeting' the work with organizational members can proceed.[9]

Learning as individual cognition

In the Western world, learning as individual cognition is the most prevailing educational theory of a psychological nature. It is based on the idea that all human beings must acquire the culture they are born into, that is, they have to become socialized to live in society. The purpose of learning may be seen as transmission of a cultural heritage and transfer of cultural knowledge. Socialization is necessary to ensure that societies can function the way they do. The individual (biological) person meets a cultural world which she or he has to be socialized into, that is to say, learn to adapt to and internalize.[10]

I argue that learning as individual cognition has inspired the approach to OL/LO as a management tool. Here, learning is considered a part of our biological heritage, of our genes, so to speak. But, apparently, the heritage has been lost, and it is necessary to dig it out anew. To quote Senge:

> Learning organizations are possible because, *deep down*, we are all learners. . . . Learning organizations are possible because not only is it our *nature* to learn but we *love* to learn. (1990: 4, emphasis added)

It is quotations like these and the prevalent use of concepts such as individual, mental models that can be 'worked with', changed and aligned to organizational visions etc., in *addition* to the absence of a social learning theory which make me suggest that this approach to OL/LO is based on an individual learning theory, which may be termed learning as individual cognition.

The purpose of the learning process is to develop a capacity for systems thinking, which requires 'a change of mind' in order to 'see the world anew' (Senge, 1990: 68). In other words, the process aims at creating a new way of thinking and new attitudes by focusing on latent capacities in (individual) human beings. Something must be done to let out our 'inner' (intrinsic) desire to learn. The desire to learn must be aroused in all organizational members to further the development of an LO. With this end in view, it is necessary to expand the intelligence, capacities and abilities of each individual organizational member. The members' abilities must be developed and their attitudes (subsequent actions) must be 'shaped' to fit organizational purposes. This is the main reason for designing an organizational vision in accordance with top management – a vision that can be transferred to and eventually internalized by organizational members into their own *mental models*.

The seminal work by Argyris and Schön (1978) on OL/LO, which they themselves term a *theory of action*, is also based on a concept of mental models (or 'maps'). According to Argyris and Schön, these models *represent* both our own actions and the organizational *actions*. As such, the models are grounded in the actual work processes as opposed to the Senge version, where the models appear to concentrate more on matters like thinking and attitudes. Argyris and Schön distinguish between two models. One model, the so-called theories-in-use, governs actions which organizational members might not be able to verbalize. The other model is the espoused (verbalized) theory in action. Organizations and organizational members 'carry' both forms of mental maps. Argyris and Schön's interventionist work with developing OL/LO is based on an organizational development tradition (OD).[11] Therefore, they have focused especially on improving *communication* skills in organizations. In terms of developing OL/LO it is necessary to make organizational members more aware of their actual theories-in-use – and any discrepancies between these and their espoused theories of action – in order to determine whether they need to be changed to improve OL/LO.

Argyris and Schön's position on OL/LO is not without problems, but at the moment space does not permit me to go more into details. I have mentioned their approach to OL/LO as an example of a position which does use the notion of mental models, maps and representations, but still considers the development of OL/LO as highly complex and difficult. It is not just a matter of designing a Master Vision that should be followed by organizational members, who are supposed to develop systems thinking. On the contrary, Argyris and Schön are very much aware of the 'room' (read: organization) for learning which is reflected in their interest in social communication structures. This brings us right into the social realm, but not quite as far as I would like to go in the pursuit of OL/LOs. That is why I have chosen to introduce the concept of situated learning in the following section.

Situated learning

The growing interest in OL/LO has coincided with an increasing interest in describing learning as *situated* in social practice. This approach has developed in opposition to the psychological, cognitive view on learning as practised in formal and institutional settings.[12] Most writers on situated learning theories come from the field of educational research, that is, they are trying to rewrite educational theory along lines that differ from individual cognition. Their work is based on theories of everyday life and social culture.[13] It is inherent in the situated learning perspective that learning is more than information-processing and the transfer of 'right' attitudes and cultures.

When learning is viewed as situated learning processes, that is, as part of a social practice, we are in an epistemological world that differs from the approach that regards OL/LO as a (management) tool, that is to say as a variable that can be used to design organizations. We are now in the metaphorical world of interpretation. Here, the perspective on learning is not based on the individual, but on the social practice of organizational life. The bare thought of reifying social structures and processes is impossible, as they continuously are being produced and reproduced, interpreted and reinterpreted. In other words, the perception is focused on *change* rather than order and regulation.

To view learning as an inherent part of social practice, as something interpreted from the world we live in, may also be called a social constructivist approach to learning – and organizations. The approach has developed concepts such as 'learning-in-working', where learning is an inevitable part of working (together) in social settings. Work practices are viewed as social constructions, that is, as constructed through narration and story-telling (Orr, 1990). From this perspective the organization may be viewed as several *communities of practice* (Lave and Wenger, 1991).

However, the concept 'communities of practice' is not that clear, as it may connote both interactional contexts and different groups of employees. The latter, I think, might also be termed 'communities of practitioners', which would imply a focus on the actual learners/persons. I believe that Lave and Wenger deliberately do *not* use the term 'communities of practitioners', as they want to stress the interactional context and not 'only' the participants' skills, knowledge and professions. However, this is precisely where I disagree. I find that Lave and Wenger focus too much on context and too little on individual *experience*. I simply find it hard to envision an interactional context of learning that somehow is not based on the actions, interactions, experiences, emotions and thoughts of individuals – but socially shaped and shaping individuals. I shall return to this issue.

As an alternative to the individual cognition approach to learning, Lave and Wenger have developed an analytical concept, *legitimate peripheral participation* (LPP), where learning is conceived as a basically social affair, that is, as participation in practice. The concept derives from an interpretation of learning in several apprenticeship situations, that is to say situations where learning as participation in practice plays an important, if not an essential, part. However, developing the concept of LPP serves a wider purpose than to understand learning in an apprenticeship situation. In fact, Lave and Wenger argue that the concept can be used to understand all forms of learning. In a sense, LPP was developed in an effort to find a term that could be used to understand learning in situations without any visible signs of teaching activities, in LOs for example. When using LPP as a concept to understand learning there is no differentiation between participation in practice and learning. Participation in any practice implies that learning in some form or other will occur. This is my main reason for introducing LPP in a chapter on OL/LO.

LPP points out that learners inevitably are participating in communities of practice – in interactional contexts. In order that newcomers can accumulate knowledge, acquire skills and/or learn some form of profession or job in an organizational setting they must participate fully in the so-called sociocultural practices of a community, a professional community, for example. To view learning as an integral and inseparable part of social practice implies that learning a skill comes from actually *engaging* in the process of performance. The concepts of meaning, understanding and learning are all defined in relation to the actional contexts, and not merely in relation to the mind, as, for example, a 'container' that is slowly filling up.

By applying the concept of LPP, the *locus* of learning is changed. Learning takes place within a framework of (social) participation, not in the individual mind. This means that the differences in perspective (the multiple perspectives) among the co-participants are instrumental in generating learning. According to this definition it is the community that 'learns'. However, Lave and Wenger argue that the learning process does not overlook the individual, who is merely viewed as part of the community. So the learning process involves learning an identity and a profession or skill in addition to a sense of belonging to the organization.

However, as I have partly implied in my discussion of the concept of community of practice, I believe that within the LPP framework the conceptual distinction between learning and practice and between the individual and the organization has 'dissolved'. My attempts to theorize on the concept of organization and to elaborate on the concept of learning should be seen in this light. In the following, I will view organizations from an *interactionist* perspective and learning as a reconstruction and reorganization of *experience* that essentially is individual – but based on a perspective of individuals as socially shaped and vice versa.

An interactionist perspective on organizations

The focus on organizations from an interactionist perspective does basically not differ from the concept of organizations as communities of practice. Star (1992) draws a parallel between Lave and Wenger's concept, communities of practice, and Strauss' (1993) interactionist concept, organizations as *social worlds*. However, I find that the expansion of the concept of communities of practice towards the concept of social worlds removes the dilemma discussed earlier, where communities of practice connote either groups of practitioners or interactional contexts. The social worlds concept explicitly involves both people and contexts.

> This [concept of social worlds] is the same concept as that of 'community of practice' – a unit of analysis based on common activities and their attendant symbols. (Star, 1992: 401)

Strauss' theory on organizations as social worlds is based on a so-called theory of action,[14] inspired by American pragmatism, especially the work of John Dewey and George Herbert Mead, but also by the academic tradition of the so-called Chicago-trained sociologists.[15] The theory emphasizes how to conceptualize action, or rather acting as action is viewed as an ongoing process. Action/interaction and the (individual and collective) experience that is an integral part of action are viewed as a continuous process. Normally, action/interaction consists of routine activities, but they may be interrupted and lead to a reorganization. It is an important assumption that the world of social phenomena is highly complex, and that social stability and social change cannot be separated. Therefore, we should consider process and structure as constituting each other, so to speak.

The individual is not an isolated entity who encounters society, but a social being, shaped by and shaping society. Both individual and collective activities are grounded in the past, the present and the future. Actions and interactions take place between and among group members and should not be viewed merely as the actions and interactions of individuals. Owing to the different perspectives of the interactants, the same actions may result in multiple meanings. Furthermore, individuals are able to engage in self-reflection (thinking) before, during and after any overt actions. The multiple perspectives are further complicated by the variety of memberships in the social worlds. We recognize a self 'in' our own actions and in those of others, that is, we can reflect on ourselves and others.[16]

Strauss has developed the concept *trajectory*, which he regards as the central concept in his sociological, interactionist theory of action. He uses the concept of trajectory in two ways:

> (1) The course of any experienced phenomenon as it evolves over time (an engineering project, a chronic illness, dying, a social revolution, or national

> problems attending mass or 'uncontrollable' immigration) and (2) the actions and interactions contributing to its evolution. That is, phenomena do not just automatically unfold nor are they straightforwardly determined by social, economic, cultural, or other circumstances; rather, they are in part *shaped by the interactions* of the concerned actors. (Strauss, 1993: 53–4, emphasis in original)

In terms of an OL/LO project, the concept might be used to place the project in a 'before', 'during' and 'after' framework, that is, an OL/LO project will always take place in an organization with a past, a present and (hopefully) a future. The 'time' aspect will, moreover, shape the process of the project. But if we stick to the OL/LO example, following the 'historical' dimension, the acting and interacting in connection with an OL/LO project can only be viewed as a developmental process that constantly is interpreted and reinterpreted, acted and reacted upon by the individual members and groups involved, including the organization as a whole.

Strauss has also developed several so-called subconcepts, but to go into these will take me outside the theme of OL/LO. However, he has developed what he calls a *conditional matrix*, an instrument that may be used to understand the conditions of actors' interaction and the results derived from actors' memberships in social worlds and subworlds.

> Other conditions bearing on interactions can be thought of in terms of a conditional matrix, ranging from broader, more indirect conditions to narrower and more directly impacting ones. The specific relevance of conditions can be analysed by means of tracking conditional paths. (Strauss, 1993: 42)

Strauss and his colleagues have developed a methodological procedure for tracing the conditional paths in order to lay out the conditional matrix for trajectory unfolding. It is a method for tracking events through different levels of conditions from – in principle – an international level to the level of interaction and action. An event (for example, an OL/LO project) may be studied and viewed along a conditional path that may end up in the realm of global economy and international politics.

In accordance with the Chicago tradition, Strauss uses the concept of social worlds to comprehend organizational life as it unfolds among the members and in the context of the organization. It is a term that underlines how important it is to go beyond thinking in terms of social structure, that is, thinking in terms of social classes, ethnic groups, institutions etc. as determining and all-significant variables. Strauss does not dismiss the variables as irrelevant, but for him they do not encompass all human actions and interactions. Instead, he suggests that we study social worlds, which he defines as:

> groups with shared *commitments* to certain activities, sharing resources of many kinds to achieve their goals, and building shared ideologies about how to go about their business. (Clarke, 1991: 131; cited in Strauss, 1993: 212, emphasis added)

The social worlds do not represent social units or 'social structures', but a recognizable form of collective action. They are formed by *individual* commitments. When using the term situated learning, in communities of practice I think that Strauss' theory of action and his development of the concepts of trajectory, conditional matrix, social worlds and commitment may add to our understanding of 'communities of practice' by including individual (yet, socially shaped) and institutional activities.

Learning as reorganization and reconstruction of experience

Previously, I have claimed that the systems theory on OL/LO retreats from theorizing on learning as a social phenomenon, as it considers it an individual affair. Individuals are seen as part of a system and as constituting the system through their behaviour and the work they perform, which depends on the technical aspects of organizational life. I also claimed that something is missing in the conceptualization of learning in the situated learning theories. In addition, I have shown that the social worlds perspective on organizations which regards human actions and interactions as a collective phenomenon has potential as a social theory of learning for developing OL/LO.

In my analysis of this approach I will now return to the tradition of Pragmatist philosophy and especially to its study of education and learning presented by the work of John Dewey.[17] The most interesting concept in his study on learning is his notion of *experience*. Dewey's theory on learning is not as such in opposition to the situated learning approach. Rather, the two theories belong to the same field of enterprise, but stress slightly different aspects of learning.[18] However, as I feel that the *intentionality* of individuals, that is, the ability to act in a purposeful and meaningful way in learning processes, tends to disappear in the situated learning approach, I will turn my attention to Dewey's perspective on learning.

Dewey defines learning as a continuous reorganization and reconstruction of experience.[19] Learning takes place all the time and in all situations where people act and interact – reflect and think. Dewey's notion of learning, or rather *reflective experience*, grows out of a *situation* where a person is confused or in doubt, that is, confronted with a *problem* that makes her/him stop and think. His learning theory can be described as the following stream: situation>problem>inquiry>reflection>new situation. Dewey's notion of learning implies a non-dualist understanding of doing and knowing, action and thinking. The dualist separation is replaced by a continuity of acting and knowing.

According to Dewey, learning results in *growth*, or rather a growing process, that is, a continuous process as part of life's development. Although learning takes place in social situations, it is the *individual* learner who learns, and learns through reorganizing and reconstructing her/his experience. This leads us to the definition of his concept of experience, and what it means to learn from experience:

> To 'learn from experience' is to make a backward and forward connection between what we do to things and what we enjoy or suffer from things in consequence. Under such conditions, doing becomes a trying; an experiment with the world to find out what it is like; the undergoing becomes instruction – discovery of the connection of things. . . . (1) Experience is primarily an active–passive affair; it is not primarily cognitive. But (2) the *measure of the value* of an experience lies in the perception of relationships or continuities to which it leads up. It includes cognition in the degree in which it is cumulative or amounts to something, or has meaning. (Dewey, 1916(1966): 140, emphasis in the original)

Thus, experience does not derive from mere activity, mere doing, and it is not only based on change, but change which implies reflection on former actions in order to anticipate further consequences. The mere participation in practice, in action, does not create learning. A person is only learning if she/he is able to reflect upon her/his actions and reorganize as well as reconstruct experience by a continuous process of reflection – thinking – as a means of action. The idea of learning as reorganization and reconstruction of experience is not a matter of arguing for or against cognition. Learning theory, according to Dewey, involves both actions and cognition, and actions without cognition are of little value in terms of learning.

Reflecting and thinking are intentional efforts aiming at discovering specific connections between our actions and the resulting consequences to the effect that the two elements become continuous. This process allows a person to act with an end in view, that is, in a purposeful manner. We may also say that learning begins by thinking (by having an end in view, a purpose) and results in further thinking enabling the learner to come up with new aims etc. Thus, action is a necessary condition for thinking, but not a sufficient one. Thinking, however, requires a *language*. The learner needs a language to reorganize and reconstruct her/his experience. A language will enable the learner to generalize, for example, about specific actions and communicate the message through signs, words and concepts to her/himself and others.

We may also call the approach to the learning theory *problem-oriented*, as its point of departure is our encounter with a problem that makes us stop and think and by means of purposeful inquiry leads us to reflect, think, and change our practice. In other words, we discover a problem, make inquiries, reflect on the problem and solve it for the time being. However, the whole process is embedded in a social practice, which means that learning involves changes in both social practice and individuals engaged in a continuous reorganization and reconstruction of their experience – and expertise. They are engaged in personal growth processes as well as in social changes, such as organizational changes.

As the learning process – reorganization and reconstruction of experience – is embedded in social practice, the role of mediational means is important. In Dewey's study mediation is done by way of language, both in the form of 'internal' thought processes and dialogues with oneself and as 'external' communication processes with oneself and others. The nature of language is essentially social, something that people share as a (sub-) culture. It is the *tool* we use for thinking and (self-) reflection. And for Dewey, language is the 'tool of tools'. The reason is that language is a means to turn thinking into a social medium, a way of sharing our world with others. Other artifacts, such as technology, are also perceived as tools and embedded in the social world, and they also play a crucial role in developing (social) learning.

> The invention and use of tools have played a large part in consolidating meanings, because a tool is a thing used as means to consequences, instead of being taken directly and physically. It is intrinsically relational, anticipatory, predictive. Without reference to the absent, or 'transcendence', nothing is a tool. . . . As to be a tool, or to be used as means for consequences, is to have and to endow with meaning, language, being the *tool of tools*, is the cherishing mother of all significance. (Dewey, 1925/1958: 185–6, emphasis added)

When we view language as a tool of communication we establish a cooperation between partners. It is not a mere 'expression' of something antecedent or of antecedent reasoning. Language is a tool for generating meaning in cooperation with others – and in communication with oneself. As such, it may be viewed as a form of *action*.

From OL/LOs to learning communities?

The time has come for me to draw this chapter to a conclusion and tie up any loose ends. It is never easy to part with the text for now, and it is a task that always fills me with ambivalence. Partly, I feel good about a job done, and partly I am concerned whether I was able to impart to the reader what I really wanted to say. Did I elaborate on my material in the right places, and did I leave out all irrelevant stuff? But all things must come to an end, and as OL/LO is the heart of the matter, I have decided to do so by briefly discussing the contributions of a social learning theory as opposed to an individual cognitive perspective on learning.

This means that I will skip all other questions relating to this chapter and OL/LOs, as for example: Can OL flourish in a system of regulation and control? Can learning be managed? The short answer is 'no'. Learning is a deeply emotional and personal process, and unless 'brainwash' is used as a means to pursue learning, it is certain that even if many people are presented with the same problem, no one will learn exactly the same from their efforts to solve it. This difference might be due to many things, but the primary reason is that each person 'enters' a situation with her/his own – individual – experience. Let me take a positive view and try to answer my concluding question: What can we do to establish an OL/LO project when we take Lave and Wenger, Strauss and Dewey by the hand?

First and foremost, I consider Lave and Wenger's concept, *participation* in communities of practice, as an important contribution. In order to learn it is necessary to participate, be *engaged*, in the organizational project. I am deeply convinced (but have no evidence as such, if that exists within this area) that in order to create engaged participation it is necessary to include employees, middle management and other organizational members in decisions about where the organization wants to go, why and how. It is not only a matter of employing the best consultants, designing a feasible vision and then say 'go' to the rest of the organization. They must be included all the way. Does this line of thought have too much of a Scandinavian ring to it? Well, there may be a reason for that.

Secondly, and as mentioned earlier, I find Strauss' concepts, *trajectory* and *conditional matrices*, very relevant as analytical tools in a learning process aimed at developing OL/LOs. I see the concepts as tools that can help to understand the social world within the organization that aims to become an LO. In my view, the development of an LO is a fairly long process, in which organizational members will need tools to assist them in understanding their own organization. Questions raised by the trajectory concept might be: Where did we come from? Where are we now? And where do we want to go? And how do we get there? The questions relating to the conditional matrix concept may lead to a joint analysis of organizational events, situations, and the like. The questions may be: What is the problem, and how is it connected with the organizational members, the organization, and the world around it?

Finally, I believe that the notion of *experience* prevents us from focusing solely on individual cognition, although cognition is a very important part of constructing and reconstructing experience. The learning situation is expanded by trying, doing – and thinking of the consequences in order to resolve any potential problems. It is not enough that the right ideas and attitudes are presented in a nice packet (say, at a fancy course resort). It is a matter of taking part in formulating the problems and solving them within the social worlds of the organization. These themes have been very little discussed in the literature on OL/LOs, and I think it is because most research and practice are unwilling to dig right into the beef. In other words, to actually work on the issues of 'what' in the learning situation, which means to work with the tasks of the organization in order to study and improve the hows and discuss the whys. Such a process demands working with the development of an LO *in situ*, working on the actions of the organization. However, organizations consider it much more straightforward to send people off to learn, for example to learn to communicate better.

Notes

1 See also the latest book on OL/LO by Argyris and Schön (1996), where they discuss the split in OL/LO theories, although from another perspective.

2 In my interpretation of different epistemological positions within OL/LO theories I am indebted to the work of Smircich (1983) for her notion of organizational culture. Smircich distinguishes, on the one hand, between an understanding of culture as yet another variable to manage from a functionalistic perspective. On the other hand, she presents us with a social constructivist understanding of culture as something that is inherent in all organizations, and which only can be interpreted – not 'managed'. I use the same general perspective when I distinguish between OL/LO to regulate processes versus OL/LO as a term that explains organizational (learning) processes.

3 I have been inspired by the work of Lave and Wenger (1991) to use the term 'situated' learning. However, the perspective was brought into the OL/LO literature by an article written by Brown and Duguid (1991) in the Special Issue of *Organization Science* on Organizational Learning. I do not know who actually coined the notion 'communities of practice', but all the writers mentioned (Brown and Duguid; Lave and Wenger) have at one point been affiliated with the Institute for Research on Learning (IRL) in Palo Alto, California. For many years this research centre has worked with this perspective on learning.

4 To mention a few, see e.g. Argyris 1992, Argyris and Schön, 1974, 1978, 1996; Elkjaer, 1995a, 1995b; Mabey and Iles (eds), 1994; *Organization Science*, 1991; Schein, 1992; Schön, 1983a, 1983b; Senge, 1990.

5 The following articles are overview articles: Dodgson, 1993; Elkjaer, 1994; Huber, 1991; Levitt and March, 1988; Miner and Mezias, 1996; Shrivastava, 1983.

6 See Legge (1995) for an elaborated discussion of this theme.

7 Mabey and Iles (1994) even titled their reader on organizational learning *Managing Learning*.

8 Senge (1990) has been inspired by the work of Forrester, see e.g. Forrester and Senge, 1980, and later also by the work of Richardson, 1991. See also Roth and Senge, 1996.

9 I am aware that my description may not include all the subtleties in this organizational perspective, and that I may be doing a great injustice to this approach to OL/LO. But sometimes such actions are necessary in order to further an understanding of the more basic, underlying values and assumptions in theoretical positions.

10 There are many references on these processes under many different names and titles, but mainly they are disguised under themes such as developmental or educational psychology. See e.g. Jensen, 1980; Lave, 1988; Nielsen and Webb, 1991. The work of Jean Piaget (e.g. 1967) and his emphasis on adaptation as a sort of process of equilibrium between the individual and the environment has had a great influence on the cognitivists, see e.g. Prawat, 1995.

11 See e.g. Hollway's work (1991) on the OD tradition.

12 First and foremost, I think of Lave, 1988; Lave and Wenger, 1991; but also of Brown and Duguid, 1991; Orr, 1990; as well as other writers who are in one way or another connected with the work on situated learning processes. One may also refer to the work on distributed cognition, see e.g. Salomon (ed.), 1993.

13 Their work has a Danish counterpart based upon critical theory, see e.g. Nielsen and Webb, 1991; Olesen, 1985.

14 Strauss does not have the same understanding of the concept 'theory of action' as Argyris and Schön (1974). It will be too complicated to go into further details about the differences here.

15 See Clarke, 1991 for an excellent account of this approach to organizations.
16 See also Strauss, 1959.
17 I refer primarily to Dewey's work on learning and education: see Dewey, 1916/1966; 1933 (ed.)/1910; 1938/1963.
18 See Garrison, 1995 for an excellent discussion of this issue.
19 Dewey uses the term 'education' instead of learning, but a more up-to-date version of his theory would probably use the term 'learning'.

References

Argyris, Chris (1992) *On Organizational Learning*. Oxford: Blackwell.

Argyris, Chris (1996) Unrecognized defenses of scholars: impact on theory and research. *Organization Science*, 7 (1): 79–87.

Argyris, Chris and Schön, Donald A. (1974) *Theory in Practice. Increasing Professional Effectiveness*. San Francisco: Jossey-Bass.

Argyris, Chris and Schön, Donald A. (1978) *Organizational Learning: a Theory of Action Perspective*. Reading, MA: Addison-Wesley.

Argyris, Chris and Schön, Donald A. (1996) *Organizational Learning II. Theory, Method, and Practice*. Reading, MA: Addison-Wesley.

Bjørn-Andersen, Niels and Chatfield, Akemi (1996) Driving Organizational Transformation through the Use of Inter-Organizational Systems (IOS). Invited plenary presentation. Ninth International Conference on EDI–IOS, Bled, Slovenia, June 1996.

Brown, John Seely and Duguid, Paul (1991) Organizational learning and communities-of-practice: toward a unified view of working, learning, and innovation. *Organization Science*, 2 (1): 40–57.

Clarke, Adele E. (1991) Social worlds/arenas theory as organizational theory. In: David R. Maines (ed.), *Social Organization and Social Process. Essays in the Honor of Anselm Strauss*. New York: Aldine de Gruyter. pp. 119–58.

Dewey, John (1916/1966) *Democracy and Education. an Introduction to the Philosophy of Education*. New York: The Free Press.

Dewey, John (1925/1958) *Experience and Nature*. New York: Dover Publications.

Dewey, John (1933 (rev.)/1910) *How We Think: a Restatement of the Relation of Reflective Thinking to the Educative Process*. Boston, MA: D.C. Heath.

Dewey, John (1938/1963) *Experience and Education*. New York: Collier Books.

Dodgson, Mark (1993) Organizational learning: a review of some literatures. *Organization Studies*, 14 (3): 375–94.

Elkjaer, Bente (1994) Arbejde som kontinuerlig læreproces? (Work as a continuous learning process?) *LOKE. Om arbejdsmiljø, teknologi, samfund, uddannelse*, 12: 3–5.

Elkjaer, Bente (1995a) Learning is an active and personal process. In: Cristina Zucchermaglio, Sebastiano Bagnara and Susan Stucky (eds), *Organizational Learning and Technological Change*. Berlin: Springer. pp. 75–95.

Elkjaer, Bente (1995b) Learning as the New Form of Labor. Paper presented at the AERA (American Educational Research Association) Conference in San Francisco. Department of Informatics and Management Accounting Working Paper.

Forrester, Jay W. and Senge, Peter M. (1980) Tests for building confidence in system dynamics models. *TIMS Studies in the Management Sciences*, 14: 209–28.

Garrison, Jim (1995) Deweyan pragmatism and the epistemology of contemporary social constructivism. *American Educational Research Journal*, 32 (4): 716–40.

Hollway, Wendy (1991) *Work Psychology and Organizational Behaviour. Managing the Individual at Work*. London: Sage.

Huber, George P. (1991) Organizational learning: the contributing processes and the literatures. *Organization Science*, 2 (1): 88–115.

Jensen, Jørgen Pauli (1980) *Udvikling og Livsvilkår*. (Development and Conditions of Life). Copenhagen: Gyldendals pædagogiske bibliotek.

Lave, Jean (1988) *Cognition in Practice*. Cambridge: Cambridge University Press.

Lave, Jean and Wenger, Etienne (1991) *Situated Learning. Legitimate Peripheral Participation*. Cambridge: Cambridge University Press.

Legge, Karen (1995) *Human Resource Management. Rhetorics and Realities*. Houndmills: Macmillan Business.

Levitt, Barbara and March, James G. (1988) Organizational learning. *Annual Review of Sociology*, 14: 319–40.

Mabey, Christopher and Iles, Paul (eds) (1994) *Managing Learning*. London: Routledge.

Miner, Anne S. and Mezias, Stephen J. (1996) Ugly duckling no more: pasts and futures of organizational learning research. *Organization Science*, 7 (1): 88–99.

Nevis, Edwin C., DiBella, Anthony J. and Gould, Janet M. (1995) Understanding organizations as learning systems. *Sloan Management Review*, Winter: 73–85.

Nielsen, Jørgen Lerche and Webb, Thomas W. (1991) An emerging critical pedagogy. Rethinking Danish educational philosophy in the light of changing concepts of culture. *Humanistisk Årbog*, no. 4 (Roskilde Universitetscenter), pp. 157–208.

Olesen, Henning Salling (1985) *Voksenundervisning – hverdagsliv og erfaring*. (Adult teaching – everyday life and experience). Copenhagen: Unge Pædagoger.

Organization Science (A Journal of the Institute of Management Sciences) (1991) *Special Issue Organizational Learning: Papers in Honor of (and by) James G. March*. 2 (1).

Orr, Julian (1990) Sharing knowledge, celebrating identity: community memory in a service culture. In: David Middleton and Derek Edwards (eds), *Collective Remembering*. London: Sage. pp. 169–89.

Piaget, Jean (1967) *Intelligensens psykologi* (The Psychology of Intelligence). Copenhagen: Hans Reitzel.

Prawat, Richard S. (1995) Misreading Dewey: reform, projects, and the language game. *Educational Researcher*, 24 (7): 13–22.

Richardson, George P. (1991) *Feedback Thought in Social Science and Systems Theory*. Philadelphia: University of Pennsylvania Press.

Roth, George L. and Senge, Peter M. (1996) From theory to practice: research territory, processes and structure at an organizational learning centre. *Journal of Organizational Change*, (9) 1: 92–106.

Salomon, Gavriel (ed.) (1993) *Distributed Cognitions. Psychological and Educational Considerations*. Cambridge: Cambridge University Press.

Schein, Edgar H. (1992) *Organizational Culture and Leadership*, 2nd edn. San Francisco: Jossey-Bass.

Schön, Donald A. (1983a) *The Reflective Practitioner. How Professionals Think in Action*. New York: Basic Books.

Schön, Donald A. (1983b) Organizational learning. In: G. Morgan (ed.), *Beyond Method. Strategies for Social Research*. Beverly Hills, CA: Sage. pp. 114–28.

Senge, Peter M. (1990) *The Fifth Discipline. The Art and Practice of the Learning Organization*. New York: Doubleday Currency.

Shrivastava, Paul (1983) A typology of organizational learning systems. *Journal of Management Studies*, 20 (1): 7–28.

Smircich, Linda (1983) Concepts of culture and organizational analysis. *Administrative Science Quarterly*, 28 (3): 339–58.

Star, Susan Leigh (1992) The Trojan door: organizations, work, and the 'open black box'. *Systems Practice*, 5 (4): 395–410.

Strauss, Anselm L. (1959) *Mirrors and Masks. The Search for Identity*. Glencoe, IL: The Free Press.

Strauss, Anselm L. (1993) *Continual Permutations of Action*. New York: Aldine de Gruyter.

PART TWO

EVALUATIONS OF PRACTICE

---

6 The Role of Evaluative Enquiry in Creating Learning Organizations

Hallie Preskill and Rosalie T. Torres

In this chapter we propose that traditional forms of evaluation practice within organizations be reconceptualized as 'evaluative enquiry' for organizational learning. Evaluative enquiry requires that organization members critically consider what they think, say and do in the context of the work environment. Evaluative enquiry is an approach to understanding, improving and changing organizational life where the beneficiaries of enquiry are the enquirers. It implies both thought and action, as well as cognitive, behavioural, and affective processes that influence the way we make decisions, solve problems, adapt to change, and meet learning and performance challenges. The processes we have identified as the core of evaluative enquiry are:

- Asking questions
- Identifying and challenging values, beliefs and assumptions
- Reflection
- Dialogue
- Collecting, analysing and interpreting data
- Action planning
- Implementation

The seven evaluative enquiry processes facilitate learning by helping individuals and teams develop new knowledge, insight, skills and appreciation.

The ideas expressed in this chapter are discussed in greater detail in *Evaluative Inquiry for Learning in Organizations*, 1999, Thousand Oaks, CA: Sage.

Asking questions helps individuals and teams clarify issues, identify misconceptions and determine what additional information is needed. *Identifying and challenging values, beliefs and assumptions* encourages individuals and teams to make public how and why they think the way they do. At an organization level, identifying the assumptions under which the organization operates creates opportunities to change old routines and structures. Engaging in *reflection* creates the freedom for organization members to consider the impact of theirs and others' behaviours with the hope of creating deeper understanding about an issue and each other. Through *dialogue* a team shares ideas and experiences that lead to new ways of thinking and perceiving. When team members share the results of dialogue with others in the organization they act as translators of learning between themselves and other organization members. When teams *collect, analyse and interpret data,* they engage in a collective enquiry process that produces information on important organizational issues and concerns. *Action planning* involves taking what has been learned by organization members and developing a plan for what should be done. Finally, *implementation* exemplifies the need to act on members' learning, to test out new methods, processes, procedures, products and services.

An organization can start with any one of the enquiry processes and employ any of the others as appropriate. It is the interaction among these processes that creates double-loop and deutero learning (Argyris and Schön, 1978, 1996). That is, as these processes are implemented, individuals collectively begin not only to question current practices and what they have learned, and how their values and assumptions have changed from enquiry, but they continually reflect on *how* they have learned.

The underlying premise of the evaluative enquiry approach and specific processes is based on the following assumptions:

- enquiry informs learning for and about performance;
- enquiry is the process and energy of learning;
- enquiry facilitates collection and analysis of data that supports learning;
- enquiry should be embedded in organizational culture, structures and processes.

We argue that evaluation as currently practised is more likely to be conceived and implemented as a product-oriented event, rather than as an integral, on-going process that contributes to individual, team and organizational learning. And, as continuous change becomes the normal state in organizations, evaluators will need to broaden their purpose and corresponding set of tools if they wish their work to contribute significantly to the future success of organizations.

As a way to begin, we feel it is important to acknowledge our position about learning in organizations. The ideas expressed in this chapter are a result of our education and experiences in conducting programme evaluations in government and education agencies, and business, industry and healthcare organizations for the past 20 years. We became interested in the concept of organizational learning as we increasingly encountered instances where our work went unused and realized what little impact traditional evaluation practice was having on organizational change efforts. What follows is a framework of learning in organizations that uses the lens of enquiry and evaluation theory and practice. It will be clear to readers that our thinking has been significantly influenced by many noted writers on individual, team and organizational learning. Our recent research on evaluation communicating and reporting strategies and evaluation use with evaluation practitioners, and the interviews we have conducted at five US (learning) organizations has further strengthened our convictions about the role of evaluative enquiry and organizational learning (Torres et al., 1997). Throughout this chapter we have interwoven quotations from our interviewees as a means to illustrate the nature, role and barriers to evaluative enquiry and organizational learning.

Individual, team and organizational learning occur when:

- There is an acknowledged need for information.
- A spirit of enquiry exists.
- There is a need to focus on current issues or problems.
- There is a willingness to make explicit the values, beliefs and assumptions of organization members.
- Current assumptions are questioned.
- Past experiences are valued.
- There are opportunities to reflect on experience.
- There is an understanding that learning how to learn is as important as what is learned.
- Risks can be taken without fear of punishment.
- There are opportunities to share knowledge, skills and creative abilities which create new understandings and meanings.
- There is a climate of trust.
- Open and honest communication is honoured.
- There is widespread generation of, access to, and use of information.
- Data are turned into useful knowledge.
- Information is collectively interpreted.
- There is an established process for planning and decision-making.
- There is a high degree of involvement in determining how the learning will be applied.
- Change is seen as an opportunity for growth and improvement.
- Learning is applied to solve problems and resolve issues.
- There is an urgency to act.
- Determining what worked and what did not work is rewarded.

The role of data collection and information gathering has also been cited as central to organizational learning efforts. Learning organizations:

- are hungry for information and strive to communicate that knowledge with organization members who may benefit from it (Wick and Leon, 1993);
- continually measure how well they are doing and hold organization members accountable for progress (Brooks and Supina, 1992);
- involve the acquisition of new information and the ability to analyse that information creatively, learn from it, and apply that learning in useful ways (Thompson, 1995: 95).
- provide 'information regarding the bigger picture – information relevant to how the various parts fit together' (Mohrman et al., 1995: 182).

We now discuss how evaluative enquiry can be the catalyst for individual, team and organizational learning.

What it means to enquire evaluatively

While the term evaluation is not used by authors on organizational learning, there is sufficient evidence to suggest the powerful role evaluation could play when fully integrated into an organization's culture. Evaluation is described as 'a process of systematic enquiry to provide information about some object – a programme, project, process, organization, or product' (Torres et al., 1996: 1), that concerns judgements about the merit, worth or value of something. It seeks to answer questions of concern to programme or organizational members which includes understanding the values, standards and assumptions of those involved with what is being evaluated. Its ultimate goal is to provide meaningful information to intended users that can be used to support decision-making processes.

Summative forms of evaluation attempt to answer questions such as, 'Should the programme be continued?', 'Should more resources be allocated to a product's development?'. Formative evaluations, on the other hand, are used to make instrumental, usually immediate, improvements to the object being evaluated. We believe that evaluation can assist organizations in developing a culture of information, 'where information collection, development and utilization becomes a matter-of-fact, ongoing activity for all those working in the organization' (Bhola, 1995). To this end, 'we see the most realistic role for evaluative information as one that contributes in an evolutionary way to both understanding and decisions' (Torres et al., 1996: 48).

We see evaluative enquiry as a process for learning *in* organizations. The evaluative enquiry processes we propose are interdependent and relational; for evaluative enquiry to be effective, each of these processes must be engaged. As a set of interrelated processes, evaluative enquiry sustains and institutionalizes learning in organizations. We believe that regardless of the model used to conceptualize organizational learning, 'it is how this change is processed and managed that separates successful from less successful attempts to develop learning organizations' (Preskill, 1994: 293). We offer this approach and specific evaluative enquiry processes as one attempt to build a bridge between theory and practice that has been lacking in the organizational literature to date (Kilmann, 1996).

Evaluative enquiry processes

In the next section we present a definition and rationale for each of the seven enquiry processes. While many organizational learning researchers have written about one or more of these processes, we turn the kaleidoscope another revolution, to achieve a new perspective that adds the evaluative enquiry lens to our understanding of individual, team and organizational learning.

Asking questions

> Asking the proper question is the central act of transformation . . . (Chawla, 1995: 505)

Asking questions is a fundamental characteristic of organizations that learn. It is also one of the first tasks evaluators engage in when beginning an evaluation project. Yet, asking questions has not been highly valued in many organizations' cultures. Too often, asking questions has been seen as challenging authority, a means of evading someone else's question, or as a way to place blame, test someone, or make judgements. After analysing the taped conversations of executive meetings, Ryan (1995) found that hardly a question had been asked in several hours of meetings. She asks, '*What if we valued the questions we hear as much as the answers we worship in our allocation of time?*' (1995: 282, emphasis in original). The point is, when we fail to ask questions, we lose the opportunity to gain information, insight, clarity and direction that would resolve problems more efficiently and effectively. In short, we miss out on learning at deeper levels.

Examples of not asking questions can be seen in any organizational environment where we leap from the problem to the solution without questioning what happened. In business organizations we see it in new programmes such as Total Quality Management and Business Process Re-engineering that are embraced with great fanfare, and within one or two years are dismissed as failures without knowing how, why and in what ways they may have failed. We see it in organizations' training departments where trainers are asked to design and develop training programmes without conducting needs assessments. In our schools educators have too often determined that a school's curriculum should be built around Howard Gardner's (1983) multiple intelligences model without carefully considering the implications and consequences of such actions. In evaluation practice, evaluators see it when at the beginning of an evaluation the client suggests conducting a survey without having clearly identified the purpose, audiences and expected uses of the evaluation findings.

Ultimately, the kinds of questions we should be asking in organizations are empirical questions that bring us closer to achieving the organization's mission, goals and supportive learning culture. We should be asking what, where, how, when and why questions of all we do. Most of the time these questions will emerge as a result of a problem, issue or concern one or more might have about a particular process, product, service, policy or procedure. These questions are not the type that lead to yes or no answers or one correct answer. Rather, these questions are truly open-ended and require reflection, dialogue and additional data to fully comprehend the range of possible actions. Only by asking questions can real change occur. Garvin (1984: 20) offers the following typology of questions:

- Broad diagnostic questions that provide a stimulus for opening up discussion, such as 'What's your interpretation [of a given situation]?' and 'What's the problem?'
- Specific questions of 'action or decision', that would ask practitioners what they should or would do in a given situation.
- Questions of extension or synthesis, such as 'How does that comment tie in [with someone else's comment]?' Another question could relate to the implications of someone's comment.
- Questions of priority or ranking, such as 'What's the most important issue?'
- Questions that challenge and test, such as 'Do you really believe that?', or asking for evidence to support a claim.
- Simple questions of clarification, such as 'What do you mean by that?'
- Factual questions that serve as fill-in-the-blank kinds of questions. These are frequently used questions that are less effective for sustaining continuing dialogue.
- Hypothetical questions, such as 'Suppose that, instead of being the smallest company, the firm were the largest – would that change your recommendations in any way?'
- Summary questions, such as 'What themes or lessons have emerged from this discussion?'

As 'enquiry practitioners' (Argyris and Schön, 1996) and 'communities of enquirers' (Ryan, 1995), asking questions develops a spirit of curiosity which serves as a catalyst for learning. As many evaluators have witnessed, the mere asking of a survey or interview question can cause individuals to change their thinking or practice even when personal enlightenment was not the evaluation's goal. Good questions awaken the curiosity, challenge our limited views, and create opportunities for dynamic learning. As Postman and Weingartner remind us,

> Once you have learned how to ask questions – relevant and appropriate and substantial questions – you have learned how to learn and no one can keep you from learning whatever you want to need to know. (1969: 23)

As organizations continue to change and evolve, the cost of not asking questions will increase. Organizations can no longer afford offering products, services and processes without knowing the extent to which their goals are accomplished. No longer can senior management rely solely on gut feelings and information from their inner circle to make decisions. Organizations that survive will be those that have cultures that support asking the hard questions and have developed methods, processes and systems to answer those questions. In Sally Helgeson's book *The Web of Inclusion* (1995), she describes how Dan Wolf, the founder and editor of the *Village Voice* newspaper in the early 1970s, 'shaped the organization by listening and asking the right questions, eliciting ideas that people hadn't even known they had' (p. 6). Some believe that the success was largely due to how employees were made to feel a part of the process. As Helgeson explains,

> This approach made everyone involved with the paper feel like participants in the debate and part of something important and always evolving. A kind of fractious togetherness developed, a good example of what *Inc.* magazine has recently called 'emancipation capitalism', an enterprise in which everyone who is part of it feels a sense of ownership – even if, in literal terms, they have none. (p. 7)

Even when questions are asked in organizations today, we find there is a strong tendency to believe that expert knowledge resides somewhere other than within the organization itself. While this tendency has created vast opportunities for external consultants who make a living out of providing advice to organizations, it has had serious consequences for those within organizations who possess expertise that goes untapped. By under-utilizing employees we create cultures of apathy, lethargy and anti-learning. The truth is, we have failed to tap the potential of organization members' knowledge and experience. We have not asked what they know, don't know and need to know, before seeking outside assistance. A manager at one organization we visited explained this dilemma in the following way:

> I think one of our biggest learning disabilities is that if you're a salaried graded 8 engineer for twenty years, then you're worthless. Because if you've been in the company for twenty years and don't have a [perk], you're obviously dead wood. Well that's [expletive]. Maybe that person has been there twenty years and has the knowledge that no one will ever learn if we don't tap it. (FD, DB)

While there are definite times it is necessary and valuable to engage a consultant to add expertise, we have too often overlooked the knowledge, skills and experiences of people closest to the problem.

On the other hand, there are times we are too quick to assume that we 'know' something fully when in fact we hold only a piece of the puzzle. The tendency not to acknowledge the limits of our own knowledge has been referred to as pre-reflective reasoning (King and Kitchener, 1994). Such reasoning is characterized by individuals asserting that what they have seen is true, and what is perceived is all that exists. While there may be several intellectual and ethical developmental reasons for this kind of reasoning, there are also organizational barriers that limit question-asking in organizations. As one human resources consultant explained to us,

> We don't ever talk about what it is we don't know and need to learn. We always talk about everything we know. We don't talk about what we don't know because I suppose there's this fear that we'll look really stupid. I don't know that I've ever heard any of our top management say, 'I don't know the answer to that.' (LOL, JT, p. 24)

Another interviewee added, 'There's not a lot of places where you're rewarded for saying, "I don't know". It's typically you either know or you fake it, or say, "I'll get back to you on that"' (FD, GJ, p. 11).

Asking questions about individuals' knowledge and experience is an important method for exploring the capacity of organization members. More and more organizations are beginning to find ways to capture the expertise of their employees. At *Fortune Magazine*, when employees log on to their e-mail bulletin board each day, they typically see the message, 'Does anyone know . . .?' The editor explains that this is part of a trend at the magazine to 'accumulate the knowledge of individual employees into an organizational asset' (Allerton, 1996: 8).

Evaluative enquiry requires that people carefully consider their current level of knowledge and understanding about the problem or issue at hand and determine what other information is needed. The consistent and ongoing questioning about the practices, processes and outcomes of our work stimulates continuous learning, a sense of connectedness, and improved individual, team and organizational performance.

Identifying and challenging values, beliefs and assumptions

Inherent in any questions or solutions that may be offered are the values, beliefs and assumptions people hold. These dispositions have been developed over time and are what guide people in their everyday life. They are the taken-for-granted behaviours by which we function. As Brookfield asserts, 'we *are* our assumptions' (1995: 2). Yet, for organizations to learn, individuals and teams must learn how to continually question, test and validate these values, beliefs and assumptions in a public way. Mental models, knowledge structures, cognitive maps, schema, frames and paradigms have all been used by organizational theory and learning researchers to describe how individuals interpret information. They have also been used to understand the role of memory in learning and how future action is predicted. Without exploring what underlies our thinking, we are prone to continue operating in old ways – limiting the potential for learning and change.

To understand individuals' underlying values, beliefs and assumptions with regard to an issue or problem, it is critical that members establish a climate of safety and trust. This includes not only determining ground rules of acceptable group behaviour, but ensuring that the physical environment guarantees the necessary privacy. The goal is to understand why and how someone believes the way they do about a particular issue. Specific activities can be used to help individuals uncover their values, beliefs and assumptions with respect to a particular issue facing the organization. For instance, group members can be asked to write their responses individually to each of the following questions:

- What are my roles/responsibilities with respect to this issue?
- How did I become involved in these roles/responsibilities?
- What experiences have I had with respect to this issue? Were they positive, negative, or neutral?
- What experiences in other settings have I had with respect to this issue? Were they positive, negative, or neutral?
- Have I had an experience with this issue where my expectations were not met? If so, why were they not met?
- What are my opinions about how this situation can be improved?
- Based on my answers to these questions, what underlying assumptions/values does my perspective on this issue reflect?
- In what ways might my values influence my position on this issue?

Sharing responses can help group members more clearly see their value-position as one among many in the organization (Torres et al., 1996). The following example illustrates what can happen when individuals' assumptions are not explored.

Early into an evaluation that one of the authors conducted of a multi-year educational reform effort, she learned that the four lead teachers, who were called a 'team', had never discussed what it meant to be a team. From the outset, they simply assumed that they knew and agreed on what it meant to work as a team. During the school's experimental three years the teachers met almost daily to discuss and resolve various issues that the school was experiencing. Yet, they found themselves in almost constant conflict about how these issues should be resolved. By the end of the school's third year, the teachers' relationships with each other had deteriorated to a point where they barely spoke to each other. What became clear to the evaluator was that the teachers were operating from very different mental models about teamwork and that this situation contributed to the group's inability to work together more effectively. For one teacher, being part of a team meant coming together only to decide on obviously significant issues. For another teacher it meant daily meetings to decide on most of the school's operating policies and procedures by consensus. For another, it meant socializing with the staff during and after school, and building a close-knit adult community. The effect of the teachers' different assumptions about teamwork was disastrous for the long-term future of the school. At the end of the three years the lead teachers all transferred to different schools and left those behind feeling bewildered, frustrated and confused. Once touted as a school of the future, the school now functions much like any other school. It would be wrong to conclude that the teachers' failure to define teamwork led to the school's failure at reform. However, it is likely that their inability to work as a team contributed to many of the problems the school faced in its first few years.

Identifying individuals' and teams' values, beliefs and assumptions helps organization members appreciate why people talk and behave the way they do. In addition, it helps people understand why an individual or group has trouble moving forward when there is disagreement about direction. As one of our interviewees explained, 'If I start talking and somebody says, "oh, that's just a mental model", we all know what we're talking about. It diffuses the situation. It takes the emotional side out of it' (FD, GJ). By acknowledging people's assumptions, others can understand without saying it is right or wrong, or that they agree or disagree. This enquiry process helps further the dialogue by valuing and respecting individuals' history and opinions.

Reflection

Over the past 60 years, many writers have offered definitions of what it means to engage in reflection (for example, Brookfield, 1995; Dewey, 1933; Mezirow, 1991). Most agree that reflection is a process whereby we carefully consider the knowledge, beliefs, assumptions, actions and processes that influence our behaviour in order to understand our experiences. Mezirow (1991) suggests there are three types or foci of reflection. The first, *content reflection*, refers to reflection on the content or description of a problem or issue. The second, *process reflection*, involves analysing the methods and strategies that are being used to resolve the problem. The third type of reflection is *premise reflection*. This kind of reflection focuses on the underlying assumptions or beliefs we hold of the problem and asks us to consider why the problem is a problem in the first place.

Unfortunately, however, barriers to reflection permeate the work environment. These barriers include 'performance pressure' (time for reflection is a luxury and ill-afforded), competency traps (it is quicker and easier to keep doing what we are already doing even if it is not in the best interests of the organization), and absence of learning forums or structures (the leadership and culture do not reward learning) (Shaw and Perkins, 1991). An example of a performance pressure barrier was provided by one of the companies we studied. While the Vice-President of Information Systems firmly believes in reflection as a tool for organizational learning, and has trained his team in a reflection process, he laments the fact that his employees are so busy that they haven't had time to reflect on their work. He explains,

> Part of the problem we have right now is everybody is so busy that to take time out to reflect, it's almost a burden because now I've got to work after hours or another Saturday morning to get my job done. We have been for two years under the gun – task, task, task. That's the biggest reason. And we just plain haven't taken the time. (LOL, MW)

A perceived lack of time is in part due to the larger organizational culture which has not yet made the shift from short-term to long-term thinking. Yet the value of critical reflection can not be overlooked:

> To learn from our experiences we must become competent in taking action while simultaneously reflecting on that action. To effectively initiate, implement, and sustain transformation, we must reflect on the values behind our actions. We must be willing to reflect critically on what we are doing. Theories should guide practice, and then practice should inform theory. We should always be learning and analysing as a way of organizational life. (Mink et al., 1993: 8)

When practitioners reflect on their beliefs and resultant actions, they begin to understand how and why things happen the way they do in organizations. When they engage in reflection with others, they can gather more information with which to interpret their own experiences. Reflection enables us to interpret individual behaviour within a holistic framework – seeing how our own behaviour is affected by others and at the same time, how our own behaviour affects other organization members.

There are various times and ways in which reflection can stimulate enquiry and learning. Reflection may occur either during practice, after practice or for future practice. Reflection while we are engaged in some task occurs when we watch ourselves as we act out certain thoughts and actions. It is often likened to an 'out-of-body' experience and happens most when we try to see what we are doing from a different perspective. An example would be the trainer or teacher who constantly monitors and assesses how well the programme is going and makes adjustments as she goes along. Reflection that takes place after we have completed a task provides opportunities to revisit or recall what occurred in practice. Reflection on underlying premises challenges individuals to consider their mental models and assumptions that influenced their practice. And finally, reflection for future action or practice focuses on predicting how we will use what we learned in the reflection process (Saban et al., 1994; Schön, 1983, 1987; Schwandt, 1995). While reflection is often viewed as an individual activity, the outcomes of reflection are enhanced when done collectively.

To engage practitioners in reflection, Saban et al. (1994) suggest that participants adopt a centrism point of view. That is, group members are guided through a process where they apply *egocentrism*, where actions are explored or examined from the perspective of the individual, *allocentrism*, where participants see the world and consider actions, experiences or events from someone else's point of view, and *macrocentrism*, where the focus is on how the system or organization might view certain actions, events, or experiences. Group members would develop questions for the team that represent these viewpoints and encourage members to share their thoughts. Critically reflective learners are always asking why and how. They tend to observe the dissonance between their actions and what they think and believe.

The reflection process is the way we come to know and understand ourselves. And, knowing ourselves is critical to creating new meanings that lead to personal development and change. Engaging in critical reflection as a group accomplishes an even stronger community of practice.

Dialogue

While the terms 'discussion' and 'dialogue' are often used interchangeably, we believe there are differences worth noting. For example, the purpose of discussion is to tell, sell or persuade. It is an attempt to find agreement, defend one's assumptions, or convince someone of an idea. Dialogue, however, seeks to enquire, to share meanings, to understand the whole, and to uncover one's assumptions. Discussion is about individuals and preserving the status quo; dialogue is about communities and learning for change. It is through dialogue that individuals make connections with each other and communicate personal and social understandings that guide all subsequent behaviour. Through dialogue people learn about the organization's culture, policies, procedures, goals and objectives. It is the place where practitioners may confront contradictions that otherwise might go unchallenged and unquestioned and helps uncover one's assumptions and beliefs. It requires the suspension of defensive responses and even looks into the reasons for such defensiveness. Dialogue can be defined as,

> *a sustained collective enquiry into everyday experience and what we take for granted.* The goal of dialogue is to open new ground by establishing a 'container' or 'field' for enquiry, a setting where people can become more aware of the context around their experience, and of the processes of thought and feeling that created that experience. (Senge et al., 1994: 353, original emphasis)

Through the sharing of individuals' personal knowledge, dialogue has the potential to build capacities that dissolve resistance in times of organizational change (Brown, 1995: 157). Because of participants' varied backgrounds and experiences, individuals must engage in dialogue to identify resources, and understand, accept and appreciate individual differences in order to accomplish a group's tasks. Dialogue can also contribute to the production of new knowledge that can be shared between and among team members (Brooks, 1994). As one of our interviewees explained,

> I don't have to sit at my desk and solve a problem. In fact, that's rarely the way it happens. There's so much more when you meet with a whole bunch of different people who have different knowledge in the different areas and you talk the thing out, and the solution comes out of that dialogue. (FD, MB)

Asking for reasons behind statements, questions and actions further helps individuals weigh the pros and cons of different arguments, thereby helping them achieve a greater level of understanding. As individuals communicate and comprehend each other's viewpoints, they assimilate pieces that fit with their own way of thinking. This often results in a negotiated, new perspective that contains elements of both person's thoughts. Dialogue also helps group members deal with errors in thinking that cause people to generate faulty conclusions on which we base our behaviour. Common types of error are (1) personalization, (2) overgeneralization and (3) polarization. Personalization refers to the tendency to relate all people and events to oneself. Overgeneralization is the tendency to make broad, generalized conclusions based on a single incident or piece of information. And, polarization is the tendency to see things as right or wrong or black or white, where there is no middle ground (Phillips and Phillips, 1995). Dialogue has the potential to make these distortions public and explicit, allowing a group to correct them.

As team members engage in dialogue there will eventually be disagreements. Dialogue does not necessarily require agreement or consensus from group members. However, how disagreements are managed is critical to the future functioning of the group. When group members disagree, instead of arguing over who is right, it might be more worthwhile for members to develop a means for testing their disagreement. As Schwarz (1994) suggests, they should ask themselves two questions: 'How could we both be correct?' and 'How could we each see the same problem differently?' (p. 50). As anyone who has ever been part of a team can attest, conflict is an unavoidable part of working together. Instead of seeing conflict as a barrier to learning, or as a failure to establish relationships, dialogue incorporating different viewpoints should be viewed as a method that pushes members to question existing premises – to reconceptualize their assumptions in order to create new meanings from their experiences. While maintaining and accepting differences in one another, team members may come to some understanding about each other's perceptions. This appreciation also contributes to the building of a learning community.

Collecting, analysing and interpreting data

As groups or teams work together on a project or seek to accomplish some goal, they often discover that they do not have all of the information they need in order to proceed. Sometimes this occurs when two or more people disagree about what is causing the problem, how it might be resolved, or the direction the group should take. This realization is typically the result of question asking, identifying and challenging values, beliefs and assumptions, reflection, and dialogue among group members. When a group realizes that it needs more information, a means for collecting, analysing and interpreting data should be established. This enquiry process should be embedded in all group work.

It is important to first distinguish, however, what we mean by the terms 'data' and 'information'. Data are the results of enquiry. They may be in the form of numbers, such as percentages or mean scores from Likert scale survey items or test questions. Data may also be qualitative, in the form of words or pictures as would be gathered from interviews, observations, photographs, videotape or drawings. Until we assign an interpretation and meaning to the data, they do not inform us or tell us what might be done to address the issue. Information, then, is data that have been assigned meaning.

With increasing use of technology and easy access to data, many organizations are besieged with facts and figures. The problem is not that there is not enough data with which to answer our questions, learn and make decisions, but that the quality, timeliness and content of the data do not meet the learning and performance needs of organization members. Furthermore, most organizations lack the necessary information systems and channels to ensure that those who need information can retrieve it quickly and easily.

The collection, analysis and interpretation of data should be viewed as ongoing processes that respond to the information needs of organization members. This evaluative enquiry process is most closely associated with traditional evaluation practice. As questions arise from a group's involvement in evaluative enquiry, the most appropriate and effective methods of data collection need to be identified. The key task at this point is to clearly link the information needs to the questions and the kind of data that will best inform potential users of the information. While an evaluation consultant might facilitate this process, it is important that practitioners learn evaluation skills as well so that evaluation processes and skills are used and shared by all organization members.

> Instead of thinking in terms of evaluation as an activity orchestrated by evaluators, why couldn't knowledge production about a program be linked explicitly to the collective objectification of experience and self-reflection which intimately informs and is informed by program practice? (McTaggart, 1991: 20)

This point is critical to the creation and maintenance of a learning organization.

The commitment to collecting, analysing and interpreting data is central to evaluative enquiry. Through this process organizational uncertainties may be reduced, the dissonance between individual and group assumptions can be illuminated, and alternative viewpoints representing the multiple realities that exist can be surfaced. By collecting, analysing and interpreting data, issues will ultimately be better understood.

A group's involvement in collecting, analysing and interpreting data enables each person to see how their particular information needs are being met. Once a group's questions have been identified, the group then discusses potential uses of the information and who would be most affected by the results of the enquiry. It is at this point that appropriate and useful evaluation methods would be identified. Determining how these data would be collected and analysed, and by whom, would be a group decision. As team members consider the data in light of their own values, beliefs and assumptions, and what they have learned from and about each other, they create new learnings, relationships and understandings about the issue being explored.

The collection, analysis and interpretation of data need not be a terribly cumbersome and complex task. What is important is that the team establish a method for implementing this process in ways that are efficient and produce trustworthy, usable information. The quality of data is only as good as the methods used to collect and analyse them. Therefore, it is important that team members be trained on data collection and analysis strategies, and that all information collected be documented. Often, this training can be facilitated by an external evaluator who may develop a long-term relationship with the organization. The systematic, planned and rigorous collection and documentation of data are what distinguish true evaluation activity from anecdotal, unplanned and less credible forms of data collection.

As new learning emerges from collecting, analysing and interpreting data, the evaluative enquiry process is recycled by asking additional questions, identifying values, beliefs and assumptions, and reflecting on, and engaging in dialogue, about the findings. The continuous process of evaluative enquiry further nourishes individual, team and organizational learning.

Action planning

Action planning is where learning is applied. It is the process of using information resulting from any of the evaluative enquiry processes. Action planning takes place when the organization believes it has learned enough to take action – to change behaviour, to accomplish some indicated goal or task. As described earlier, this action might entail making minor adjustments to a programme, process, or product; or substantially changing an entire programme or department's purpose and procedures.

A key element of successful action planning is waiting long enough for this phase to begin. It is indeed tempting to begin planning and committing to the specifics of a change before issues, concerns and underlying values, beliefs and assumptions have been given sufficient chance to surface and become part of the planning process. At any one time most thinking individuals in an organization will have considered issues about and potential solutions for the dilemmas facing the organization – just as a matter of their own daily observations and reflections. (And indeed, making this kind of observation and reflection a collective, organizational learning process is precisely the point of evaluative enquiry.) As individuals participate in the enquiry processes prior to action planning, it can work well to provide an opportunity for them to record their early thinking about solutions as a 'running sidebar', visible to all participants. This procedure serves two purposes: (1) to allow this thinking to be acknowledged and free the person to move on to other kinds of, perhaps more integrative, thinking about a problem area and its solution; and (2) to provide for later comparison of early thinking about solutions with later, more deeply informed thinking about solutions. Where later thinking is observed to be more incisive than earlier thinking, the comparison can substantiate the merit of engaging in evaluative enquiry processes.

Once the dedicated action planning process begins, identifying barriers to implementation and developing plans for minimizing them are fundamental. Of particular concern is the fact that implementation of an action plan almost invariably requires the participation of a wider range of organizational members than have been involved in the action planning and prior enquiry processes. Care must be taken to proceed with planning in such a way that other organizational members can approximate the same ownership to the plan that its original developers would have. In fact, while the initial action planning work may involve a core group, it should progress with the involvement of as many organizational members as possible. For instance, action planning sessions might be held with each department involved (or representatives, in the case of very large organizations) to present a draft plan for their review, discussion and modification. This process can be very fruitful for identifying (1) organizational members' values, assumptions and beliefs regarding key elements of the plan; and (2) barriers to implementation unknown to the original action planning group.

Another potential barrier to successful implementation is inadequate training, information, and support for major new initiatives. Obviously, the bigger the change in behaviour the initiative requires of organizational members, the more training and support will be needed. Means for providing this help should be well articulated within the action plan. And finally, any action plan should include a clear delineation of specific activities or tasks, persons/departments responsible, timelines, and means for gauging success.

Implementation

Once a plan of action has been agreed to, the plan is implemented. During implementation, the evaluative enquiry process continues by developing new questions about the effectiveness and impact of the actions taken. However, one of the biggest challenges, particularly for organizations which have newly embraced an evaluative enquiry approach, will be to maintain it throughout the implementation of a new initiative. That is, having invested substantial energy in asking questions, examining values and assumptions, reflecting, dialoguing, collecting, analysing and interpreting data, and action planning, organizations may be tempted to relax during the implementation of what they have worked so hard to develop. Yet, at this time, an organization's enduring faith in enquiry as a means of continuous learning is critical. The following kinds of questions should be regularly addressed:

- How is actual implementation paralleling intended implementation, and what can be learned from the discrepancies?
- What new issues are surfacing that impact the success of the change being made?
- What adjustments are necessary and what is the best way to make them?

Addressing these questions might be the central focus of an implementation team made up of representatives of all departments/areas of an organization impacted by the change or new initiative being implemented. In fact, as it focuses on a specific change or initiative to monitor and ensure its success, this team will likely be engaging, to some degree, in all of the prior enquiry processes.

With successful implementation, ultimately the change or initiative will become part of the organization's standard operating procedure. At this time the organization, or some department, team or group within it, will re-engage its energy into more broadly defined enquiry processes in its quest for continuous, iterative learning.

Outcomes of individual, team and organizational learning

Several critics as well as proponents of organizational learning believe that we still do not know very much about the various effects organizational learning concepts and processes have on individuals, teams and organizations. Some are concerned that if we do not begin to make more concrete the benefits of organizational learning, then it too will fall prey to the 'flavour of the month' organizational change mentality that has caused many change interventions to suffer untimely deaths.

We propose that by identifying possible instrumental and conceptual outcomes of evaluative enquiry for learning in organizations, we can more accurately measure organizational learning efforts. Instrumental outcomes, which are usually pragmatic and evolutionary, reflect changes in the organization's structures, systems, products, services or processes. They may also be related to individual and team performance where individuals and teams use information to solve problems, improve how their work is managed and organized, and find more effective methods for accomplishing their work. They are typically implemented in the name of organization development and competitive advantage (DeGeus, 1988). Such outcomes are often tangible, measured through quantitative methods and are considered a direct result of the organizational learning process and related systems.

Conceptual outcomes reflect changes in individuals' growth and development with respect to how they think, feel and act in the work environment. They are a result of the interactions between individuals and their engagement in the organizational learning process. Such changes may enhance individual self-esteem, promote better communication, bring people closer together, and result in organization members' willingness to take greater risks. These kinds of outcomes have been called 'aspirational' in that an organization aspires to develop a world-wide learning community that is inherently communal, dialogical and cooperative. and leads to organizational harmony and sustainability (Binns, 1994; Burgoyne, 1992). An example of this type of change is provided by one of our interviewees:

> One of the most important things is that it has created stronger bonds between the people. There's less of that feeling of isolation – of I'm in this all by myself and the ship is going down, and my life's so hard. There's much more of a team sense that we're in this together, and if I'm having trouble, I know other people I can go to for help. There's very much a sense of extended family in a way. (FD, KS)

Conceptual outcomes are usually less tangible, need more time to take effect before being measured, and are often evaluated through qualitative methods. The following is a list of outcomes that are frequently associated with individual, team and organizational learning efforts.

Outcomes related to individual and team learning

Individuals and team members:

- understand how their actions affect other areas of the organization;
- tend to ask more questions than give solutions/answers;
- develop greater sense of personal accountability and responsibility for the organization's outcomes;
- are more self-directed learners;
- take higher risks;
- are more consultative, more coaching;
- are more likely to ask for help;
- are more effective listeners;
- use information to act;

- develop creative solutions (willingness to do something different);
- share the work that needs to be done.

Outcomes related to organizational learning

Organizations:

- develop new products and services;
- increase productivity;
- have higher morale, improved organizational work climate;
- experience less turnover;
- experience less waste/sabotage/error;
- experience improved financial performance;
- experience increased efficiency and less redundancy (workers understand how each job contributes to the organization's success);
- provide more effective service to clients/customers;
- are able to change more quickly.

While we firmly believe that these outcomes can be maximized through evaluative enquiry processes, we acknowledge that an organization must develop and maintain a supportive learning infrastructure for organization-wide learning to take place. This infrastructure should ensure that organizations develop a clear vision, mission and purpose, offer continuous learning opportunities, establish open and system-wide communication processes, develop integrated systems and structures, and have leaders that model continuous learning. Critics will argue that there are many organizations which do not possess the elements of this infrastructure. Should such organizations not attempt to use an evaluative enquiry approach and/or to become learning organizations? In fact, many organizations without this infrastructure are already utilizing some of the processes we outline in this chapter – to varying degrees, and we would argue, with varying overall success. The point is that we believe organizations can expect to be successful at learning through evaluative enquiry to the extent that they have a supportive infrastructure. In some cases, the approach must begin in some part of the organization before others, including leaders, can be convinced of its merit.

Issues for evaluators and researchers

Evaluative enquiry as described in this chapter poses two significant challenges for practising evaluators: (1) the evaluator's role and (2) the purpose of evaluation. While there has been considerable research on participatory, empowerment and collaborative forms of evaluation during the past ten years, and there is evidence of a growing interest in organizational learning in the evaluation community, only a few evaluation researchers have attempted to link the two disciplines (Cousins et al., 1996; Forss et al., 1994; Owen and Lambert, 1995; Preskill, 1994; Torres, 1994a,b; Torres et al., 1996). The results from a recent survey of North American evaluators interested in evaluation use ($n = 278$) from the American Evaluation Association (Preskill and Caracelli, 1998), indicate that 87 per cent of the respondents agree that the purpose of evaluation is to 'facilitate organizational learning'. Over three-quarters of the respondents (81 per cent) suggest that evaluators should 'take responsibility for facilitating organizational learning'. We find these results rather startling in that they represent a significant shift in many evaluators' thinking and roles.

The field of evaluation, as traditionally practised, has seldom identified evaluators as primary agents of change, or facilitators of learning. Indeed, many evaluation professionals believe that both external and internal evaluators should be objective observers, judges and experts of programmes they evaluate; their role should be confined to collecting the necessary information for the client to use in making judgements and decisions. Once the findings have been delivered, it has been up to the client to use the evaluation results.

Evaluative enquiry, however, implies a role for evaluators that is very different from traditional evaluation practice. It asks both internal and external evaluators to be collaborators, facilitators, interpreters, mediators, coaches and educators of organizational learning and change processes. It asks external evaluators to develop longer-term relationships with organizations so that their members can also become knowledgeable and skilled in evaluation theory and practice. And, it requires that all evaluators develop additional knowledge and skills in conflict resolution, team development, group dynamics, group processes and intercultural communications. The purpose of evaluation shifts from making formative and summative decisions with evaluation being an event, to evaluation being a process that facilitates on-going learning in organizations.

These changes will not be met without criticism of many in the evaluation field. Yet, as our society and organizations become ever more complex and dynamic, evaluation as a discipline must find ways to evolve and contribute to individuals within these changing contexts. Evaluative enquiry offers evaluators a new way to be part of the future.

The issues for organizational learning researchers are somewhat different from those of evaluators. Given the great number of definitions, models and theories that now exist about the learning organization and organizational learning, we would be negligent if we did not begin to adjust our gaze from model and theory building to empirical research and evaluation studies that seek to validate the models and processes we have put forward. One area of study that could yield fruitful results would be on the outcomes identified in the previous section. Just what difference does a learning organization make? In our research with organizations we found that virtually no studies had been undertaken to determine whether the organization's learning processes were producing the desired results. For example, one interviewee reflected:

> I would say that to the extent a turnaround has been achieved, much of it is attributable to the culture changing. I believe a great deal of the culture changing has to do with the learning organization. Not all of it by any means. But a great deal of it. (FD, MR)

Another person at the same company added,

> We do have hard measurables that they have launched new products more quickly under budget – those type of things that you can count and touch and feel. Beyond that, I don't know that we have any measurables to know that it's [learning organization] really working. (FD, PM)

While some we interviewed were quite certain that dialogue, for example, has contributed significantly to organization members' efficiency and quality of work, they have little data to support this claim.

As organizations continue implementing organizational learning models and processes, it is going to be increasingly important to measure the effects of these efforts. Management will want to see how an organizational learning approach to organizational change and growth is different from other change efforts that have come and gone over the years.

References

Allerton, H. (1996) A different sort of corporate merger. *Training and Development*, 50 (6): 8.

Argyris, C. and Schön, D.A. (1978) *Organizational Learning: A Theory of Action Perspective*. Reading, MA: Addison-Wesley.

Argyris, C. and Schön, D.A. (1996) *Organizational Learning II*. Reading, MA: Addison-Wesley.

Bhola, H.S. (1995) Informed decisions within a culture of information: updating a model of information development and evaluation. *Adult Education for Development*, 44: 75–85.

Binns, P. (1994) Organisations, values and learning. In: J.G. Burgoyne, M. Pedler and T. Boydell (eds), *Towards the Learning Company: Concepts and Practices*. London: McGraw-Hill.

Brookfield, S.D. (1995) *Becoming a Critically Reflective Teacher*. San Francisco: Jossey-Bass.

Brooks, A.K. (1994) Power and production of knowledge: collective team learning in work organizations. *Human Resource Development Quarterly*, 5 (3): 213–35.

Brooks, A. and Supina, J. (1992) Reframing HRD: insights from research on the development of exemplary managers. *Studies in Continuing Education*, 14 (2): 156–65.

Brown, J. (1995) Dialogue: capacities and stories. In: S. Chawla and J. Renesch (eds), *Learning Organizations: Developing Cultures for Tomorrow's Workplace*. Portland, OR: Productivity Press. pp. 153–64.

Burgoyne, J.G. (1992) Creating a learning organisation. *Royal Society for the Arts Journal*, CXL (5428): 321–32.
Chawla, S. (1995) Conclusion: reflections of learning from a gathering. In: S. Chawla and J. Renesch (eds), *Learning Organizations: Developing Cultures for Tomorrow's Workplace*. Portland, OR: Productivity Press. pp. 501–8.
Cousins, J.B., Donohue, J.J. and Bloom, G.A. (1996) Collaborative evaluation in North America: evaluators' self-reported opinions, practices, and consequences. *Evaluation Practice*, 17 (3): 207–26.
DeGeus, A. (1988) Planning as learning. *Harvard Business Review*, 66 (2): 70–4.
Dewey, J. (1933) *How We Think*. New York: Heath.
Forss, K., Cracknell, B. and Samset, K. (1994) Can evaluation help an organization to learn? *Evaluation Review*, 18 (5): 574–91.
Gardner, H. (1983) *Frames of Mind: the Theory of Multiple Intelligences*. New York: Basic Books.
Garvin, D.A. (1984) Asking questions is the key skill needed for 'discussion teaching'. *Chronicle of Higher Education*, July 25, p. 20.
Helgeson, S. (1995) *The Web of Inclusion: a New Architecture for Building Great Organizations*. New York: Currency/Doubleday.
Kilmann, R.H. (1996) Management learning organizations: enhancing business education for the 21st century. *Management Learning*, 27 (2): 203–37.
King, P.M. and Kitchener, K.S. (1994) *Developing Reflective Judgment*. San Francisco: Jossey-Bass.
McTaggart, R. (1991) When democratic evaluation doesn't seem democratic. *Evaluation Practice*, 12 (1): 9–21.
Mezirow, J. (1991) *Transformative Dimensions of Adult Learning*. San Francisco: Jossey-Bass.
Mink, O.G., Esterhuysen, P.E., Mink, B.P. and Owen, K.Q. (1993) *Change at Work: a Comprehensive Management Process for Transforming Organizations*. San Francisco: Jossey-Bass.
Mohrman, S.A., Cohen, S.G. and Mohrman, A.M. (1995) *Designing Team-Based Organizations*. San Francisco: Jossey-Bass.
Owen, J.M. and Lambert, F.C. (1995) Roles for evaluation in learning organizations. *Evaluation*, 1 (2): 237–50.
Phillips, R.I. and Phillips, A. (1995) *Cognitive Distortions: Barriers to Change. TQM Network News*. Spring. Alexandria, VA: American Society for Training and Development.
Postman, N. and Weingartner, C. (1969) *Teaching as a Subversive Activity*. New York: Delacorte.
Preskill, H. (1994) Evaluation's role in enhancing organizational learning: a model for practice. *Evaluation and Program Planning*, 17 (3): 291–7.
Preskill, H. and Caracelli, V. (1998) Current and developing conceptions of use: evaluation use TIG survey results. *Evaluation Practice*, 18 (3): 209–25.
Ryan, S. (1995) Learning communities: an alternative to the expert model. In: S. Chawla and J. Renesch (èds), *Learning Organizations: Developing Cultures for Tomorrow's Workplace*. Portland, OR: Productivity Press. pp. 279–91.
Saban, J.M., Killion, J.P. and Green, C.G. (1994) The centric reflection model: a kaleidoscope for staff developers. *Journal of Staff Development*, 15 (3): 16–20.
Schön, D.A. (1983) *The Reflective Practitioner*. New York: Basic Books.
Schön, D.A. (1987) *Educating the Reflective Practitioner*. San Francisco: Jossey-Bass.
Schwandt, D.R. (1995) Learning as an organization: a journey into chaos. In: S. Chawla and J. Renesch (eds), *Learning Organizations: Developing Cultures for Tomorrow's Workplace*. Portland, OR: Productivity Press. pp. 365–80.
Schwarz, R.M. (1994) Ground rules for groups. *Training and Development*, 48 (8): 45–53.

Senge, P.M., Roberts, C., Ross, R.B., Smith, B.J. and Kleiner, A. (1994) *The Fifth Discipline Fieldbook*. New York: Doubleday.
Shaw, R.B. and Perkins, D.N.T. (1991) Teaching organizations to learn. *Organization Development Journal*, 9 (4): 1–12.
Thompson, J.W. (1995) The renaissance of learning in business. In: S. Chawla and J. Renesch (eds), *Learning Organizations: Developing Cultures for Tomorrow's Workplace*. Portland, OR: Productivity Press. pp. 85–99.
Torres, R.T. (1994a) Concluding remarks: evaluation and learning organizations. Where do we go from here? *Evaluation and Program Planning*, 17 (3): 339–40.
Torres, R.T. (1994b) Linking individual and organizational learning: the internalization and externalization of evaluation. *Evaluation and Program Planning*, 17 (3): 327–37.
Torres, R.T., Preskill, H.S. and Piontek, M.E. (1996) *Evaluation Strategies for Communicating and Reporting: Enhancing Learning in Organizations*. Thousand Oaks, CA: Sage.
Torres, R.T., Preskill, H. and Piontek, M. (1997) Communicating and reporting: concerns of internal and external evaluators. *Evaluation Practice*, 18 (2): 105–25.
Wick, C.W. and Leon, L.S. (1993) *The Learning Edge*. New York: McGraw-Hill.

7 Learning Across Organizational Boundaries: a Case Study of Canadian Museums

Nancy Dixon

This action research study attempted to determine the extent to which six museums, all of which faced similar environmental and financial constraints, could learn from each other how better to deal with those constraints. The design of the study was based on six principles of collective learning (Dixon, 1994):

1. *Teams/organizations as the unit of learning* – The practices of organizations are not simply the sum of members' individual competence, there is also competence and knowledge that is a product of the collective. For an organization to learn new system level competencies, it must learn as a collective – a unit.
2. *Organizational assumptions are limiting* – An organization's ability to be effective is limited by its assumptions. Yet groups are often unaware of the assumptions they hold or of the ways those assumptions serve to limit their practice (Argyris and Schön, 1978).
3. *Co-inquiry* – Learning across organizations is most effective when all parties are in a learning role rather than when one party is viewed as an expert and the other(s) as students (Freire, 1994).
4. *Collective intelligence* – The world is knowable by ordinary people and their knowing can be collectively and meaningfully organized to address the serious organizational issues that they face. When people of good will think together they can create new and powerful solutions that none could have constructed on their own (Weisbord, 1992).
5. *Learning occurs over time* – System change happens over a period of months – thus learning also needs to happen over that time period. Learning is not only planning to act; implementing, reflecting on the implementation and re-planning are also acts of learning (Revans, 1982).
6. *Collaboration and alliances* – There is a new spirit of collaboration among organizations that is a recognition that there is much one organization can learn from another. In the corporate world this collaboration is manifested in an increase in benchmarking, study visits and supplier and customer training.

Canadian museums face dramatically changing social, economic and cultural realities. Reduced government funding, increased competition for donations and earned revenue, changing demographic realities and community expectations – all challenge museums to rethink their roles and operations.

This project, Learning Across Organizational Boundaries (LAOB), was developed to support participating museums as they work to reinvent themselves in light of these economic and social changes. The project was designed as an intervention and a research study with the dual goals of: (i) strengthening the capacity of individual institutions to reinvent themselves and adapt to change; and (ii) exploring how museums might collaborate and support one another in this change process.

Project description

Learning Across Organizational Boundaries took place over a period of 18 months and was anchored by three events where representatives of participating museums came together face-to-face. Between these events support was provided via telephone, fax, e-mail and electronic conferencing. The three events were:

- **The Planning Forum**. The Planning Forum brought together a representative of each museum to plan the project. The group met for two days during which a range of project details was confirmed.
- **The Learning Forum**. The Learning Forum brought together teams from each participating museum for three days to learn from and with each other. The insights acquired at the Learning Forum were to be taken back to participating organizations and applied. Following the Learning Forum, interaction among participants was facilitated by a variety of means including electronic conferencing and exchange visits.
- **The Reflection Forum**. At least one member from each team met for two days to consider the lessons learned over the preceding months within their organization and from the interorganizational learning. The group identified competencies needed to address change in museums. The learning outcomes of the Reflection Forum were made available to the wider museum community through reports and conference proceedings.

A five-person design team was established to guide the project. The role of the design team was to obtain funding, identify museums as potential participants, design the specifics of the three major events of the project, facilitate the events and identify the study findings.

The Planning Forum

The Planning Forum was a two-day event attended by one or more representatives from each of the potential museum partners. The purpose of the Planning Forum was to allow the potential museum partners to determine whether each wanted to participate in the project and to co-design the project, including the Learning Forum. Representatives, who were primarily upper level managers, from six museums were present at the Planning Forum. The learning principles proposed for the project were discussed. During the two-day meeting participants spoke about the challenges they were facing in their own institutions and what they hoped to achieve from the project. Some of the recurring themes included:

- the need for more entrepreneurial perspectives to exploit opportunities, including revenue potential;
- the need to build organizational capacities – making better and faster decisions, separating low-value from high-value work to leverage change;
- changing attitudes – overcoming the fears and insecurities that accompany change;
- how to *see* (rather than do) things differently – re-framing issues in fundamental ways in order to bring about radical or breakthrough change.

Outcomes of the Planning Forum

There was general endorsement of the collective learning principles as the framework for the project overall and, more specifically, as a guide to designing the Learning Forum. Several specific concerns were, however, identified:

- some doubt that teams had adequate skills to do this kind of work;
- concern that teams might be reluctant to discuss sensitive human resource issues in a public forum;
- the need for ground rules so that discussion at the Learning Forum would not degenerate into a complaint session;
- the recognition that museums have only limited access to the computing technology needed to exchange ideas electronically.

Three broad themes also emerged that were to become recurring project tensions and ambiguities for the project as a whole. Both before and during the Planning Forum the design team struggled with the question of how fully to pre-define the project. In the spirit of co-enquiry and collective intelligence the design was left sketchy in the hope of securing stronger input and commitment from participants. Yet, as the Planning Forum proceeded it became apparent that it had been unrealistic to ask the museum representatives to generate designs in keeping with abstract learning principles, many of which were quite new to them. Despite several attempts by the design team to describe the project in pre-meeting materials, those attending the Planning Forum voiced confusion about 'what LAOB was really all about'.

A second ambiguity centred on the task each team would undertake. Ideally the task was to be one that was central to the organization and its reinvention efforts (as opposed to being new or additional work). Concerns were raised as to whether all teams should be working on similar tasks: if each team had a unique task would learning across organizations occur?

In addition, it was difficult for the representatives, who were themselves in management roles, to believe that teams of employees would really be able to assist each other through the challenges they faced. Several representatives suggested it would be advisable to bring in an outside expert to provide useful answers. This concern was expressed in various ways, such as a suggestion that teams should have representatives from corporations on them (corporations having already successfully addressed these issues) and the need to have a forceful speaker who could lay-it-on-the-line in telling team members that they needed to change if their institutions were to survive. Still others seemed convinced that the answers to problems were *already* clear; the challenge was to bring people 'in line' by convincing them that the institution's survival depended on them thinking and acting in new ways.

In retrospect, the Design Team's own enthusiasm about the potential of interorganizational learning as a tool for better understanding and managing change in museums clouded their appreciation of how nebulous or abstract a concept this was for many participants. Compounded by high levels of stress and anxiety in the participating institutions, there was genuine difficulty establishing a level of comfort about the project, its goals and requirements. This discomfort was later to translate into reluctance to commit to LAOB reporting and reflecting.

The Learning Forum

The Learning Forum was a three-day event with six teams attending. There was considerable variation in size, geographic location and mission among the participating museums. Two of the six were relatively small museums with less than five full-time staff, while the largest museum had a staff of 175. One team was unique in that it operated a network of museums located throughout the Province (see Table 7.1).

In response to the concerns of participants and team coordinators some modifications were made in the activities, for example, adding evening sessions and including appreciative enquiry as an additional 'skill'. A description of each of the major Learning Forum activities is provided here along with the relationship of each to the learning principles (Table 7.2).

TABLE 7.1 *Teams involved in the project*

	Members present/ number of members	Project goal	Previous work as a team
Team A	4/4	Development of a Human Resource Strategy • role and composition of the Board • role of the CEO and the • organizational structure	The members had not met as a team before attending the Learning Forum
Team B	6/14	Exploration of alternative work models that would be more flexible, and participative	Team had been meeting for 8 months
Team C	7/7	How to operationalize a new mandate to serve as the Cultural and Heritage division of the City with no new resources	The members had not met as a team before attending the Learning Forum
Team D	7/7	A cross-functional team charged with building a 5-year programme based on institution-wide themes rather than more traditionally exhibition-based	The team had been meeting for 10 months
Team E	6/6	Building a more integrated organization linking geographically dispersed sites	The members had not met as a team in advance of the Learning Forum
Team F	4/6	Development of a performance management system which would align professional goals with work unit and organizational goals and which would recognize and reward the accomplishment of those goals	The team had been meeting for 6 months

Community dialogue The community dialogue brought the whole group together in a circle for a period of 30 minutes. The guidelines provided for community dialogue were to:

1 Speak the truth of your experience.
2 Listen with your heart.
3 Slow things down so more may happen.
4 Notice your inner voices.

The purpose of the community dialogue was to understand the perspective that others held and through the exchange to create shared understanding of the issues and concerns of the whole. This activity was intended to foster the collective intelligence of the group. Three community dialogues were scheduled (Bohm, 1990; Dixon, 1996).

TABLE 7.2 *Links between learning principles and design elements*

Learning principles	Design elements
Teams/organizations as the unit of learning	• Teams invited to participate rather than individuals • Activities at the Learning Forum primarily team-based • Time for teams to work on own issues
Organizational assumptions are limiting	• Paired team reflections • Appreciative inquiry
Co-enquiry	• Paired team reflections
Collective intelligence	• Joint planning for the project at the Planning Forum • Community dialogue
Collaboration and alliances	• Community dialogue to build a support system for change • Eurythmy • Computer conferencing system
Learning occurs over time	• Project length of 12 months

Paired team reflection In paired team reflection each team had the opportunity to have a mirror held up so they could 'see themselves as others see them'. Each team held a regular work session for approximately 30 minutes while their partner team observed them in action. Then the partner team offered their reflections on the critical ideas and assumptions they heard in the discussion. Finally, the work team responded to the reflection, identifying what they found helpful. Then the two teams switched roles and repeated the process. Paired team reflection was based on the principle of co-enquiry, each team being both a learner and a helper. It also served the principle that organizational assumptions are limiting, in that it worked to uncover principles on which the team might have been acting unaware.

Teams work on own issues Time was scheduled for each team to meet by itself to assimilate what it was learning and to plan how to use the ideas that it was formulating. The principle that this activity supported was that the team was the unit of learning rather than individuals. Teams needed time to discover what they were jointly learning. There were three periods set aside for the teams to meet by themselves.

Appreciative inquiry For appreciative inquiry two teams were paired to allow an individual from each team to interview an individual from the other team. Each interview lasted an hour, using a structured format. The questions were framed 'appreciatively' to elicit the core factors that give life and value to the museum as well as peak experiences individuals had in working for the museum. Each team then met to develop themes across the interviews they had conducted. Finally, each team met with their paired team to give feedback on the themes they had heard. The teams were asked to give feedback that identified for their partner team the 'life giving' forces of that team and what gave 'energy and meaning' to the team. This activity was based on the principle that organizational assumptions are limiting. The activity served to uncover assumptions of each team (Cooperrider, 1995).

Eurythmy Eurythmy, as developed by Rudolf Steiner, is the art of harmonious movement to the sounds of speech that incorporates mood, colour and story. It gives a group the opportunity to practise concentration, co-ordination and awareness of others by moving together. There were three 45 minute periods of eurythmy. The activity served the principle of collaboration.

Data collection

The initial data collection, conducted at the end of the Learning Forum, was at the individual and team level. Participants were asked to interview each other for one and a half hours, using a structured interview guide. These interviews served two purposes; first it was an opportunity for each participant to reflect on the experience they had in the three days and find the meaning in it for themselves. Past experience had shown that individuals often went into such interviews unsure of what they had learned and that much of the meaning was actually constructed during the interview experience (Dixon, 1996). The interviewer's interests and questions work to clarify and deepen the experience of the person being interviewed. The second purpose of the interview was to record the responses so that the researchers could provide back to the whole group an understanding of what people had learned together.

The second set of data was collected as team insights. On the last day of the Forum, teams were asked to spend an hour reflecting together on the following questions. What progress has your team made on its task? What insights have you gained about yourselves as a team that will help you in the future? What have you learned about learning from other organizations? What can you commit to giving and getting from other organizations? The teams briefly reported out their reflections to the full group. As with the individual interviews, the reason for the reflection was to provide time for the teams to construct meaning for themselves about the experience. Thus both the individual and team reflection periods were learning experiences for the participants as well as allowing data collection for the researchers.

Outcomes of the Learning Forum

The findings address two topics: what people learnt from the forum, and the extent to which the activities facilitated that learning.

What people learnt from the forum

Awareness of the connection between personal relationships and effective team work Both the teams and individuals reported that a more personal understanding of other team members was needed to improve work on the group task. For many participants this was a new realization, one that both surprised and pleased them. During the three days, team members came to know what other team members cared about and what they hoped for. Team members were able to be open with each other about their vulnerabilities and their concerns. Out of these more personal dialogues a level of trust developed that facilitated the team's work. This deeper relationship was reported by teams that were newly formed, but appeared to be equally powerful for the teams that had been working together for some time. Representative of the comments that reflected awareness of this relationship were:

- 'Aired issues/ potential concerns – Built trust within the group – we worked at a personal level.'
- 'Speaking from the heart – from a personal level – being able to cut through the official language.'
- 'Our working relationship is easier; we got to know each other better.'
- 'Social aspects are important to work environment.'

The deeper relationships that developed among team members also brought about a concern related to how to include the team members who had not come to the Learning Forum in the trust that had been developed. Even more broadly, the question of how to include the wider organization was troubling to the teams. The design team had not anticipated this issue, assuming that an entire team would be present at the Learning Forum, thus they did not build in help for this concern. The following comment represents the concern expressed by many participants:

> Trust was really built within the team. But now there is an uneasiness about coming back to the institution and trying to build trust within the larger group.

Reframing individual roles within the team Many participants were able to reframe their own role within their team. By seeing themselves through the eyes of other teams, they gained new insight into the impact they had on their team. As a result, some participants framed expanded roles for themselves while others became aware of ways in which their actions were a detriment to the team. Representative of the comments that reflect the reframing of roles in the team were:

> 'I am an obstacle (knew that already) Should I go? This dilemma sucks my energy, I'm tired. I am not needed in the way that I was. Can I and will I adopt a new leadership mode that I feel is needed?'

'I found out that I am a lot stronger than I thought and that I am an integral part of the collective whole and I have the ability to be supportive.'

'I have a tendency to be domineering, that I was aware of before, but it is now confirmed.'

'Being a new team member I felt outside before. The group was very willing to listen to me which allowed me to break out of that mould. I feel accepted by my team members.'

Teams learned that their problems were not unique Teams discovered that the problems they were struggling with in their own organizations were shared by other teams. Many of the participants in less senior positions would not have regularly attended professional meetings in the past and for that reason might have had little contact with other museum professionals. Thus, for many the Learning Forum was a unique opportunity to interact with other museum professionals. There was comfort in knowing that others were faced with the same issues and even greater comfort in knowing that others cared about the difficult issues that the teams were facing.

'I was moved by how much we all have in common and by how willing we all are to share our knowledge and experience; how hungry we are for each other's contribution.'

'We are not so far in left field – but are a quality organization.'

Museums learned specific 'how to' practices from other museums In creating the Learning Forum the design team took the position that a team could be most helpful to another team by reflecting on the assumptions they heard which would assist the other team in reframing the issues with which they were dealing, rather than focusing on a more traditional exchange of best practices or 'how to' information. However, during the Learning Forum the teams were clearly eager to exchange 'how to' information with each other and to learn from each other on a practical level. They felt there was not enough time built into the Learning Forum for this kind of exchange with other teams. The two evening activities that were listed on the agenda were abandoned for a more informal time to exchange information. During other activities as well, teams often turned to informational discussions.

Resources that could be called on for further help Each team identified other teams they intended to meet with in the future or with whom they agreed to exchange further information. Through spending the three days together, the teams came to know what the resources were in the larger group. The community that was formed among the six teams gave them assurance their enquiries would be welcomed.

> 'We talked with Team E about sharing our team process; Team A, HR projects; Team C, Strategic Planning and measurement; Team B, communicating over distances; Team F, brainstorming.'

The extent to which the activities facilitated that learning

Community dialogue This had the greatest impact of all the activities of the Learning Forum. It was evident both from the comments at the close of the dialogue reflection and from subsequent comments that many people had been moved by the ideas that had been expressed. The dialogues seemed to create a sense of community and support that allowed people to be more open with each other and therefore more available to new ideas and support.

Paired team reflections The teams found the paired reflections of considerable assistance. They were able to reframe some of their tasks in ways they found more beneficial, as these comments reflect:

> 'I realized that the team had limiting assumptions and that some members were unaware of the organization's problems.'

> 'Refocused it [the team's task] – something that continues over time – on-going need to develop communication organization wide.'

> 'We saw calmness demonstrated in Team C.'

The benefit of the paired reflections came as much from the perspective gained by *observing others*, as it did from the reflections of others on the team's work. As the last quote above notes, one team was struck by the difference between the way they normally functioned and what they referred to as the 'calmness' of Team C. This observation opened to them the possibility that there was another, and perhaps more effective, way to function. As another example, an observing team noticed that management had relinquished power to the team, a phenomenon the observing team had assumed was not feasible or had taken for granted was unlikely to happen in a museum setting. However, the interaction they witnessed helped them to see that it was possible for management to empower a team and allowed them to consider the possibility that their organization might also be able to achieve such a goal. In this way the paired reflections provided needed perspective, although that perspective may have come less from the direct identification of assumptions and more from seeing another team in action.

Appreciative inquiry Using appreciative inquiry at the beginning of the Learning Forum was helpful in that the one-on-one interviews created a bonding across teams. It also provided a non-critical way for the teams to have their first in-depth interaction. Several teams noted that the experience of looking for themes in the interviews had an impact itself. As in the paired team reflections, the opportunity to look closely at another museum may have engendered perspective in a way that had not been anticipated by the design team.

Many of the participants noted that appreciative inquiry was a technique that they would take back and use in their own organizations. Comments that represented this view were:

> 'Will use certain techniques from weekend, appreciative inquiry – to help lessen negativism.'

> 'Group decided to take Appreciation Inquiry and use it in the institution.'

Eurythmy Eurythmy was the most controversial of the activities of the Learning Forum. The intent was to build a community among the 40 participants through a physical medium, given that most of the Learning Forum was cognitive. The participants who engaged in the Eurythmy sessions felt it had enhanced their experience of the Learning Forum. However, many opted out after the first of the three experiences. Those who continued appeared to be fully engaged and frequently expressed disappointment when the session was over. Yet there were few comments in the reflections that related to Eurythmy. It is possible to explain the absence of comments in two ways: either that Eurythmy was viewed as simply a pleasant physical diversion in an otherwise sedentary day, or that participants were influenced by the Eurythmy but could not put into words the way in which it assisted their learning.

Social interactions The teams made extensive use of the evening hours to socialize. Activities ranged from going out to dinner, to parties in the residence, to contra dancing. Many participants noted that the socializing had been important to them in building trust within the teams and across the teams within the community as a whole.

> 'Opportunity to socialize with the team is rare.'

> 'Opportunity to meet one-on-one other people doing the same thing. Growing the differences and similarities. This happened as much in social situations as in the structured ones. Building friendships and connections.'

Equity in openness An unplanned event that proved valuable to participants was the design team members publicly reflecting on their own experience of facilitating the Learning Forum. On the second afternoon, a number of participants suggested that the design team take a turn in the 'fishbowl'. These requests had a aggressive edge to them, suggesting an underlying anger or sense of inequity on the part of the participants making the suggestion. The design team agreed, and talked for about 20 minutes in the fishbowl, primarily about the things they had misjudged in the planning process, such as not communicating the activities fully or accurately. Following the fishbowl discussion, participants offered their reflections, which indicated that they found the discussion helpful in terms of clarifying the project objectives and that prior to the design team fishbowl they had felt they were being asked to make themselves vulnerable, while the design team was protected by their role. The tone in the meeting changed palpably after the design team fishbowl. Comments that reflected this change include:

> 'I was moved by the facilitators being willing to discuss openly the plans for the process and perhaps the part they missed in the planning process.'

> '. . . when facilitators reflected together in front of the group. Felt empathy, had never seen facilitators do that before. Insight that conference has been learning for the facilitators. This has made conference better for everyone.'

Between Learning and Reflection Forums

The design team had intended that regular progress reports, prepared monthly and circulated among teams, would facilitate learning across the organizations. With some prompting four of the six teams prepared one interim report between the Learning and Reflection Forums.

There was also very limited use of the electronic conferencing system designed to enable participants to take part in discussions with other LAOB participants on a number of topics. An explanation of electronic conferencing took place at both the Planning and Learning Forums. After the Learning Forum the design team established a number of topics linked to issues that had emerged at the event. Immediately following the Learning Forum there was a modest number of contributions posted. However, a number of technology constraints reduced participation, including the lack of access to the software required and in some cases the lack of access to computer equipment.

All these factors shaped the design of the Reflection Forum. Teams were contacted and asked to appoint a representative. Prior to the Reflection Forum this person was asked to meet with their team and reflect on what they had achieved within their own institution – the task and process outcomes of the project for their own team as well as what they had continued to learn from other teams. The team representative was asked to report on these issues at the Reflection Forum.

The Reflection Forum

The Reflection Forum was a two-day event attended by a representative from each of the teams as well as members of the planning team. The purpose of the Reflection Forum was to assess what had been learned by each team and to reflect on the extent to which the museums were able to assist each other.

Each of the six teams reported substantial progress on their task. The teams reported functioning in turbulent environments that included significant legal issues, the loss of senior leadership in the museum, severe budget cuts, unexpected tasks or responsibilities. The teams credited the cohesiveness and trust that had been developed during the Learning Forum with sustaining them through such times. Several of the teams noted the personal and leadership growth that members of the team had achieved. In one situation the designated leader became ill and members surprised themselves with how well they were able to continue functioning. For some tasks team members had to step outside of their area of expertise to get the task accomplished and that also produced personal growth and confidence.

Several representatives noted that their teams were viewed as exemplary within their organization – a group which could get things done, which 'had its act together'. There was a sense of pride in this identity as well as the acknowledgement of additional burdens on top of already busy schedules. However, the teams also acknowledged that they had made few attempts to learn from each other after the Learning Forum ended. Some contact between individuals on different teams had occurred (to obtain a reference or piece of information), but the site visits that teams anticipated holding did not happen. Likewise, the electronic conferencing system was little used and seen as of little help.

The reasons representatives gave for this were that each team saw themselves as very different from the other teams attending the Learning Forum; one team saw themselves as being far ahead of other teams; another viewed their task as unique – very unlike the tasks that other teams were engaged in; one team believed that their size differentiated them. In each case these teams determined that they had little to learn from the other teams, thus they failed to pursue contact. However, listening to the reports from other teams at the Reflection Forum, representatives retrospectively were able to see a great deal of similarity between tasks and issues that each had been dealing with. Many renewed their intentions to make contact with the other teams.

Conclusions

This project set out to accomplish the following goals: (i) to explore how individual institutions can reinvent themselves and adapt to change in this difficult time, and (ii) to explore how museums might collaborate and support one another in this change process.

The first of these goals was very successful. Participants were able to form teams that exhibited a high degree of cohesiveness and were able to function effectively within very turbulent environments. These teams became exemplary within their own organizations. Participants increased their sense of competence and were able to exhibit leadership in difficult situations. Through observation and reflection on the interactions of others, teams were able to identify assumptions that were limiting them and to discover different ways that their own team could function. What was gained at the Learning Forum about their own team stayed with the groups and they were able to capitalize on what they had learned back in their home environment.

The second of the two goals was less successful. After the Learning Forum, teams learned little from each other, nor did they actively offer each other assistance. The three days together at the Learning Forum were not a long enough period to cement relationships across teams. What had been learned from and about other teams was lost between the Learning Forum and the Reflection Forum. At the Learning Forum teams acknowledged the similarities between the problems they were facing, yet by the time of the Reflection Forum, this had been forgotten and was, in fact, relearned in that setting.

For the teams that attended the Learning Form the idea of one team helping another was feasible, but primarily in relation to practical ideas about how to accomplish a task or where to get information about something. Although this kind of practical help was not built into the design of the Learning Forum, participants found ways to ask their questions of each other and obtain the answers they sought, not, however, without considerable frustration aimed at the design team. The organizational learning principles were too abstract to have much meaning to the participants, including the idea of uncovering assumptions about self and team. Paired reflection and appreciative inquiry was viewed as interesting, but not very practical.

The only type of assistance seen as practical to the teams was task- and project-based information-gathering and analysis. Given that each team viewed itself as unique, it is not surprising that there were few efforts made to continuing learning from each other after the Learning Forum. In reality the teams benefited greatly from the process-based learning activities of the Learning Forum, but it was only in retrospect that they were able to recognize this learning.

Perhaps a most important lesson to be taken from this project is that 'learning across organizations' is too abstract a goal to be offered to groups; the goal is better identified with a business outcome and learning used as means to reach the outcome.

References

Argyris, C. and Schön, D.A. (1978) *Organizational Learning: a Theory of Action Perspective*. Reading MA: Addison-Wesley.

Bohm, D. (1990) *On Dialogue* (transcript). Ojai, CA: David Bohm Seminars.

Cooperrider, D. (1995) An interview with David Cooperrider on appreciative inquiry and the future of OD. *Organization Development Journal*, 13 (3): 5–13.
Dixon, N.M. (1994) *The Organizational Learning Cycle: How We Can Learn Collectively*. New York: McGraw-Hill.
Dixon, N.M. (1996) *Perspectives on Dialogue: Making Talk Developmental for Individuals and Organizations*. Greensboro, NC: The Center for Creative Leadership.
Freire, P. (1994) *The Pedagogy of the Oppressed* (rev. edn). New York: Continuum Publishing.
Revans, R. (1982) *The Origins and Growth of Action Learning*. Bromley: Chartwell-Bratt Ltd.
Senge, P. (1990) *The Fifth Discipline*. New York: Doubleday.
Weisbord, M. (1992) *Discovering Common Ground*. San Francisco: Berrett-Koehler.

8 The Concept of the 'Learning Organization' Applied to the Transformation of the Public Sector: Conceptual Contributions for Theory Development

Matthias Finger and Silvia Bürgin Brand

In this chapter we want to make a theoretical contribution to the concepts of the 'learning organization' and 'organizational learning'. We do this by referring to public sector organizations in general, and the Swiss Postal Service in particular. We hope that the so-developed theoretical contributions will be useful to private sector organizations as well. Indeed, in our view, public sector organizations are not qualitatively different from private sector organizations, but they operate in a more difficult environment, which makes their functioning and their management *more complex*. For historical reasons, public sector organizations are generally also more bureaucratic than private sector organizations. As a result, public sector organizations constitute a particular challenge for people who seek to put the concept of the learning organization into managerial practice.

This chapter is structured into five sections. First, we will discuss why the concepts of the learning organization and organizational learning are particularly useful in the case of public sector organizations. We will show the differences and the similarities when it comes to arguments for the learning organization, and will develop additional arguments for the learning organization in the case of public sector organizations. The specificity of the public sector of course also affects the practice of the learning organization. Here we will argue why public sector organizations are particularly slow to change, and why, as a result, transforming the public sector needs to be conceptualized as a collective learning process. Secondly we will discuss the main concepts of the learning organization and organizational learning. After clarifying these concepts in respect to their intellectual origins, we will show their pertinence when applied to public sector organizations. This will lead us to sharpen the concepts used in the case of the Swiss Postal Service. In a third section, we will present one example of such an application in the Swiss Postal Service, and draw lessons from it. This application will also highlight the main weaknesses of the concept, that is, in particular the inability to distinguish between means and goals. A fourth section, will therefore propose an additional conceptualization of the learning organization. This will lead us to developing key indicators of organizational learning. In the conclusion we will offer some indications of how the idea of the learning organization can be inbuilt into an overall management information system.

The learning organization in the public sector

By 'public sector organizations' we mean public enterprises as well as units of public administrations. We will argue that both can and should be transformed into learning organizations. We will begin here by recalling the main arguments why today's organizations need to become learning organizations. We will then compare whether these arguments apply in the public sector, and develop additional arguments. This will lead us to clarify the aspects one needs to pay particular attention to when it comes to transforming public sector organizations into learning organizations.

Arguments for the learning organization

Without almost any exception, people writing about the learning organization refer to private sector organizations. It appears that in the private sector change is a given. Watkins and Marsick for example: 'Organizations are realizing that they will not survive if they don't change' (1993: 4). However, this argument is not as straightforward in the public sector, where better arguments why change is necessary still need to be developed. Given the fact that 'change' is generally just taken as a given, these arguments are unfortunately scarce in the literature.

In the next section we will distinguish between two basic theoretical orientations among the authors writing about the learning organization. Let us state here simply that there are on the one hand those authors who originate in workplace learning and human resources development. They basically write about learning *within* the organization. On the other hand, there are those authors who originate in *systems (management) theory*, and conceptualize the learning organization from a *macro-systems perspective*. For the latter, the concept of the learning organization mainly makes sense within a global context of increasingly rapid competitive pressures. A competitive advantage in such an environment, it is said, will result from producing, transforming and implementing information faster than the competitors (Garratt, 1987; Probst and Büchel, 1994). In short, collective and collaborative learning is seen, by these authors, as being key for survival in the future. The crucial element, for them, is therefore *time* and *speed*, which, they say, have become the key competitive factors of the global economy. For authors originating in *workplace training and learning* instead, the main reference is knowledge (knowledge society, knowledge economy) and the *changing nature of work* (and its consequences in the workplace) (Dixon, 1994; Watkins and Marsick, 1993). Here the need for higher qualifications and better skills and for continuous learning is invoked as being the main reason for the learning organization.

It is probably fair to say that for most authors the learning organization must be seen in relation to a combination of change and competition, both of which are taken as a given. In an increasingly rapidly changing environment, the only competitive advantage left, it is said, is to learn faster than the others. Learning, in the literature, is therefore almost synonymous with change. In short, a learning organization is one that is open to change, or even more so, one that can change from within itself. Implicitly, therefore, the learning organization's underlying idea is an *adaptive* or even *reactive* one: adaptation or reaction to environmental pressures lead an organization to change and perhaps to learn, and learning and/or changing faster than others will increase an organization's chances to survive. The *arguments why change is occurring*, however, are hardly developed. Change is simply assumed to result from globalization and the corresponding competitive pressure, as well as from the changing nature of work, which itself is said to be a result of technological progress. Yet, when it comes to change in the public sector, these quite simplistic arguments are, in our view, not sufficient.

Arguments for the learning organization in the public sector

It is obvious that in the public sector we need a better argumentation for why change is necessary or inevitable. Also, if in our view the (poorly developed) arguments of the private sector certainly do apply in the public sector, there exist, however, additional and even more compelling reasons why the learning organization is a 'must'. And this even more so if one considers the specificities of public sector organizations when it comes to change and transformation.

For public sector organizations, the point of departure is in fact the same as for private businesses. Because of globalization, economic and financial activities are increasingly unrelated to (national) territories. Technological progress, especially in the areas of informatics and communications, adds to this phenomenon, leading to additional capital and other mobility. This increasingly 'global playing field' opens up unprecedented possibilities for big enterprises, which had started to encounter the limits of national economies. As a result, financial and economic globalization lead to new and unprecedented pressures on the public sector. Nation-states enter into competition with one another, especially when it comes to attracting investments and jobs. Being more and more in competition with one another in order to obtain a share in the global economy, the nation-states are also gradually losing control over the industrial development process, which now has a dynamics of its own. In addition, being less able to control industrial development, and thus their tax revenues, nation-states also face a growing legitimation problem, as they can no longer pay for the social and other services their citizens used to expect. This legitimation crisis is reinforced by the fact that the nation-states are increasingly unable to respond to growing global threats (environment, unemployment, health, etc.), as well as to the growing demands of their own citizens. As a result, public service organizations are exposed to a *double challenge* of growing competitive pressure on the one hand and the erosion of the nation-state on the other.

Let us illustrate this first global pressure 'from above' in the case of the Swiss Postal Service: with economic globalization new competitors emerge, and these multinational corporations are competing with public sector organizations even on their traditional, national territory. This is, for example, the case of Fedex and DHL, but even other national postal services which have 'gone global'. These emerging multinationals are moreover creating political pressure that liberalization be extended to the entire public sector and to the entire world. As a result, public enterprises are increasingly under pressure from competitors, especially in their most profitable segments. Their challenge thus is to compete against multinationals, while at the same time offering (non-profitable) public service domestically (Rey and Finger, 1995).

The second pressure to public sector organizations comes, so to speak, 'from within': indeed, the nation-states are gradually losing the means of their policies, as well as their legitimation in the eyes of the citizens. As a result, politicians are increasingly putting pressure on their own public sector organizations to improve quality of service. In addition, nation-states as a whole have abandoned some of their decision-making power to international and multilateral organizations, especially in such areas as global trade and financing. Organizations such as the IMF (International Monetary Fund) or the WTO (World Trade Organization) are now pressuring for deregulation of the public sector, as well as for the withdrawal of the public sector from productive (and profitable) areas. Consequently, politicians are more and more considering their own public organizations, especially public enterprises, as either a burden which is too expensive to entertain, or as an opportunity whose sale will bring badly needed cash. Therefore, for some, privatization of public sector organizations appears as a (temporary) financial solution, while at the same time being in line with the dominant neo-liberal ideology. For others, deregulation is simply a means to introduce competition, which is said to increase efficiency and customer-orientation. In short, public enterprises, but also *many of the public sector organizations*, are thus simultaneously under pressure from their own national governments, from the increasingly global market, and from their clients.

Having been used to stability and protection, public sector organizations are now particularly challenged to adapt to this new and rapidly evolving context. They must develop the capacity to analyse this new context, to adapt to it, and to transform themselves accordingly. They therefore need to develop their collective learning capacity and become learning organizations. The above pressures have reached public enterprises sooner and stronger, yet they are increasingly also becoming a reality for all public administration. Indeed, the entire public sector is coming under financial pressure due to the diminishing tax base, and the inability to raise revenue directly through the commercialization of services. It also runs into a legitimation problem, as citizens increasingly want to be treated as clients entitled to an efficient and effective public service.

Public sector organizations are therefore subject to the same pressures as are private sector organizations. This is particularly the case for *competitive pressure resulting from a globalized economy.* In addition, the changing nature of work, resulting from technological progress, of course also applies to public sector organizations (Coriat, 1990). However, in addition to these two arguments for the learning organization, there is a third argument which is unique to public sector organizations, and that is the pressure for legitimation, resulting from the erosion of the nation-state. Indeed, public sector organizations today are in particular need of legitimation from their citizens. Treating their citizens as 'clients' appears to be one of the means to restore at least part of this legitimation. But treating citizens as customers and clients obliges public sector organizations to undergo a substantial transformation of their identity and culture, and develop some sort of 'corporate identity', which for most of them is totally unprecedented.

The specificities of public sector organizations when it comes to learning

It thus becomes clear why the learning organization represents an ideal form of organization towards which public sector organizations should transform themselves in order to face these new challenges. However, there is, in the public sector, a series of factors or obstacles that make its transformation particularly difficult, and actually leave no alternative other than a learning approach to this transformation. We will distinguish here between environmental factors, organizational factors and public sector constraints.

The first type of factors are *environmental constraints* and pertain to the fact that public sector organizations operate in a political and public context. This context makes their functioning and their management, if not different, yet much more complex. Indeed, public sector organizations operate in a political environment with political actors on one side and citizens and society on the other. Both sides are more than stakeholders to public sector organizations. Their public mission, the role of public interests, their responsibility towards the citizens, or their mode of financing all imply that public sector organizations are part of a larger system. This also means that their transformation relates to the transformation of the larger system, as well as to the changing relationship among the different elements of this system.

While from a purely *organizational perspective* public sector organizations are very similar, if not identical to private sector organizations, their history, nevertheless, makes them today look unique. History is thus a second factor defining the specificity of public sector organizations. Indeed, having been sheltered from competition and even from comparison, mainly because of their monopoly position, public sector organizations have become quite bureaucratic. This tendency towards bureaucratization was and still is reinforced by specific administrative rules and regulations. But, to be sure, the tendency towards bureaucratization is an organizational phenomenon and not specific to the public sector. It can therefore also be found in private sector organizations, especially the ones who enjoy a monopoly or cartelized position. Nevertheless, in the public sector organizations have been particularly overprotected, so that they find themselves today facing dramatic change. Organizational change for them therefore often takes the form of a threat, as it must often occur in a radical way and in a very short time period. Moreover, such organizational change often goes to the heart of public sector organizations, as their very identity and culture has become bureaucratic in nature.

The same historical considerations also apply in the case of *public sector constraints*, a third factor defining the specificity of public sector organizations. We think here in particular of the fact that the unions hold a very strong position in public sector organizations, which is the result of a historical compromise concluded between the technocrats and the civil servants to the detriment of the customer (Stoffaës, 1995). In most of Europe, the existence of public and administrative law, as opposed to civil and private law, often constitutes an additional constraint, especially in the areas of personnel and financial management. Nevertheless, we consider that these constraints should and can be minimized, the objective being to more clearly separate management areas and issues from political and public questions and issues (see below).

At this point let us state the following: though public sector organizations must respond to the above identified pressures, that is, global competition, the changing nature of work and the legitimation crisis, they will do so as part of a particular (i.e. political) environment, and with a specific historical background. While pressure on public sector organizations is particularly fierce, their response, because of these reasons, will be particularly complex. More specifically, the transformation of public sector organizations will require, in our view, that particular attention be paid to at least the following three aspects:

- In order to account for public sector organizations' specific political and public environment, their transformation will require a particularly *global* look and approach. Indeed, it will not be enough simply to introduce new management tools without simultaneously transforming the entire system within which public sector organizations are embedded, that is to say, without including politicians and citizens.

- In order to account for the historical dimensions of public sector organizations which have made them particularly bureaucratic and entrenched, a much more *organizational* look and approach must be adopted. This is a kind of look which traditional management 'science' has mostly ignored so far. One thinks here in particular of the approach Michel Crozier and his associates have developed, one which, unlike dominant organizational theory, takes into account power relationships and the various actors' specific strategies (Crozier, 1963, 1987; Crozier and Friedberg, 1977).
- In order to account for both the specific context and the particular history of public sector organizations, a *processual* look and approach seems to be the only way to get these organizations to change. Indeed, only a processual approach, as opposed to an interventionist one, offers the necessary patience to deal with bureaucracies, while at the same time allowing for a global and contextual view.

All these arguments pertain to public enterprises as well as to organizational units with a public administration. They lead us to the conclusion that the only conceivable way of transforming public sector organizations today is in terms of a collective learning process. Indeed only such a collective learning approach can take into account the factors mentioned above. Only a collective learning process permits the integration of all actors of the system (and a transformation of their relationships), allows the necessary attention to be paid to all organizational dimension (in particular the cultural dimension), and allows for a processual approach (pragmatic, iterative) (Finger and Bürgin, 1997). This collective learning process must lead, among others, as we will show, to a growing capacity of the organization to learn and increasingly to function like a learning organization. But before developing our conceptualization any further, let us first clarify some of these concepts.

Conceptual clarification

There is a great deal of conceptual confusion around the terms organizational learning and learning organization. We therefore find it helpful to clarify the difference between organizational learning and the learning organization. In our view, the *learning organization* is an ideal, towards which organizations have to evolve in order to be able to respond to the various pressures identified above. It is important to note that the learning organization is an *ideal*. Pedler says: 'the learning company is an aspirational concept that . . . constitutes a "view of what might be possible"' (Pedler, quoted in Burgoyne, 1995: 22). This ideal organizational form is characterized by the fact that individual and collective learning are key. On the other hand, *organizational learning* is the *activity* and the *process* by which organizations eventually reach this ideal of a learning organization.

We will focus in this section in particular on the process and less on the activities. Organizational learning is therefore, in our view, a particular form of a process of organizational transformation. Individual and collective learning – fostered by concrete and measurable learning activities (see below) – play a key role when it comes to furthering this (organizational learning) process. Organizational learning, in our definition, is therefore a transformational process to which the organization's stakeholders, individually and collectively, contribute through their learning.

Despite this conceptual distinction, the dominant literature often confuses 'organizational learning' and the 'learning organization' (for example, Dixon, 1994; Senge, 1990; Watkins and Marsick, 1993). It also assumes that organizational learning necessarily leads to a learning organization, and that the learning organization inevitably results from previous organizational learning. Both assumptions are, in our view, not necessarily true, as one can imagine that organizational learning can take place without a learning organization resulting from it. And one could also imagine, at least in theory, that a learning organization is being created without organizational learning having taken place (for example, through a process of organizational transformation like re-engineering, initiated by top management and with little focus on learning). The conceptual clarification one has to make here is between *means* (organizational learning) and *ends* (learning organization), and the additional element to introduce is *organizational strategy*: indeed organizational learning is only a means to achieve organizational strategies, like, for example, increased profitability or customer satisfaction. The learning organization then becomes one of these strategic objectives of an organization. Finally, when it comes to the organizational learning process, the confusion between process and activities leads most authors to conceptualize organizational learning as an intervention (for example, Argyris, 1992), rather than as a *process* of organizational transformation. Only recently have authors who traditionally write about organizational transformation started to conceptualize this transformation as a learning process (Mohrman et al., 1989; Nadler et al., 1995).

Schools of thought

In addition to distinguishing between a strategic objective (learning organization) and the process (and activities) to reach it (organizational learning), we also must distinguish between different schools of thought. At this point we would like to distinguish a systemic from a psychosociological approach and differentiate between three conceptions of learning on which they build (cognitive, humanist and pragmatic).

The *systemic* approach to the learning organization finds its roots in the change that has taken place in management theory during the 1980s towards systemic and holistic thinking, a change which is inspired by developments in computer science, physics and biology (for example,

Ulrich and Probst, 1998). With Senge and his collaborators, who popularized the concept of the learning organization, the organization became seen as a 'learning system' (Nevis et al., 1995; Senge, 1990). This system is interacting with its environment and has to adapt to it and permanently change in order to survive. More precisely, the organization is conceptualized as an information processing system, a system which performs certain necessary functions such as the generation of information, as well as the diffusion, the storage and the utilization of this information . This systemic approach aims at describing the way an organization can learn as a system. Several, especially technical, tools can help, such as, for example, computer models and simulations. This school of thought is based on a *cognitive* framework, which conceptualizes individual learning as a structured developmental process. Furthermore, it is based on the assumption that a few members of the organization – the managers or the top managers – can understand the system and its collective underlying assumptions, and by doing so help it evolve (for example, Argyris' idea of double-loop learning: Argyris and Schön, 1978). In our view, this school therefore focuses mainly on 'management learning', rather than on organizational learning. There exists a German version of this systemic school of thought, based on the same cognitive conception of learning. Transposing this conception to the systems level, these authors focus mainly on the evolution of an organization's 'knowledge basis' (Klimecki et al., 1994; Pautzke, 1989; Probst and Büchel, 1994) (see Table 8.1).

The *psycho-sociological* approach to the learning organization can be traced back to theories of Human Resources (HRD) and Organizational Development (OD) (for example, Burke, 1982; Pedler et al., 1991; Whyte, 1991). This school of thought conceptualizes the organization as a set of 'resourceful humans'. Increasingly referring to humanistic psychology, it considers that adequate conditions must be created within an organization in order to make maximum use of the individuals' capacities to learn and grow, referring here of course to a *humanistic* conception of learning. The learning organization, in this conception, is one that fosters individual and collective learning in order continuously to transform itself (Burgoyne, 1995: 25). In this approach, adult educators and HRD professionals have come to define their work as a contribution to the learning organization. In this humanistic tradition, they consider themselves as fostering the learning of all members of the organization, as opposed to only the learning of managers.

An original branch of this psycho-sociological tradition is based on a *pragmatic* conception of learning. This conception can be traced back to American pragmatism. It is intellectually rooted in John Dewey's theory of learning from experience. More recently, Kolb (1984) has conceptualized what he calls 'experiential learning' as stemming from a learning cycle. Nancy Dixon (1994) has built on this tradition and developed her own and original conceptualization of the learning organization: she sees organizational learning as the activation of such an experiential learning cycle, both

TABLE 8.1 *Conceptions and levels of learning*

Conception of learning	Level of learning		
	Individual	Group	Organization
Cognitive	Development of knowledge and assumptions		Evolution of the organizational 'knowledge basis'
Humanistic	Personal growth	Conditions fostering personal growth (learning culture)	
Pragmatic	Experiential learning cycle	Collective learning cycle	Conditions fostering the collective learning cycle

individually and collectively. The originality of her approach stems from the fact that the learning cycle is conceptualized as a collective one seeking to link individual and collective learning. According to Dixon, the activation of this learning cycle involves, on a collective level, the following four steps:

1 the widespread generation of information;
2 the integration of information into the organizational context;
3 the collective interpretation of information;
4 responsible action based on the interpreted meaning.

This conceptualization is in our view particularly appropriate on a group level. Table 8.1 summarizes these different conceptions and their relevance for the various levels of learning.

In the cognitive and humanistic conceptions, learning appears to be basically an individual endeavour. If the cognitive approach has a highly developed conceptualization of individual learning, the humanistic tradition instead confuses learning with personal growth. Both cannot convincingly relate such individual learning to organizational change and development. This is also why both schools of thought cannot conceptualize organizational change or learning in other ways than through interventions. In the case of the cognitive approach, intervention mainly takes the form of education and training in order to increase an organization's knowledge basis, as well as in order to question underlying organizational assumptions. In addition, different management tools can be used in order to manage the organization's knowledge basis (planning, controlling, etc.). In the case of the humanistic approach, intervention mainly takes the form of group or inter-group interventions, such as team-building, conflict resolution, and others. The pragmatic approach of Dixon, with its focus on collective learning, appears to us as being a particularly promising one. Unfortunately, this approach remains, at least with Dixon, conceptualized as an intervention. This is in our view mainly due to the fact that the concept of the learning organization has been applied so far only to private sector organizations. Before we can show below how we have applied it in the case of the Swiss Postal Service, we will briefly argue why such a pragmatic approach is, in our view, the only possible one in the case of public sector organizations.

Organizational learning/the learning organization and public sector organizations

We have seen above that public sector organizations display some particular features which make them different from private sector ones and which make their transformation more complex. Therefore, anybody concerned with the transformation of public sector organizations has to pay particular attention to the process of their transformation, to their organizational context, and to their particular, mainly political environment. Let us briefly examine whether and to what extent the three approaches presented above to the learning organization and organizational learning can take these specificities into account.

In public sector organizations, the creation of a learning organization must be seen as a *process* of organizational change and profound organizational transformation, involving culture, structure and, most importantly, the organization's relationship to its political environment. Therefore, a set of interventions cannot be sufficient. Only the pragmatic conceptualization of the learning organization has, in our view, the potential adequately to address this processual requirement. Unfortunately, Dixon, referring primarily to private sector organizations, has not yet developed such a processual conceptualization.

We have seen that today's public sector organizations, as a result of their history, are still very bureaucratic, even though this might well disappear in the future. For the time being, however, this history considerably shapes these organizations. Therefore, one must pay particular attention to the *organizational dimensions* of change, transformation and learning (structure, culture, leadership). Paradoxical as it sounds, none of the above three approaches is able to take these organizational dimensions adequately into account. There is therefore a need to further conceptualize and theorize organizational development when it comes to linking collective learning with the organizational dimensions of change and transformation.

Finally, we have seen that public sector organizations are much more influenced than private ones by the mainly political *environment* which shapes much of their behaviour and developments. If the humanistic approach cannot deal with the environment in a way other than as conditions that foster learning, the cognitive approach can at least take it into account in terms of a larger knowledge basis. The pragmatic approach instead has, in our view, the ability to deal adequately with the organization's specific environment. So far, the only experience in doing so stems from the private sector, where this has been done by defining and taking into account the various stakeholders. However, in the public sector, this stakeholder approach will have to be adjusted in order to account for 'public stakeholders', such as political parties and non-governmental organizations. Nevertheless, the pragmatic approach is, in our view, perfectly capable of doing so.

In conclusion, we note that from the three approaches to organizational learning and the learning organization identified above, that the pragmatic one comes close to the particular needs of public sector organizations. In the next section, we will therefore build on this pragmatic approach and present how we have conceptualized and practised so far the learning organization and organizational learning in the case of the Swiss Postal Service. More precisely, we will not take Dixon's learning cycle as a prescriptive tool, whose optimal conditions must be realized, but rather as a research instrument, helping us to identify the organizational obstacles to the learning organization, that is to say, to Dixon's learning cycle.

Conceptualization and practice of the learning organization in the case of the Swiss Postal Service: lessons learned

In this section we will show how, since 1992, we have put this pragmatic idea of the learning organization into practice in the case of the Swiss Postal Service, and what lessons we have learned from it for improving the concepualization of the learning organization. In order to do this, we proceed in the following four steps: first we briefly present the Swiss Postal Service and the challenges before it. This will help understand why the Swiss Postal Service wanted to become a learning organization to begin with. Secondly, we will present the conceptualization of the overall transformation of the Swiss Postal Service. Thirdly, we will then show how our practice of the learning organization fits into this overall conceptualization. Fourthly, we will critically assess this practice and draw lessons for further developing the concept of the learning organization.

Why the Swiss Postal Service wanted to become a learning organization

In 1992 the Swiss Postal Service started a process by which it seeks to transform itself from part of a public institution to an autonomous, efficient and competitive public enterprise. With its top management, we see this as an organizational learning process and conceptualize the outcome as a 'learning organization'. To our knowledge, the Swiss Postal Service – with its approximately 39,000 employees being the second largest enterprise in the country, is one of the first large public sector organizations among the industrialized countries to seek to become a learning organization.

The triggers of this process are multiple, though they do not yet explain the objective (learning organization) and the nature of the process (organizational learning). Indeed, until 1992 the Swiss Postal Service and Swiss

Telecom were integral parts of the Swiss PTT (a public institution with little autonomy from politics, no budgeting autonomy, etc.). Under the pressure of the global liberalization of telecommunications – starting in the USA in the 1970s – and anticipating the European Community's telecom deregulation on 1 January 1998, the Swiss government passed a new law on telecommunications in May 1992. This law liberalized some sectors of the Swiss Telecom and by the same token forbade the heavy cross-subsidy of the Postal Service by the Telecom as of 1 January 1997. The Swiss Postal Service, with a sizeable annual deficit, was thus heavily challenged. Moreover, in the context of the crisis of the Swiss public finances and given the shift to the right in Swiss national politics and the corresponding calls for liberalization, deregulation and privatization, the threat to the Swiss Postal Service was its privatization or the decline of public service or both.

But there is also growing market pressure: indeed, not only is the deficit unacceptable, but moreover the Swiss Postal Service was losing market share at an accelerated pace, and this especially in its most profitable businesses, namely the international express and the parcel services which were increasingly being lost to global competitors (TNT, FedEx, DHL, UPS, etc.). In short, without substantial changes, there was no chance that the Swiss Postal Service would ever become an efficient public enterprise.

With all these considerations in mind and a heightened sense of urgency, the newly appointed director of the Swiss Postal Service initiated in January 1992 a profound transformation which was intended to lead the Swiss Postal Service to become a fully fledged learning organization.

Conceptualization of the transformation of the Swiss Postal Service

As we have argued above, the transformation of public sector organizations requires a specific approach, in particular a holistic approach which takes into account the organization's changing relationship with the political environment, a processual approach, and an approach that pays particular attention to organizational (cultural and structural) dimensions. Mindful of these specificities, we have conceptualized the transformation of the Swiss Postal Service as having to take place on three different levels simultaneously: the autonomization from politics, internal structural changes and cultural transformations. As we will see in the next section, the learning organization concept pertains mainly to the cultural dimension, whereas the way we have conceptualized the overall organizational learning process takes all three dimensions into account and links them together. In the case of the Swiss Postal Service, a strategic decision was made to engage internal structural changes first, followed immediately by cultural transformations, while initiating the autonomization from politics only three to four years later.

In the beginning, and under the influence of the literature, we considered that the learning organization pertains, before all, to an organization's cultural transformation. Nevertheless, it was clear to us that cultural and structural changes are, in the case of the Swiss Postal Service at least, closely linked: the transformation towards a learning organization was engaged only after the structural changes were set in motion. As for the cultural dimension of this transformation, we broke this process down into the following four steps or rather stages, as one builds on the other.

- *Unlearning* is the first and particularly important step in the transformation of a public administration into a learning organization. In this step the dominant administrative or bureaucratic culture is critically questioned and the main *cultural obstacles* to a learning organization are identified. Our practice of the learning organization with top managers of the Swiss Postal Services pertains precisely to this first step (see below).
- Only after this step is it possible to turn to what we call *conversion learning*, that is, to turn to the customer and to the market, and to learn from them. It is indeed the customer who – according to the idea of Total Quality – not only defines quality, but furthermore obliges the organization and its members to think in terms of processes rather than administrative sectors and divisions. Part of our practice of the learning organization in the case of the Swiss Postal Service, but which we will not present here, pertains to this second step, and consist mainly of 'converting' – through training – *all* collaborators to the new philosophy of customer and market orientation.
- While conversion learning is a unique step in the organizational learning process, comparable to a one-time intervention, the next step, called *continuous improvement*, will be permanent. At this stage, the organization and its members will have to learn to continually improve themselves, by adapting to the changing market on the one hand and by learning from errors on the other.
- Many private sector organizations will consider that achieving the stage of continuous improvement is identical to being a learning organization. However, in the case of the Public Service in general and the Swiss Postal Service in particular – and probably even for private enterprises – this will not be enough in order to qualify for a learning organization. As argued above, in this fourth step, therefore, a *learning culture* similar to a corporate or 'public service identity' will have to be created. At this point, learning will become an organizational principle. If by steps two (conversion learning) and three (continuous improvement), the organization learns to become more flexible and more efficient, step four (learning culture) will add (public service) cohesion and identity.

Practice of the learning organization in the case of the Swiss Postal Service

In order to promote the learning organization at the Swiss Postal Service, several initiatives mainly related to training have been undertaken since late

1992 (Finger and Bürgin, 1996: 254–5), and most of them pertain to the first step of 'unlearning'. We would like to present here a top management learning initiative whose goal it was to foster unlearning by collectively identifying – and hopefully removing – the obstacles to creating a learning organization. In this section we will describe this initiative, make a first assessment, and in the next section draw conclusion for the further conceptualization of organizational learning in public sector organizations.

This top management learning initiative was conducted in Spring 1995 and took the form of two one-day seminars, a month apart. The seminar was inspired by the pragmatic conceptualization of the organizational learning cycle, as developed by Dixon (1994) in two different ways. First, we wanted not to define the optimal conditions for the learning as does Dixon, but to identify the main organizational obstacles prevailing in the Swiss Postal Service, and which prevent the full realization of this pragmatic learning cycle. Secondly, we conceived of the removal of these obstacles as being itself a collective learning process. The concrete objectives of this management learning seminar were thus the following:

- to familiarize the managers with the pragmatic concept of the learning organization;
- to identify the impediments or obstacles to the learning cycle (and thus the full realization of the learning organization) in the case of the Swiss Postal Service; and
- to remove these impediments or obstacles.

The top managers of the Swiss Postal Service, numbering approximately 100, were gathered in five groups within their respective organizational units (for example, Human Resources, Finances and Strategy, Marketing, Logistics, Postal Network, Giro, Postal Buses). In preparation for the first session, they had to fill out a questionnaire listing the positive and negative aspects of their everyday work at the Swiss Postal Service. The answers to these questionnaires where analysed and used as an input for the seminar.

The first session started with a presentation of the conceptual framework of the learning organization – mainly the arguments for the learning organization, the idea of the collective learning cycle, and the conceptualization of the process of transformation – as adopted by the Swiss Postal Service. We then proceeded to the identification of the impediments to the learning organization, as perceived by the managers. First, the features identified in the questionnaires that would have a positive influence on the learning organization were presented. Secondly, in small groups, the managers had to analyse critical or negative statements extracted from the questionnaires and relate them to the different steps of the organizational learning cycle. In this way the various impediments to the learning cycle were identified. Back in the plenary session, the so identified impediments were discussed and prioritized. A co-generated typology of impediments to the learning organization was then collectively consolidated for each of the five groups. This typology turned out to be very similar for each group and consisted mainly of cultural obstacles to the learning cycle, such as subservience to regulation, fear of risk, perfectionism, fear of conflict, and linear thinking. Obstacles of a more structural nature were compartmentalization, opaque decision-making processes, and communication problems (Finger and Bürgin, 1996: 256–8).

The second day of the seminar, one month later, aimed at collectively addressing and hopefully removing these impediments. In order to have a concrete basis for discussion, we had asked the participants to elaborate, during this month and in teams, concrete and creative projects that would move the Swiss Postal Service forward on the road to becoming a learning organization. The participants did not have to consider limits of resources (personnel, finances). Each project was presented to the rest of the group, who had to reflect critically and argue why, at the current state of the Swiss Postal Service, these projects were not feasible. A list of the main obstacles to implementing these projects was generated and only then compared with the previously elaborated typology of impediments to the learning organization. Both lists appeared to be very similar, and highlighted that 'political' obstacles were considered the most serious impediments to creating a learning organization (for example, the unpredictability of external influences, as well as the uncertainty about the future of the Swiss Postal Service). At the conclusion of the seminar, the identified impediments or obstacles to the learning organization were presented and discussed with the director of the Swiss Postal Service. During this discussion, all participants, including the director, were asked to conceive of themselves as being part and parcel of these impediments to the learning organization, which they collectively had to overcome.

Even though this seminar was not able to lift most of the identified obstacles to becoming a learning organization, we managed to identify the key impediments in the case of the Swiss Postal Service, and we also managed to create a climate conducive to collective learning. Indeed, the point of departure was the concrete experiences of the Postal Service managers. All exercises and discussions were rooted in their experiences, and the workshop was set up in such a way that the idea of the learning organization was practised at the same time. At this point, we would like to draw the following lessons from this particular learning initiative, before offering a more general assessment of the practice of the learning organization in the case of the Swiss Postal Service:

- First, the success of the last part, namely, the collective confrontation of the various perspectives on impediments, shows that such opportunities to discuss trans-hierarchically and trans-sectorally are a necessary condition for the learning organization. Such opportunities for dialogue have therefore to be institutionalized.
- Secondly, this initiative confirms that in order to solve problems collectively, the constitution of the groups has to be thought through

from the perspective of the problem and not from the perspective of the organization. The hierarchical and sectoral logic that still prevails in the organization should therefore be countered by the more systematic creation of problem-solving teams.

- Thirdly, this initiative has shown the importance of cultural obstacles to the learning organization, at least in the case of the Swiss Postal Service. Such cultural traits are in fact more generally present in public sector organizations. This confirms the need for cultural transformation in a public sector organization in order for it to be able to respond to its new context. Such transformation, however, cannot be imposed, but can only result from a collective learning process. But if organizational culture heavily determines whether organizational learning can take place or not, cultural change is also the outcome of organizational learning. As a follow-up of this initiative, we therefore consider it necessary to regularize and to institutionalize periodical critical assessments of cultural and other impediments to organizational learning.

Critical assessment

On the basis of the above assessment, and on the basis of assessments of other learning initiatives within the Swiss Postal Service, we unfortunately have to conclude that it is not possible to transform a bureaucratic organization by such learning initiatives alone. If we have been able, through our various initiatives and activities, to make the concept of the learning organization more acceptable in the Swiss Postal Service, we have however only made little progress on the road to creating a fully-fledged learning organization. Overall, we can say that we have been able, by referring to the concept of the learning organization, to *make change less threatening* and more acceptable to the collaborators and to management. However, individual and collective learning which has undoubtedly taken place has not really been connected to organizational change and transformation. This might be in part due to our own shortcomings, but it is certainly also due to some shortcomings in the pragmatic conceptualization of the learning organization we have adopted. We think that it is therefore necessary to enlarge and further develop the concept of the learning organization in order to overcome the weaknesses we have identified. The following are the shortcomings we have identified so far and the remedies we propose.

- The concept of the learning organization focuses mainly on the cultural dimension, and does not adequately take into account the other dimensions of an organization. Indeed, the transformation of an organization's culture cannot be achieved without simultaneously transforming the structures and the organization of work. Also, focusing exclusively on training activities in order to foster learning, which we have done so far, favours this purely cultural bias. This shortcoming speaks in favour of a better connection between individual learning and collective change, as well as between learning and institutional transformation.

- The concept of the learning organization favours individual and collective learning processes at all levels of the organization, but does not connect them to the organization's strategic objectives, even though the assumption certainly is that such a connection exists. It is therefore imperative, in our view, that the link between individual and collective learning and the organization's strategic objectives be made. All currently existing theories on the learning organization, including Dixon's collective learning cycle, simply assume such a link, without making it explicit how this link works, nor what the exact strategic outcomes are for the organization. This shortcoming speaks in favour of some form of measurement of organizational learning, so that one can assess whether and to what extent such learning contributes or not to the organization's strategic objectives.
- The concept of the learning organization remains rather vague. Indeed, in order to establish a link with the organization's overall objectives, the exact function(s) of organizational learning need to be more clearly defined. In our view, organizational learning is just a means in order to achieve strategic objectives. But creating a learning organization is also a goal, since the ability permanently and collectively to learn is a necessary condition for thriving in the new context. Therefore, the capacity of an organization to learn, that is, to function like a learning organization, needs to be made more concrete and institutionalized, so that the management of such learning can be made more effective.
- Finally, there is a need to develop a true management system of an organization's evolving learning capacity. This can be achieved by defining indicators of individual and collective learning, and by connecting them to all other indicators that help monitor the progress towards an organization's strategic objectives.

In order to respond to the above shortcomings, we propose to develop, in the next section, a clearer conceptualization of an organization's learning capacity, and to connect this conceptualization to the existing theories on organizational learning and the learning organization.

The capacity of an organization to learn

In order to conceptualize an organization's learning capacity, we need to come back to the distinction made earlier between process and goal. To recall, if the objective is to create a learning organization, the means to do so must be conceptualized as a collective learning process. There are various learning activities that can contribute to moving this process along. During this process, an organization's learning capacity should be increased, leading ultimately to a fully-fledged learning organization. We will therefore distinguish here between the various learning activities, the organization's capacity to learn, which should grow as a result of these activities, and indicators measuring such evolving capacity to learn.

Learning activities

Learning activities are elements, contributions, or interventions into the organizational learning process which should contribute to achieving the organization's strategic objectives. As argued above, one of these strategic objectives can – but not necessarily must – be to create a learning organization. Moreover, we define a learning organization as an organization which has a strong learning capacity and is improving it constantly. We therefore focus in this section on those (learning) activities which contribute to enhancing an organization's capacity to learn. The following learning activities can be distinguished: traditional educational and training activities, the active use of internal learning sources, the active use of external learning sources, as well as the creation of an environment conducive to learning. This includes structural, as well as cultural, and more generally organizational environmental conditions. These learning activities can pertain either to the entire learning cycle, or just to one of its steps. We also note that education and training are just one among many possible learning activities contributing to an organization's learning capacity. Let us describe here each of these activities in a little more detail.

- *Educational and training activities*: we think here in particular of training activities in the spirit of the learning organization, that is, activities that take place 'on-the spot', 'just-in-time', 'on the job', etc.
- *The active use of learning sources inside the organization*, which includes, among others, job rotation, the circulation of information, open access to statistical data, audits, self-directed learning teams, mentoring, quality circles, best-practice seminars, morning meetings, management information systems, performance standards.
- *The active use of learning sources outside the organization*, which includes, among others, customer panels, feedback loops, analysis of complaints, market research, benchmarking, analysis of the press, cooperation, joint ventures.
- *The creating of an environment conducive to learning*, which includes, for example, free spaces for learning, collective rewards, selection and promotion criteria rewarding collective learning, participation of collaborators, management by objectives.

The list of these learning activities is, of course, not complete, and will probably always only remain a list. Each organizational unit must, in our view, decide by itself which learning activities are most appropriate in order to enhance its learning capacity. Moreover, it must be kept in mind that each of these learning activities will always also contribute to other objectives than simply enhancing the organization's capacity to learn. Other such objectives are, for example, increasing customer satisfaction or profitability. As we will see below, these learning activities will have to be measured both in terms of quantity and in terms of quality, so that they can be put in relation with those indicators that measure an organization's growing learning capacity, as well as with all other indicators measuring the achievement of the strategic objectives. Only such measurement will make it possible to assess whether and to what extent such learning activities do in fact make a difference.

The dimensions of an organization's learning capacity

We seek here to define more precisely the various dimensions of an organization's hopefully growing capacity to learn. On the one hand, this definition will lead to developing indicators measuring organizational learning. On the other hand, it can also contribute to tailoring learning activities to particular needs. To recall, an organization's learning capacity is defined as its ability to learn individually and as a collective unit. We conceive of this hopefully evolving ability as an aggregate indicator measuring an organization's progress towards becoming a learning organization. Obviously, this ability or this indicator, is itself composed of a variety of different aspects or dimensions. The goal of this section is to identify these dimensions more clearly.

We opted above for the pragmatic approach to the learning organization, defining, with Dixon (1994), organizational learning as a continuous cycle of generating information, of integrating it into the organizational context, of collectively interpreting it, and of taking action on the basis of it. We also argued that in order to become a learning organization, one has to develop a learning culture and a learning structure, not to mention the fact that work should be organized in a way which favours learning. We now go back to this conceptualization of a learning organization in order to define more concretely the dimensions of an organization's learning capacity. This capacity is constituted, in our view, by individual and collective capacities to learn, but must include also organizational dimensions. As a result, we can distinguish the following six dimensions of an organization's learning capacity:

- individual learning capacities;
- collective learning capacities;
- structural learning capacities;
- cultural learning capacities;
- capacities resulting from the organization of work; and
- the capacity of the leadership to learn and to promote learning.

It is the combination of these six learning capacities which make up for an organization's capacity to learn in a continuous way. Focusing only on one of these aspects will be insufficient. Therefore, for example, it will be useless to develop a high individual capacity to learn, without putting into place structures that favour collective learning. Indeed, without corresponding structural changes, highly aware individuals might simply become cynical.

Indicators measuring an organization's evolving capacity to learn

Referring to our conceptual framework of organizational learning, that is, the four steps of the learning cycle, as well as to our own empirical observations, we can now break down each of the above six dimensions into more precise elements. Considering, for example, an individual's capacity to learn, we can now distinguish between his or her capacity to generate information, to integrate it, to interpret it, and to take responsible action on the basis of it. For each of these elements one can define corresponding learning activities, as well as indicators measuring whether such a learning capacity exists. Though in many cases this is probably a too detailed approach to elaborating indicators, it might nevertheless be useful to keep the entire learning cycle in mind when it comes to defining more precisely each of the six above learning capacities. The following list is not complete, but will offer insights into the various possible indicators measuring progress along each of the six learning capacities.

- The *individual capacity to learn* corresponds to an individual's ability and competence to learn. These are, for example, the ability to think systemically, the ability to think critically, the ability to put oneself in the mind of somebody else, the openness of mind, and others. One could imagine indicators measuring each of these abilities separately, as well as an aggregate indicator measuring an individual's overall capacity to learn.
- The *collective capacity to learn* characterizes, before all, groups of individuals. Indeed, as organizational learning theory argues, an organization's learning capacity results in part from successful interaction among individuals. Such capacities are, for example, group spirit, multi-functionality, the capacity to dialogue, the capacity to deal productively with conflict, etc. Again, each of these capacities can either be measured separately or as an aggregate.
- The *structural capacity to learn* corresponds to those structural characteristics of an organization which favour (or impede) individual and collective learning. These are, in particular, decentralized structures allowing for participation, flattened hierarchies, small units interacting with each other, the integration of central functions into the line and so on (for example, Dixon, 1994; Ducan and Weiss, 1979; Hall and Fukami, 1994; Hedberg, 1981). These capacities are more difficult to measure, and corresponding indicators must be based, in our opinion, on (participatory) observation.

- The *cultural capacity to learn* refers to the fact that an organization's norms and values influence individual and collective learning processes. Individual and collective learning is, for example, favoured by a culture of dialogue, of communication, of openness, of transparency, of trust, of risk taking, of comparison with the best, and so on (for example, Argyris and Schön, 1978; Dixon, 1994; Probst and Büchel, 1994). This cultural capacity can easily be measured through questionnaires.
- The organization's *capacity to learn resulting from the organization of work* implies that the production processes be organized in a way that individual and collective learning is favoured and not impeded. This is, for example, the case when the organization uses project groups, information systems, information on results, experimentation, decentralized control, job rotation etc. (Dixon, 1994). Here, specific criteria will have to be developed, so that precise indicators can be measured.
- The *capacity of the leadership to learn and to promote learning* is another important element of an organization's learning capacity. Indeed, through their behaviour, their management style, their ways to reward (and to punish), but also through their ability to coach, to mentor, to accept critique and alternatives, to question dominant views, the leaders have a significant influence on individual and collective learning (for example, Dixon, 1994; Nyström and Starbuck, 1984). This capacity can, for example, be measured through questionnaires among the leaders' collaborators.

Above, we have identified four types of activities which promote an organization's learning capacity, namely, educational and training activities, the active use of internal and external sources, and the promotion of a learning environment. We now propose to break down each of these learning activities according to the four steps of the learning cycle. This indicates which learning activities need to be undertaken in order to promote each of the six dimensions of learning. And this will also serve as a basis to define the various indicators more precisely. Table 8.2 summarizes this idea.

Conclusion

In this chapter we wanted to show that by putting the learning organization into practice in public sector organizations a significant contribution can be made to further developing organizational learning theory. Indeed, public sector organizations oblige one to pay particular attention to the processual dimension of their transformation, to their various organizational dimensions, as well as to their particular (political) environment. Taking the processual dimension of organizational learning seriously, we have clarified here the distinction between organizational learning, and the learning organization, as well as the distinctions between

TABLE 8.2 *Dimensions of an organization's learning capacity and its characteristics*

	Characteristics applying to the . . .				
Dimensions:	Entire learning cycle	Generation step	Integration step	Interpretation step	Action step
Individual learning capacity	• System thinking	• Capacity to assimilate new information • Capacity to enter into contact with environment • Self-observation • Attention	• Multi-skilling • Openness • Capacity to integrate new information	• Creativity capacity to think (analytical, synthetic, abstractly, etc.) • Empathy • Tolerance • Courage • Humour	• Capacity to transfer • Enthusiasm • Capacity to take responsibility • Openness to change
Collective learning capacity	• Team capacity		• Multi-functions • Helpfulness	• Capacity to dialogue • Capacity to face conflicts • Diversity	• Capacity to implement
Structural learning capacity	• Decentralization		• Flat hierarchies • Integrate staff into line	• Small organizational units • Frequent interactions	
Cultural learning capacity	• Problem solving	• Concern for measurement • Active attitude towards information • Openness towards the outside	• Transparency • Trust • Culture of continuous information	• Culture of dialogue and communication • Openness to multiple perspectives • Spirit of comparison and competition	
Learning capacity of organization of work		• Monitoring feedback loops • Self-correction experimenting	• User-friendly information media • Job-rotation limit specialization • Integrate staff into line	• Task forces, work in teams	• Decentralized control • MbO • Few specifications
Leadership learning capacity		• Give responsibility for information generation	• Reward for pertinent information	• Egalitarian conditions	• Coaching

the goal (the learning organization, that is, the build-up of an organization's learning capacity), the process (organizational learning) and the various learning activities. Looking at the learning process, it became obvious that indicators need to be developed, so that progress along this process can be evaluated and that learning can be managed. Addressing, then, the organizational dimensions of organizational learning, we came to clarify the various dimensions of an organization's growing capacity to learn. We also felt that the pragmatic approach to organizational learning – as opposed to the cognitive and the humanistic approaches – was better suited to public sector organizations.

In this conclusion, we would now like briefly to address the third, that is, the contextual or environmental dimension of organizational learning. We have already indicated above that the pragmatic approach is well suited to include the various stakeholders into the organization's learning process. We will not pursue this idea any further here, but we would like to highlight how public sector organizations must respect and pursue multiple strategic objectives. In particular, we would like to show here how this fact influences the management of organizational learning. Indeed, so far we have treated the creation of a learning organization – that is, the building up of an organization's capacity to learn – as being the only strategic objective. This is evidently not the case in public sector organizations, and we doubt that it is the case in private sector organizations either. As a matter of fact, any organization always pursues various strategic objectives. In the case of the Swiss Postal Service, for example, the four key strategic objectives are profitability, customer satisfaction, collaborator satisfaction and development of the organization's learning capacity. The objective of creating a learning organization is thus only one among other strategic objectives. Moreover, organizational learning can and must contribute to achieving all these objectives (and not just the objective of creating a learning organization).

Along the process of organizational transformation, management undertakes various and multiple efforts or interventions in order to achieve its strategic objectives. If one looks only at the strategic objective of creating a learning organization, one would probably focus on some of the learning activities outlined in the previous, fourth, section and which contribute to developing each of the six dimensions of an organization's learning capacity, as shown in Table 8.2. Yet, management has to consider more generally all strategic objectives of an organization. Therefore, it undertakes generally much more comprehensive organizational initiatives, such as for example MbO (Management by Objectives), TQM (Total Quality Management), BPR (Business Process Re-engineering) etc. Some of these organizational interventions might actively contribute to fostering a learning organization (along one or several of its dimensions), while others might well represent a step backwards. This is, in our view, the case with ISO certification for example, which, at least in public sector organizations, has a tendency to cement hierarchical structures, reinforce administrative procedures and strengthen bureaucracy more generally. As creating a learning organization has become an important strategic objective next to profitability, customer satisfaction and collaborator satisfaction in the case of the Swiss Postal Service, it is important to measure whether and to what extent such organizational interventions move an organization closer to achieving its strategic objectives. Ideal interventions would be the ones which enhance several, if not all strategic objectives simultaneously, and which moreover build on each other. For example, one organizational intervention enhances an organization's learning capacity in a way that the next organizational intervention is made much easier, and so forth. The indicators developed in the previous chapter will enable us to measure progress towards a learning organization. In parallel, other indicators will have to assess progress towards customer satisfaction and profitability, for example. The indicators measuring progress towards the learning organization must therefore be fully integrated into the overall management information system, and be put into relationship with all other indicators. Only then will it be possible for management to transform the organization into a learning organization, while at the same time achieving the other strategic objectives as well. We think that these contextual considerations, derived from public sector organizations, and which make us link organizational learning with progress towards other strategic objectives, are also valid in the case of private sector organizations.

Bibliography

Argyris, C. (1983) *Reasoning, Learning and Action: Individual and Organizational.* San Francisco: Jossey-Bass.

Argyris, C. (1992) *On Organizational Learning.* Oxford: Blackwell.

Argyris, C. and Schön, D. (1978) *Organizational Learning: a Theory of Action Perspective.* Reading, MA: Addison-Wesley.

Auditor General of Canada (1992) *Report of the Auditor General of Canada to the House of Commons*, chapter 5: *The Learning Organization*, Ottawa, pp. 143–57.

Bergquist, W. (1993) *The Postmodern Organization. Mastering the Art of Irreversible Change.* San Francisco: Jossey-Bass.

Burgoyne, J. (1995) Feeding minds to grow the business. *People Management*, 21 September, pp. 22–5.

Burke, W. (1982) *Organizational Development: Principles and Practices.* London: HarperCollins.

Chawla, S. and Renesch, J. (eds) (1995) *Learning Organizations. Developing Cultures for Tomorrow's Workplace.* Portland, OR: Productivity Press.

Coriat, B. (1990) *L'atelier et le robot. Essai sur le fordisme et la production de masse à l'âge de l'électronique.* Paris: Christian Bourgois Editeur.

Crozier, M. (1963) *Le phénomène bureaucratique.* Paris: Seuil.

Crozier, M. (1987) *Etat modeste, Etat moderne. Stratégies pour un autre changement.* Paris: Fayard.

Crozier, M. and Friedberg, E. (1977) *L'acteur et le système.* Paris: Seuil.

Dilworth, L. (1996) Institutionalizing learning organizations in the public sector. *Public Productivity and Management Review*, 19 (4): 407–21.

Dixon, N. (1992) Organizational learning: a review of the literature with

implications for HRD professionals. *Human Resource Development Quarterly*, 3 (1): 29–49.
Dixon, N. (1994) *The Oganizational Learning Cycle. How We Can Learn Collectively*. London: McGraw-Hill.
Dodgson, M. (1993) Organizational learning: a review of some literature. *Organizational Studies*, 14 (3): 375–94.
Duncan, R. and Weiss, A. (1979) Organizational learning: implications for organizational design. *Research in Organizational Behavior*, 1: 75–123.
Finger, M. and Bürgin, S. (1996) Steps towards the learning organization. In: K. Watkins and V. Marsick (eds), *In Action: the Learning Organization*. Washington, DC: American Society for Training and Development. pp. 251–61.
Finger, M. and Bürgin, S. (1997) Apprendre le changement dans le secteur public. In: M. Finger and B. Ruchat (eds), *Pour une nouvelle approche du management public*. Paris: Seli Arslan.
Finger, M. and Hofmann, A. (1995) Umgang mit Veränderungen in Organisationen. In: R. Arnold and H. Weber (eds), *Weiterbildung und Organisationen. Zwischen Organisationslernen und lernenden Organisationen*. Berlin: Erich Schmidt Verlag. pp. 143–58.
Fry, B. (1996) Learning in a public organization: the case of OIR. Paper presented at the 57th National Conference of the Society for Public Administration, Atlanta, GA, 29 June–3 July.
Galbraith, J.R., Lawler III, E.E. and Associates (1993) *Organizing for the Future: the New Logic for Managing Complex Organizations*. San Francisco: Jossey-Bass.
Garratt, B. (1987) *The Learning Organization*. London: HarperCollins.
Garvin, D. (1993) Building a learning organization. *Harvard Business Review*, 71 (4): 78–91.
Hall, D. and Fukami, C. (1979) Organizational design and adult learning. In: B. Staw (ed.), *Research in Organizational Behaviour*. Greenwich, CT: JAI Press. pp. 125–67.
Hedberg, B. (1981) How organizations learn and unlearn. In: F. Nyström and W. Starbuck (eds), *Handbook of Organizational Design*. New York: Oxford University Press. pp. 3–27.
Klimecki, R., Lassleben, H. and Riexinger-Li, B. (1994) Zur empirischen Analyse organisationeller Lernprozesse im öffentlichen Sektor: Modellbildung und Methodik. In: W. Bussmann (ed.), *Lernen in Verwaltungen und Policy-Netzwerken*. Berne: Paul Haupt. pp. 9–38.
Kolb, D.A. (1984) *Experiential Learning*. Englewood Cliffs, NJ: Prentice-Hall.
Lewin, K. (1951) *Field Theory in Social Science*. New York: Harper.
Marquardt, M. (1996) *Building the Learning Organization*. New York: McGraw-Hill.
Marquardt, M. and Reynolds, A. (1994) *The Global Learning Organization*. New York: Irwin.
Marsick, V. (1994) Trends in managerial reinvention: creating a learning map. *Management Learning*, 25 (1): 11–33.
Mohrman, A.M. et al. (eds) (1989) *Large-Scale Organizational Change*. San Francisco: Jossey-Bass.
Mohrman, S.A. and Mohrman, A.M. (1993) Organizational change and learning. In: Jay Galbraith et al. (eds), *Organizing for the Future: the New Logic for Managing Complex Organizations*. San Francisco: Jossey-Bass. pp. 87–108.
Nadler, D., Shaw, R., Walton, E. and Associates (1995) *Discontinuous Change. Leading Organizational Transformation*. San Francisco: Jossey-Bass.
Nevis, E., DiBella, A. and Gould, J. (1995) Understanding organizations as learning systems. *Sloan Management Review*, Winter: 73–85.
Norman, R. (1985) Developing organizational capabilities for learning. In: J.

Pennings et al. (eds), *Organizational Strategy and Change*. San Francisco: Jossey-Bass. pp. 217–48.

Nyström, P.C. and Starbuck, W.H. (1984) To avoid organizational crisis, unlearn. *Organizational Dynamics*, Spring: 53–65.

Pautzke, G. (1989) *Die Evolution der organisatorischen Wissensbasis: Bausteine zu einer Theorie des organisatorischen Lernens*. Herrsching: Verlag Barbara Kirsch.

Pedler, M., Burgoyne, J. and Boydell, T. (1991) *The Learning Company. A Strategy for Sustainable Development*. London: McGraw-Hill.

Probst, G. and Büchel, B. (1994) *Organisationales Lernen. Wettbewerbsvorteil der Zukunft*. Wiesbaden: Gabler.

Reinhardt, R. (1993) *Das Modell organisationaler Lernfähigkeit und die Gestaltung lernfähiger Organisationen*. Berne: Haupt.

Rey, J.-N and Finger, M. (1994) *Die Zukunft der Post – Die Post der Zukunft*. Zürich: Orell Füssli.

Rey, J.-N. and Finger, M. (1995) The Swiss Postal Service: towards a learning organization. *Union Postale*, No. 4: 84–8.

Sattelberger, T. (ed.) (1994) *Die lernende Organisation. Konzepte für eine neue Qualität der Unternehmensentwicklung*. Frankfurt: Gabler.

Senge, P. (1990) *The Fifth Discipline: the Art and Practice of the Learning Organization*. New York: Doubleday Currency.

Shrivastava, P. (1983) A typology of organizational learning systems. *Journal of Management Studies*, 20 (1): 7–28.

Solomon, C. (1994) HR facilitates the learning organization concept. *Personnel Journal*, November: 56–64.

Stoffaës, C. (1995) *Services publics. Question d'avenir*. Paris: Odile Jacob.

Ulrich, H. and Probst, G. (1988) *Anleitung zum ganzheitlichen Denken und Handeln. Ein Brevier für Führungskräfte*. Berne: Haupt.

Useem, M. and Kochan, T. (1992) Creating the learning organization. In: T. Kochan and M. Useem (eds), *Transforming Organizations*. New York/Oxford: Oxford University Press. pp. 391–406.

Watkins, K. and Marsick, V. (1993) *Sculpting the Learning Organization*. San Francisco: Jossey-Bass.

Watkins, K. and Marsick, V. (eds) (1996) *Creating the Learning Organization*. Washington, DC: American Society for Training and Development.

Whyte, W.F. (1991) *Social Theory for Action. How Individuals and Organizations Learn to Change*. London: Sage.

9 Learning, Trust and Organizational Change: Contrasting Models of Intervention Research in Organizational Behaviour

Amy Edmondson and Bertrand Moingeon

To remain viable in an environment characterized by change and uncertainty, organizations must be able to continue to change themselves. To do this requires considerable self-scrutiny and effort, and organizations often fail to adapt effectively, as is well documented in the literature (for example, Mirvis and Berg, 1977). These issues have been explored under the broad rubric of organizational learning by a growing number of researchers, including practising managers (for example, DeGeuss, 1988; Stata, 1989) and scholars from fields as diverse as organizational behaviour (Argyris, 1982; Huber, 1991; Levitt and March, 1988; Schein, 1992), operations management (Hayes et al., 1988), strategy (Collis, 1996; Redding and Catalanello, 1994) and system dynamics (Senge, 1990). Understandably, given this diversity, the resulting literature is fragmented, with multiple constructs and little cross-fertilization among researchers (cf. Fiol and Lyles, 1985; Huber, 1991; Shrivastava, 1983). Some study the ways organizations change or fail to change; others propose and sometimes implement approaches to creating change (Moingeon and Edmondson, 1996). Elsewhere, we have presented a framework that organizes these diverse approaches to organizational learning into meaningful categories and discussed the distinction between descriptive and intervention research in this field (Edmondson and Moingeon, 1998). Here, we focus exclusively on intervention-oriented research as an important subset of the literature. Our aim in this chapter is to foster discussion and understanding of what intervention research is as well as what it accomplishes, and to focus on the role of trust as a way of highlighting differences across approaches to conducting this kind of research. Trust is not selected arbitrarily for special focus; rather, we argue that it is central to the core of managers' willingness to allow or participate in any kind of field research conducted by organizational scholars.

Is trust a prerequisite to intervention research? Or, conversely, does intervention research give rise to a climate of trust? This chapter proposes an affirmative answer to both questions, but finds that the emphasis shifts from prerequisite to outcome depending on which model of intervention is employed. Our conclusions are based on analyses of data we collected in interviews with two leading scholars who conduct intervention research, Chris Argyris and Michel Crozier, and with members of organizations in which they intervened. Our analysis of the work of these two scholars suggests that trust plays an important and different role in each approach. Below, we first define trust and briefly discuss its relationship to organizational learning, followed by descriptions of the theory and intervention research of Argyris and Crozier as explicated in interviews and in the researchers' own scholarly writings. Finally, we analyse the different role of trust in each approach and discuss implications for conducting intervention research in general.

Organizational learning and trust

We define trust as the belief that relinquishing some degree of control over a situation to one or more others will not lead to personal loss or harm – a definition similar to those presented in Lorenz (1993) and in Mayer et al., (1995). Trust, as a cognitive state, is the willingness to place resources at others' disposal; this willingness is based on an expectation that they will not be used in a way that will leave the truster worse off. Several decades ago social psychologists showed that trust was an essential prerequisite to persuading others to change their views (Hovland et al., 1953). More recently, trust has been implicated as vital to the maintenance of productive supplier relationships (Lorenz, 1988) and to the implementation of self-managed work teams (Lawler, 1992). In a recent empirical study, Edmondson (1999) showed that work groups with high levels of trust among members are more likely to engage in learning behaviours than other groups.

The issue of trust arises when a decision or an action needs to be taken in a situation involving some degree of uncertainty and risk (Gambetta, 1988; Johnson-George and Swap, 1982; Lorenz, 1988). In both intra- and interorganizational relationships, uncertainty is related to the unpredictability of others' behaviour. In general, as organizations become flatter and more geographically dispersed, there is greater uncertainty and the ability to use traditional management controls is somewhat curtailed; thus Handy (1995) predicts that control must be replaced by an ability to trust individuals and groups to carry out critical organizational tasks without close supervision. In short, trust functions as a substitute for other, more explicit controls (Larson, 1992), and is thus a source of efficiency (Arrow, 1974). Moreover, although contracts and control systems are designed to reduce the risk of self-serving behaviour that harms the organization, many have commented on the limits and inefficiency of such practices (Argyris, 1994; Donaldson and Davis, 1991; Sitkin and Roth, 1993), suggesting that trust does and will continue to play a critical role in the management of organizations.

The above definition of trust leaves some flexibility about the nature of situations in which trust applies. Managers who say they trust a subordinate, or team members who trust each other, may mean quite different things, such as a belief that another is capable of producing a desired outcome or in contrast a belief that another can be relied upon to behave in ways that support the interests of the truster. The former involves *trust in competence* and, the latter, *trust in intentions*. Although these two types of trust may often co-occur, they are conceptually distinct. Trust in competence refers to the belief that another has the ability to do a task or fulfil a responsibility, while trust in intentions refers to the belief that another is sincere in his or her espoused commitment to carry out a task or responsibility.

Organizational learning, by its nature, is called for in situations in which much is unknown and uncertain (Senge, 1990), creating a need for trust to enable experimentation, reflection, or action. More generally, trust is needed in periods of change. For example, when a significant change is announced in an organization, the announcement creates uncertainty that often leads people to reject or block the change. It is particularly clear in such cases that direct orders are inadequate for ensuring new behaviours; for real change to be implemented the degree of perceived uncertainty must be offset by an increase in trust. In summary, trust in both intentions and competence comes into play in producing significant organizational learning and change. Finally, although there is an extensive literature on trust in organizations, along with some related work on consulting relationships (for example, Schein, 1988), there has been little work on the role of trust in intervention research. Here we focus primarily on the relationship between organization members and the researcher; elsewhere (Moingeon and Edmondson, 1998) we have used this framework to analyse trust among organization members.

Intervention research: Chris Argyris and Michel Crozier as exemplars

An empirical study constitutes intervention research if it leads to the production of valid scientific knowledge *and* is undertaken with the aim of improving the situation under study. Accomplishing these two aims together is an ambitious if not daunting prospect, which may explain the small number of organizational scholars who undertake intervention research. As a step toward increasing researchers' awareness of this kind of work, this chapter presents two models of intervention research. To do this, it focuses on the theories and methods of two prominent intervention researchers, Chris Argyris and Michel Crozier, whose high-quality work has earned both a world-wide reputation beyond the borders of their own nations, the United States and France respectively. The publications of both scholars are often regarded as reference works. For both, the theories they have developed seek to reach a better understanding of organizations – government departments, private firms and state-owned undertakings – in support of improving organizational effectiveness. To differing degrees, both Crozier's 'sociological approach to organizations' and Chris Argyris' 'theory of action' are concerned with enhancing learning in organizations by intervening in them. However, intervening in organizational systems is a complex undertaking that necessarily affects interpersonal and interdepartmental relationships in ways that are not always known at the outset of the intervention.

Chris Argyris: theory of action

Over 20 years ago, Chris Argyris, in collaboration with Donald Schön, formulated a theory of individual and organizational learning that he has continued to develop ever since (see in particular Argyris and Schön, 1974, 1978, 1996; Argyris, 1990, 1993). This theory, referred to as 'theory of action', grew out of Argyris' earlier research on the relationship between individuals and organizations (Argyris, 1957, 1962, 1964). As discussed below, Argyris' approach differs from that of Crozier, in that it is highly prescriptive and includes the introduction of very specific skills for organizational learning. Argyris and Schön (1978) defined learning as detection and correction of error, and distinguished between 'single-loop learning' (detecting error without questioning underlying policies) and 'double-loop learning' which involves questioning and changing governing conditions in order to achieve desired results. In his intervention research, Argyris' broad objective is to help develop organizations capable of double-loop learning. The underlying theory, supported by years of empirical research, is that the reasoning processes employed by individuals in organizations inhibit the exchange of relevant information in ways that make double-loop learning difficult – and all but impossible in situations in which much is at stake. This creates a dilemma as these are the very organizational situations in which double-loop learning is most needed.

How do individuals' reasoning processes create organizational failure to learn? Argyris and Schön (1978) observed that in all organizations – government departments, private firms and state-owned undertakings – individuals confronted with interpersonally threatening situations rely on tacit 'theories in use' for how to be effective, which have the unintended consequence of preventing them from learning. This is in part because of a gap – of which the individual actors themselves are unaware – between how they believe they behave (their espoused theory) and how they actually behave (driven by their theory-in-use). The problem is compounded by the fact that observers often *are* aware of that gap in others' behaviour (and blissfully unaware that they too have a gap between espoused and in-use action strategies). According to the theory, all people utilize a common theory-in-use in difficult interactions, which Argyris and Schön (1978) have called 'Model I'. Model I involves making inferences about another person's behaviour without checking whether they are valid and advocating one's own views abstractly without explaining or illustrating one's reasoning; this strategy has the unintended consequence of communicating that one is not interested in understanding others' points of view, giving rise to self-sealing interpersonal dynamics in which no one mentions their silent attributions and thus no one learns. Model I theories-in-use are shaped by a set of implicit values, including the desire to retain unilateral control over a situation, to maximize winning and minimize losing, and to avoid embarrassment. Model I behaviour is inherently driven by a defensive mindset, of which the actor is typically unaware, which gives rise to 'defensive routines' in the organization. These routines are implicitly designed to prevent individuals and organizations from experiencing embarrassment or threat, but they have the unintended consequence of avoiding changing the root causes of problems. Finally, only by examining and modifying the values governing one's actions, is it possible to produce new action strategies that enable learning. This reflective process exemplifies double-loop learning.

In numerous studies Argyris has shown how the Model I theory-in-use leads to entrenched defensive routines at individual, group and organizational levels. Face-saving actions are one kind of defensive routine. For instance, participants at meetings may avoid addressing real problems in a situation when a colleague stands to lose face. Thus many important problems from which much can be learned to enable the organization to improve its effectiveness become undiscussable and thereby insoluble. Additionally, they may generate other problems, that in turn remain undiscussed, and so on. For example, participants may feel that the meetings they attend are ineffective, but the defensive routine will prevent them from discussing this problem, thereby not addressing the problem of time wasted in ineffective meetings. Over time, the climate may deteriorate further, the degree of involvement may diminish and discontent and frustration may rise. Another way of expressing this is that individuals using Model I will create Organizational I (O-I) learning systems, characterized by 'defensiveness, self-fulfilling prophecies, self-fuelling processes, and escalating error' (Argyris, 1982: 8). And, O-I systems are resistant to change; a web of feedback loops make organization assumptions and behavioural routines self-reinforcing – inhibiting 'detection and correction of error' and giving rise to mistrust, defensiveness and self-fulfilling prophesies. This web is itself 'caused by the theories of action that human beings use to deal with such problems' (Argyris, 1985: 93). In short, the problem is that *individuals* 'cause' their social systems to malfunction by virtue of their theories-in-use – and at the same time *O-I social systems* 'cause' individuals to reason and act as they do.

In Argyris' model, the only way to improve this self-sealing non-learning system is to change the way in which individuals think and behave, by adopting a 'Model II theory-in-use'. The core aim in Argyris' intervention strategy is therefore to develop an organization's capability to engage in

Model II. The central research question is to what extent is this possible, a question he engages organization members in answering with him. The Model II theory-in-use explicitly draws on and refers to observable data (such as what is actually said in a conversation or letter) to draw inferences; Model II also involves extensive inquiry into the views and experiences of others, thereby allowing learning about others' views and minimizing defensiveness. When employing Model II, advocacy of views must be supported by explanation and illustration of one's reasoning (Argyris, 1982). While it is not difficult to agree with these premises, employing Model II in difficult interpersonal interactions requires profound attentiveness and skill for human beings socialized in a Model I world.

When Argyris carries out intervention research, he typically begins by observing meetings of senior management. The data he collects are both what is said and how discussions are conducted, especially in discussions of difficult issues. His intervention starts at the top of the organization, because he believes that change must be backed by senior management to succeed. Top managers not only serve as an example but also must be aware of the difficulty of the task at hand and willing to allocate the necessary resources (particularly time) to promote new thinking throughout the organization. After gathering data through meetings and observation, he draws up an action map that depicts how organizational values and norms are giving rise to behaviours that preclude double-loop learning and produce undesired results; that is, it shows the web of causal relationships that hold counterproductive patterns in place. It also points out managers' personal and collective responsibility for the dysfunction. Argyris submits this chart to managers at a meeting and invites them to voice any criticisms or alternative interpretations of data (for a more detailed account of an action map presentation, see Argyris, 1993: 98–9).

The ensuing research process involves generating and analysing qualitative data together, drawn largely from interactions among individual managers. So that these managers feel a sense of responsibility for these data, they are asked to contribute 'cases', which reveal their own tacit strategies in working through a tough problem. Through analysing these cases together, they discover the discrepancy between their actual and their espoused interpersonal strategies. In this process, organization members learn to explain their thinking, invite others to question it, and to check with others on inferences they are making, even if the issues are potentially threatening. This kind of collective learning helps to break the vicious circle and combat defensive routines. It enables the organization to question the values and political choices that govern its actions and achieve double-loop learning. Through this diagnostic process and longer term through developing its members' skill, the organization becomes better able to engage in tough self-scrutiny as needed to create and sustain change.

The role of trust in Argyris' intervention research

This analysis is based on data gathered in tape-recorded interviews we conducted with Argyris and with five directors and consultants from The Monitor Company, a large strategy consulting firm in which Argyris intervened as a researcher. Each interview lasted at least one hour. To understand this research project, we also draw from a book written by Argyris (1993). We asked the company participants to describe to us their experiences and reactions to the intervention process, as well as to tell us about the state of the company at the time of the interviews, which was several years later. The project results are described elsewhere (Moingeon and Edmondson, 1996); the role of trust, which was not our specific focus at the time of the interviews, surfaced as a critical issue later. In re-analysing the tapes for this chapter, we listened for references to trust and noted the participants' implicit theories about the role of trust, and we also listened for other factors they considered important in promoting or inhibiting the success of the change effort. We used these informants' explanations to supplement our analysis of Argyris' writings and own explanations, to develop our own theory of the role of trust in the intervention process. Overall, these data suggest that trust plays a central role, including both trust in competence and trust in intentions.

We found evidence that trust in competence is highly influenced by organization members' perceptions of the researcher's ability to understand their organization and to take into account its unique attributes and concerns (Argyris, 1993). For example, in an interview with the authors, one of the directors of Monitor explained that he decided to commit himself and to allocate part of his most scarce resource, his time, to the intervention process after seeing Argyris present an action map that captured interpersonal and organizational dynamics of the firm. The competence revealed by the accuracy and insight of this diagnostic map convinced the director to participate fully. More centrally, to build trust in competence, the theory of action researcher must demonstrate the interpersonal skill required to behave in a Model II way when dealing with difficult issues. A growing understanding that the researcher is using these skills to help them allows organization members to engage in a more extensive self-diagnostic process and to explore such sensitive issues as how their own behaviour inhibits learning in their organization. Trust in competence is also important for relationships among the organization's members, as Argyris (1985) claims. If organization members mutually believe that others are not competent enough to change their behaviour, or if the researcher holds such an assessment of the organization's members, this kind of intervention will probably not appear attractive.

Trust in competence is insufficient, however. To build trust in intentions, the researcher must demonstrate that he or she does not work solely for the CEO's interests but rather to serve the whole firm's interests; otherwise, the intervention process could be perceived as an attempt to manipulate them. Similarly, members must believe that confidential company issues will not be revealed to others, and so the researcher must stress that confidentiality is very important both externally and within the firm. In summary, trust in intentions is needed for organization members to risk the personal vulnerability created by participation in this kind of intervention research.

Argyris (1995 personal interview) uses three 'structural devices' to help establish trust in both competence and intentions before engaging in an intervention project. First, when the CEO invites him into the organization, he asks for a meeting with other senior executives to give them an opportunity to critique the proposed process, and then to choose whether or not to participate; 'that way they can't say "this was the CEO's idea", but instead must take responsibility for their participation. Second, he tells the group explicitly that 'if they ever hear that I am bad mouthing them, or feel I am not behaving in a way that is consistent with what I say, to bring it out in the open, publicly'. Third, is a 'fifty-second contract – in fifty seconds they can kill it, or I can kill it. . . . These are all structural devices to build trust.' Further, as alluded to above, Argyris explains that he is careful not to appear to 'take sides' with the CEO in meetings and he endeavours to illustrate with his behaviour that he is working to help everyone. He tells participants repeatedly that he wants to be confronted by them if they have any concerns or doubts. Thus, the essence of his strategy for building trust is to try to demonstrate competence by acting in ways that are consistent with Model II even under some degree of stress (Argyris, 1995 personal interview). In short, the primary mechanism for building trust is 'through my actual behaviour, especially when I say things that would be somewhat embarrassing or threatening to them, such as about the way they manipulate each other, and they can see that I am consistent with Model II in these situations.' The key to consistent Model II behaviour in difficult situations is to maintain a learning orientation; in Argyris' words, 'when I was challenging them and they were challenging me, how I challenged them and how I dealt with their challenge was critical – that is, did I maintain a learning orientation, or did I become as Model I as they did.'

In Argyris' model, the intervention researcher also requires a certain level of trust in the organization members' intentions and in their capacity for change. Are they ready to really involve themselves in the project? Are they likely to divert the process for political ends? Do they want to use it to manipulate the other actors? 'I do not require trust to be completely established at the outset but I need to make an assessment of the likelihood that adequate trust can be developed' (Argyris, 1997, personal interview). For instance, before starting a major project, Argyris meets with the senior managers of the organization to make these questions discussible and to make sure they are ready to participate in the process.

Increased trust is one of the outcomes of intervention research aimed at making a company more of a learning organization (Argyris, 1990, 1993). Members of the same team or organization engaged in a learning process tend to increase the level of trust they have in their ability to change and to work together. A virtuous circle can then be set in motion, with each achievement further supporting their trust in themselves and each other. The same is true of trust in intentions, which grows as events confirm the rightness of the decision to trust – a self-reinforcing process. This can result in reducing transaction and control costs within the organization (Larson, 1992) and increasing organizational efficiency. In interviews, directors of The Monitor Company stressed the positive consequences of Argyris' intervention in their organization. They explained that they are now able to tackle controversial subjects productively that previously were impossible to discuss. 'We are better at working out problems internally because we can diagnose them and figure out ways to avoid them.' The ability to examine causes of interpersonal tension, as well as to experiment with new behaviours, creates sizeable savings in consultants' time – as 'being stuck in behavioural dynamics costs money'. Another director explains that 'several years ago, we found ourselves faced with classic professional-services-firm nastiness, and we decided to try to change it.' Through working with Argyris, 'we learned – and are still learning – how to diagnose and fix these dynamics, which are a significant source of ineffectiveness'. This illustrates how trust functions as an outcome of the process.

As noted above, there is a minimum degree of interpersonal trust, below which intervention research cannot be carried out. On the other hand, too much trust can be detrimental to an intervention's success. How does this work? If a company's members have excessive trust in the competence of the intervention researcher, they risk becoming dependent on him and blind to possible weaknesses in his approach. As Argyris points out, the intervention researcher can make mistakes, especially in interpreting data. It is therefore important that organization members be willing to identify and correct these mistakes. Similarly, within an organization, excessive trust in past and current competence frequently leads to a failure to question existing practices. Organizations can be trapped by previous learning experiences that are retained in the form of routines (Levitt and March, 1988). Overreliance on existing routines prevents new solutions from being discovered and stifles innovation and change (Levitt and March, 1988; Moingeon, 1996). Members of an organization who place excessive trust in routines are, by and large, unconscious of their own behaviour. By getting them to examine and alter theories-in-use (Argyris and Schön, 1978), the intervention researcher can help them to become aware of the extent to which they take for granted – and fail to question – the organization's existing competence. The researcher's role, therefore, is to help reveal the negative consequences of excessive trust in the status quo by demonstrating to the managers that they contribute to the problems they themselves deplore.

Michel Crozier: the sociological approach to organizations

Like Argyris, Michel Crozier has been studying organizational behaviour for the past 30 years. However, unlike his American counterpart, Crozier's intervention is meant to be non-prescriptive: 'Making an intervention does not mean that one has to be prescriptive. Personally, I am completely against anything prescriptive,' he said to us. For him, the intervention researcher's role is to help an organization's members understand how the organization works as an action system. In our analysis, this is a prescription of sorts, albeit a loose one; the prescription is that it is beneficial for organizations to engage in self-examination and reflection. This looseness is in stark contrast to Argyris' highly precise prescription for learning Model II skills, discussed above.

In our analysis of Crozier's work we have identified two periods. During the 1960s and 1970s he published a series of papers and books that have since become classic reference works. This work clearly demonstrates the relevance of his approach to an understanding of organizational behaviour, especially in the public sector. Examples include: *Le phénomène bureaucratique* (1964), *La société bloquée* (1970) and *L'acteur et le système* (with E. Friedberg, 1981). During this period, he was essentially a normal science researcher, developing descriptive theory but not yet focusing on the dual objectives of the interventionist. In 1963, he created the Centre de Sociologie des Organisations (Centre for Organizational Sociology) (CSO), which he directed for 20 years. The Centre's members, as well as the students reading for the DEA degree which he set up at the end of the 1960s, contributed to the development of the French school of organizational sociology. In his later work, since the 1980s, he has worked with consulting firms and his publications tend to stress action. Specifically, *L'entreprise à l'écoute* (1989) and *La crise de l'intelligence* (1995) examine in detail the notion of intervention. Thus, although Crozier declares himself to be 'non-prescriptive', he is in favour of an approach that he views as conducive to improving organizational behaviour. In the same vein, his colleague Erhard Friedberg considers change to be an 'open process that does not follow a pre-established model but seeks to help a group of actors develop, despite paralysing obstacles, greater openness and higher capability' (Friedberg, 1993: 325). In a footnote (note 9), Friedberg says that he accepts the argument that this observation 'contains a hidden normativeness and relies on an unstated, pre-established model built on the assumption that an organization should be "cured" of its blocks and induced to adopt more open work practices, so as to facilitate the spread of autonomous action capabilities to a larger number of people'. He explains that this normativeness is in fact the expression of values (democracy, decentralization, individual autonomy, etc.) cherished by him.

The main concepts used by advocates of the sociological approach to organizations include margin of freedom, area of uncertainty, power relationships, actors' strategies, games, concrete action systems, strategic and systemic thinking and listening. For Christine Musselin, a researcher at CSO, 'the margin of freedom is fundamental. It is not even a concept; it is an assumption, a conception of the human being, a quasi philosophy.' Crozier's sociological approach to organizations maintains that it is essential to recognize behavioural contingencies and not to view participants as completely free agents; thus it is not possible, according to this model, to adopt a strictly determinist viewpoint that requires actors to behave in a specific way in support of their organization. 'No *organizational situation ever restricts an actor completely.* He always retains a margin of freedom and negotiation. Thanks to this *margin of freedom* (which is a source of uncertainty for colleagues and the rest of the organization), *each actor retains power over the other actors . . .*' (Crozier and Friedberg, 1981: 90). An organization therefore is seen as a contingent construct, a concrete action system in which members retain a margin of freedom within the rules of the game in which they participate. By concrete action system, Crozier means 'a structured human group, which coordinates its participants' actions through relatively stable games and maintains its structure, i.e. the stability of its games and the interplay between them, by regulatory devices which constitute other games' (Crozier and Friedberg, 1981: 286).

The first stage in Crozier's intervention research involves taking a 'snapshot' of the action system, that is, a descriptive inventory of the status quo. The researcher tries to avoid interpreting, making judgements, taking sides or making recommendations. Therefore, 'Even though the researcher's essential attitude is one of general questioning of reality from an outside viewpoint, this does not provide him with any judgmental criteria, any normative basis which allows him to "evaluate the practices that he observes;" the researcher knows that all the phenomena observed "have a meaning and, from the moment they exist, correspond to a reality"' (Crozier and Friedberg, 1981: 456). The goal, which is seen as challenging, is to reconstruct the logic of situations from the actors' experience. During meetings, the researcher employs an empathic listening approach designed to discover the actor's truth. Crozier explains, 'we are interested in the orientation that each person gives to his behaviour. We are not looking for *the* truth, but for each individual truth, for what each person considers to be *his* truth' (1996, in an interview with one of the authors). The researcher collects data on the actors' experiences so as to reconstruct the logic and special properties of the concrete action system. The snapshot is meant to show the relationships between actors, the rules of power games, the stakes and rules of play, and all other elements that appear to have a role in how the action system functions (for example, the existence of barriers between organizational functions or departments). Musselin (1996, personal interview) explains, 'We acquire knowledge more through the way in which we reconstruct, than through the data itself.' This initial phase, in which the researcher builds an inventory of data, is central to this approach to intervention research; it is important for the researcher to avoid interpretation at this stage.

Presenting results of this initial analysis provides an opportunity for the researcher to present the related 'facts', to check their accuracy and relevance, and to 'transfer' the intervention's approach to the actors: 'The presentation starts with essentially descriptive elements. It then illustrates the connections between them and creates, through a series of discussions, comparisons and investigations, the conditions for a joint interpretation. The latter reveals the systemic connections between recorded facts and constitutes the learning of a new mode of thought' (Friedberg, 1993: 364).

To proceed, first the actors have to accept the report (the 'snapshot' of the action system). Only then are they welcome to comment on the snapshot and consider what actions need to be taken. The researcher's role is not to decide in place of the actors what is good or bad, or what is advisable or not, but to help them express their own criteria and norms and to clarify their objectives so that they can assess the difference between the existing and desired situation and identify actions they can take within the margins of freedom available to them. The sociological approach thus supplies its own 'methodology and tools' and produces 'concrete knowledge of the rules and fundamental structures governing co-operation between the members of an organization whose behaviour we wish to modify' (Friedberg, 1993: 347). Such knowledge can be used by the actors to embark upon a change process.

The role of trust in Crozier's intervention research

This analysis is based on data gathered in interviews we conducted with Crozier and with Christine Musselin. We also draw from a book in which Crozier describes his intervention research within SNCF (the French railways), and from interviews we conducted with an area manager at SNCF who was involved in this research. Unlike the interviews at Monitor, these interviews were conducted explicitly to help us address the goals of this chapter. We asked similar kinds of questions of the SNCF manager about his experience of the project, and we later noted all references to trust, as a way to understand his experience in this research effort. Overall, these data suggest that trust plays an important role, but one that is quite different from the role it plays in theory of action research.

Trust in intentions is more important than trust in competence for Crozier's type of intervention. Initially, those affected by the research may not see much potential for either gain or loss by participating; the competence of the researcher is likely to seem insufficiently important as to preclude allowing him or her to be interviewed or observed. However, intentions do matter and the organizational sociologists often can be regarded with suspicion about their motivation. For example, in 1987 Crozier was asked by Jacques Lesourne, adviser to the CEO of SNCF to audit the company. This audit took place after a very tough strike during which locomotive drivers blocked railways traffic in France for six weeks. As described by the area manager we interviewed, 'this strike was a manifestation of the very low level of trust between locomotive drivers and their managers. At the end of the strike, there was no more trust at all!' In this context, Lesourne had to reassure his colleagues in order to gain their agreement: Crozier recalled, 'They questioned Lesourne who told them: "Mr. Crozier is an impartial and moderate man, he is no bomb thrower." I was accepted.' But being accepted by managers was not enough. For the intervention researcher using this approach to enjoy a sufficient degree of trust, he/she must demonstrate that he/she is not taking sides with the director who contacted him/her, but acting in the interests of the company as a whole. Those at the Centre for Organizational Sociology (CSO) stress that their function as researchers observing company meetings is to be 'neutral' researchers – that is, to describe the workings of the action system but not to assess the members for the benefit of their superiors; the same principal holds for one-on-one interviews: 'the fact that we do not try to ascertain their performance at meetings, or judge them, and that we only ask them what they do and what they enjoy, creates trust' (Musselin, 1996 personal interview). Crozier's role at SNCF illustrates such a neutral position.

In Crozier's model, it is the behaviours and attitudes of empathic listening, as well as the explicit commitment to keep what is said confidential, that build trust in researchers' intentions and allow the intervention research to be carried out. 'Those interviewed easily agreed to be interviewed because of this non-inquisitorial and empathic attitude, which, rather than seeking "objective" information, takes everyone's point of view into account and assures them of the meeting's confidential nature' (Friedberg, 1993, note 8: 300). The area manager of SNCF we interviewed stressed the fact that, in a crisis situation, Michel Crozier has been able to create a dialogue with locomotive drivers thanks to his non-inquisitorial and empathic attitude. Even so, an investigation strategy that aims to guarantee the confidentiality of the information supplied has inherent limits. While it may result in an increase in the trust placed by the members of the company in the intervention researcher's intentions, it may also contribute to the maintenance of a low level of trust among the organization's members (Schwartz, 1994).

In the process of these researchers listening to participants, the act of confiding leads to an increase in trust which, in turn, produces more acts of confiding. 'By listening, if one listens attentively, your speakers begin to trust you. The human relationship thus created is essentially based on the person being reassured that he is really being listened to. If he manages to talk about things he considers important or is worried by, and the sociologist listens to what he is saying, then trust can develop' (Crozier, 1996 personal interview). Trust is nurtured during a meeting by a listening attitude that seeks to understand and show a person that his remarks are worth considering. In sum, a self-reinforcing process is generated. The more an informant trusts the sociologist, the more the sociologist will be able to help him to express himself, which in turn reinforces trust. The feedback session also plays a critical role. As explained by the SNCF area manager we interviewed, 'Michel Crozier increased the level of trust during the feedback session by proving he had carefully listened to the locomotive drivers and to their managers without taking position for one group or another. The next step was to design experiments. That has also increased trust and unlocked the situation.'

If members of the organization, and particularly its senior managers, change their way of thinking during the intervention (Crozier, 1995) and place more importance in listening, this will enable them not only to have a better understanding of the workings of this human construct, but also to increase trust in their organization. According to Crozier (1995: 58), 'trust does not solve problems; it contributes to their being experienced in a more constructive manner'. He offers as an example the director of SNCF's locomotive department, who adopted the approach used by the intervention research and developed an ability to listen to colleagues. Knowing they would be listened to, they no longer hesitated, in the event of an accident or incident, to volunteer information. This kind of behaviour was hitherto unknown: 'After the intervention, many of the staff developed sufficient trust to give their version of events, knowing that they would be listened to' (Crozier, 1995: 125) – and perhaps also not penalized for the 'bad news'. The SNCF area manager expressed a similar sentiment, but remained pessimistic about the ability to spread this kind of behaviour throughout SNCF. In his words, 'during Michel Crozier's intervention, we spent enough time to listen to people. The drama at SNCF is that it is too unusual. This has to do with our corporate culture. We think we do not have time. We always want to hurry, we want to implement solutions before having listened to all the people concerned.'

Crozier believes that the strikes in the French public sector are related to the inability of elites to reform themselves, in part due to excessive trust in their own modes of thought. This kind of trust is self-protective and can lead to lower willingness to trust others. Similarly, he calls into question the way in which the top managers are trained. In his view, the French system of *grandes ecoles* (elite schools) produces 'solution-finding machines' when the main task of managers should be 'to identify real problems'. He believes that elites must change their way of thinking and be shown the virtues of listening.

Conclusions

Researchers who intervene in organizational systems have a dual objectives: to advance knowledge in their field and to help improve the system under study. In contrast, descriptive or normal science researchers who undertake field work aim to produce new scientific knowledge through objective study of an empirical object. The object of study is assumed to be unchanged by the process of studying it. It is beyond the scope of this chapter to comment on the implications for advancing knowledge of these different approaches; the introduction in Argyris (1993) gives a thoughtful treatment of these issues. This chapter has examined how this dual objective plays out in the research of Chris Argyris and Michel Crozier.

In our analysis of these leading theorists in the development of intervention research, we found that trust plays a critical and multifaceted role in this work. We also found that it was necessary to distinguish between trust in intentions and in competence, as they were conceptually distinct and played slightly different roles in these research activities. Having sought to identify whether trust was a prerequisite or an outcome of intervention research, we discovered that it was both. However, we found differences in emphasis between the two approaches examined here. In the Argyris model, the researcher simply cannot proceed in an intervention project without the organization members placing considerable trust in both his competence and intentions, and also without them having trust in each other's intentions and abilities to change and learn. Crozier, whose research methods are at first glance less obtrusive and require less commitment from the organization members, is less likely to be precluded from intervening in an organization due to insufficient trust; this is especially true for trust in competence, whereas lack of trust in intentions may pose a barrier to participation. None the less, at the outset of such projects it is clear that an organization has less at stake in an organizational sociology project than in a theory of action project.

In both approaches, trust is likely to develop as an outcome of the research when the work is skilfully carried out. The degree of change may be greater in an organizational sociology project, as it starts with less of a foundation of trust. This is especially true if organization members are surprised by how much the process teaches them about themselves and about their organization. The unexpected nature of this insight places more emphasis on trust as an outcome in this work, whereas in Argyris' model, trust issues necessarily surface at the outset.

We also found evidence that trust can serve as an obstacle to intervention research. This phenomenon is more relevant to Argyris' work than to Crozier's, as the nature of the relationship between the researcher and organization members is more pivotal to the effectiveness of the project. Excessive dependence on the organizational sociologist is unlikely as this researcher is not offering to impart critical skills to participants; yet excessive trust in the action science researcher can limit inquiry and effort on the part of participants in ways that sabotage the project. Although there is some potential in both models for participants to accept the results of the study uncritically, the behavioural risk is greater in theory of action research because it explicitly attempts to change participants' behaviour – to Model II, which by definition requires questioning and checking until mutual understanding is reached. Figure 9.1 summarizes this comparison, using bold titles to depict the shifts in emphasis between models.

Participation in intervention research (Argyris model)				**Participation in intervention research (Crozier model)**			
Organization members' trust in researcher	***Trust as prerequisite***	*Trust as consequence*	***Trust as obstacle***	*Organization members' trust in researcher*	*Trust as prerequisite*	***Trust as consequence***	*Trust as obstacle*
Trust in competence	If members believe researcher is capable of helping firm, they will agree to participate – 'high stakes' engagement	After exposure to researcher's skills members' trust in his/her competence increases, but it was high to begin with	Excessive dependence on researcher can inhibit taking responsibility for own learning	Trust in competence	Only minimal level of trust is necessary to be willing to be interviewed by researcher – 'low stakes' engagement	After exposure to researcher's skills and insight members' trust in his/her competence is established	Excessive dependence on researcher is unlikely to occur in this kind of intervention research
Trust in intentions	If members believe researcher will not betray the firm or its members they will participate – 'high stakes' engagement	As a result of working together, members become increasingly comfortable with goodwill and integrity of researcher – fairly well established to begin with	Blind trust in his/her intentions leads members not to challenge or confront researcher thereby reducing opportunities to further their own learning	Trust in intentions	If members do not trust researcher not to betray confidential information, they simply will not reveal it, but they may still agree to participate – 'low stakes' engagement	As a result of working together, members become comfortable with goodwill and integrity of researcher	Blind trust in his/her intentions leads members not to challenge researcher's interpretation of the data, potentially diminishing the learning

FIGURE 9.1 *A framework depicting relationships between trust and intervention researcher*

This chapter adds to an extensive literature on trust in organizations by focusing on the role of trust in intervention research. It also contributes to the organizational learning literature by exploring the nature of intervention research conducted to enhance learning in an organization. We focused our analysis on the work of two leading organizational scholars as a strategy for ensuring that the insights obtained were drawn from widely accepted theory and high-quality examples of field-based research. Both in our interviews and in this small part of the literature, we found strong evidence that intervention researchers and members of organizations both view trust as centrally important to effective interventions. The primary implication of these findings for other researchers who wish to engage in this kind of work is that it is critical to pay close attention to building trust – particularly to creating an environment in which participants feel comfortable raising concerns and questions.

References

Argyris, C. (1957) *Personality and Organisations*. New York: HarperCollins.

Argyris, C. (1962) *Interpersonal Competence and Organizational Effectiveness*. Homewood, IL: Dorsey Press.

Argyris, C. (1964) *Integrating the Individual and the Organisation*. New York: Wiley.

Argyris, C. (1982) *Reasoning, Learning and Action: Individual and Organizational*. San Francisco: Jossey-Bass.

Argyris, C. (1985) *Strategy, Change and Defensive Routines*. Boston, MA: Pitman.

Argyris, C. (1990) *Overcoming Organizational Defenses. Facilitating Organizational Learning*. Boston, MA: Allyn and Bacon.

Argyris, C. (1993) *Knowledge for Action. a Guide to Overcoming Barriers to Organizational Change*. San Francisco: Jossey-Bass.

Argyris, C. (1994) Litigation mentality and organisational learning. In: S.B. Sitkin and R.J. Bies (eds), *The Legalistic Organisation*. Thousand Oaks, CA: Sage.

Argyris, C. and Schön, D.A. (1974) *Theory in Practice*. San Francisco: Jossey-Bass.

Argyris, C. and Schön, D.A. (1978) *Organizational Learning: a Theory of Action Perspective*. Reading, MA: Addison-Wesley.

Argyris, C. and Schön, D.A. (1996) *Organizational Learning II: Theory, Method and Practice*. Reading, MA: Addison-Wesley.

Arrow, K.J. (1974) Limited knowledge and economic analysis. *American Economic Review*, March: 1–20.

Collis, D. (1996) Organizational capability as a source of profit. In: B. Moingeon and A. Edmondson (eds), *Organizational Learning and Competitive Advantage*. London: Sage.

Crozier, M. (1964) *Le phénomène bureaucratique*. Paris: Seuil.

Crozier, M. (1970) *La société bloquée*. Paris: Seuil.

Crozier, M. (1989) *L'entreprise à l'écoute*. Paris: InterEditions.

Crozier, M. (1995) *La crise de l'intelligence*. Paris: InterEditions.

Crozier, M. and Friedberg, E. (1981, first edition 1977) *L'acteur et le système*. Paris: Seuil.

DeGeus, A. (1988) Planning as learning. *Harvard Business Review*, 66 (2): 70–4.

Donaldson, L. and Davis, J.H. (1991) Stewardship theory or agency theory. *Australian Journal of Management*, 21: 44–56.

Edmondson, A. (1999) Psychological safety and learning behaviour in work terms. Accepted for publication, *Administrative Science Quarterly*.
Edmondson, A. and Moingeon, B. (1996) When to learn how and when to learn why: appropriate organizational learning processes as a source of competitive advantage. In: B. Moingeon and A. Edmondson (eds), *Organizational Learning and Competitive Advantage*. London: Sage. pp. 17–37: 7–20.
Edmondson, A and Moingeon, B. (1998) From organisational learning to the learning organisation. *Management Learning*, 1 (29): 5–20.
Fiol, C.M. and Lyles, M.A. (1985) Organizational learning. *Academy of Management Review*, 10 (4): 803–13.
Friedberg, E. (1993) *Le pouvoir et la règle: dynamiques de l'action organisée*. Paris: Seuil.
Gambetta, D.G. (ed.) (1988) *Trust. Making and Breaking Cooperative Relations*. New York: Basil Blackwell.
Handy, C. (1995) Trust and the virtual organization. *Harvard Business Review*, May/June: 40–50.
Hayes, R., Wheelwright, S.C. and Clark, K. (1988) *Dynamic Manufacturing: the Making of the Learning Organization*. New York: The Free Press.
Hovland, C., Janis, I. and Kelley, H. (1953) *Communication and Persuasion*. New Haven, CT: Yale University Press.
Huber, G.P. (1991) Organizational learning: the contributing processes and the literature. *Organization Science*, 2 (1): 88–115.
Johnson-George, C. and Swap, W. (1982) Measurement of specific interpersonal trust: construction and validation of a scale to assess trust in a specific other. *Journal of Personality and Social Psychology*, 43: 1306–17.
Larson, A. (1992) Network dyads in entrepreneurial settings: a study of governance of exchange relationships. *Administrative Science Quarterly*, 37: 76–106.
Lawler, E. (1992) *The Ultimate Advantage: Creating the High Involvement Organization*. San Francisco: Jossey-Bass.
Levitt, B. and March, J. (1988) Organizational learning. *Annual Review of Sociology*, 14: 319–40.
Lorenz, E.H. (1988) Neither friends nor strangers: informal networks of subcontracting in French industry. In: D.G. Gambetta (ed.), *Trust*. New York: Basil Blackwell. pp. 194–210.
Lorenz, E.H. (1993) Flexible production systems and the social construction of trust. *Politics and Society*, 21 (3): 307–24.
Mayer, R.C., Davis, J.H. and Schoorman, F.D. (1995) An integrative model of organisational trust. *Academy of Management Review*, 20 (3): 709–34.
Mirvis, P.H. and Berg, D.N. (1977) *Failures in Organization Change and Development*. New York: Wiley-Interscience.
Moingeon, B. (1996) L'apprentissage organisationnel. *Sciences humaines*, 62 (6): 36–9.
Moingeon B. and Edmondson, A. (eds) (1996) *Organizational Learning and Competitive Advantage*. London: Sage.
Moingeon, B. and Edmondson, A. (1998) Trust and organisational learning. In: N. Lazaric and E. Lorenz (eds), *Trust, Learning and Economic Expectations*. London: Edward Elgar.
Redding, J.C. and Catalanello, R.F. (1994) *Strategic Readiness: the Making of the Learning Organization*. San Francisco: Jossey-Bass.
Schein, E.H. (1988) *Process Consultation*, Volume I: *Its Role in Organization Development* (2nd edn). Reading, MA: Addison-Wesley.
Schein, E.H. (1992) *Organizational Culture and Leadership* (rev. edn). San Francisco: Jossey-Bass.
Schwartz, R.M. (1994) *The Skilled Facilitator. Practical Wisdom for Developing Effective Groups*. San Francisco, Jossey-Bass.

Senge, P. (1990) *The Fifth Discipline: the Art and Practice of the Learning Organization*. New York: Doubleday Currency.
Shrivastava, P. (1983) A typology of organizational learning. *Journal of Management Studies*, 20 (1): 7–28.
Sitkin, S.B. and Roth, N.L. (1993) Explaining the limited effectiveness of legalistic 'remedies' for trust/distrust. *Organization Science*, 4: 367–92.
Stata, R. (1989) Organizational learning: the key to management innovation. *Sloan Management Review*, 12 (1): 63–74.

10 Project Design for Learning and Innovation: Lessons Learned from Action Research in an Aircraft Manufacturing Company

Karen Ayas

The increased pace of change in the environment surrounding organizations makes innovation a necessity rather than a choice, if one assumes that this trend is likely to continue. The increased emphasis on innovation alongside productivity calls for the creation of infrastructures where innovation can be fostered and effectively managed. This chapter is based on action research conducted in the aircraft industry to extend and apply the concepts underlying organizational learning to management of innovation. The focus is on technological innovation projects that transform a technology from an idea to a new product, namely new product development projects (NPD). Based on two and a half years of field study, the research has addressed the question 'How can innovation projects be managed and designed for maximum effectiveness of learning?' The field work was initiated by multiple case studies on NPD projects varying in size, scope and complexity to reveal what was happening with new product development at the chosen research site, Fokker Aircraft. The action research methodology proved to be effective for dealing with the research question and allowed the generation of knowledge about the processes of innovation and learning, insights about the potential contribution of learning to NPD projects, and the development of an alternative approach to project management[1] and design which treats learning as central.

In this chapter, after a glimpse into the processes of innovation and learning, the factors associated with innovation effectiveness are briefly discussed. This is followed by a section exploring the link between the organizational context, innovation and learning. After some reflections on organization design and learning, the emphasis remains on the design of large and complex projects which can create a facilitating context for learning. Next, the proposed organic network design for innovation projects is briefly described. Finally, the results following implementation of this design in NPD projects at Fokker Aircraft are discussed.

Innovation and learning

The objective of the study is the nexus between innovation and learning. The stance taken here is that *innovation may be perceived as a learning process.* A quick glimpse into the processes of innovation and learning already emphasizes the strong link between them. An innovation project embraces the cumulative effort from the creation of a new idea to its commercialization. It encompasses a sequence of multifaceted, multistage processes, which involve the dynamic interplay of many different parties at different levels of abstraction (Souder, 1987). Innovation requires more than creative capacity to invent new ideas; it requires managerial skills and talents to transform good ideas into practice (Van de Ven et al., 1989). As an innovation develops, the new idea often represents a threat to the established order. A process of change is triggered. When the innovation process is perceived as a 'change producing activity' (Zirger and Maidique, 1990), there is an additional challenge involved in the process: optimum use of the opportunity to learn and adapt.

Innovation in its essence is a process where ideas are generated, and which may lead to knowledge creation. The innovation process further involves the execution or exploitation of these ideas, that is, application or effective use of the knowledge. Since knowledge may be created with every innovation project, there exists a potential for learning. Whether this knowledge is potentially useful is dependent on both quantity and quality of learning that takes place while innovating. As Bastien argues:

> In circumstances of essential change, learning goes on whether or not the management of the organisation realizes it, but it is of low quality and inefficient without the self-conscious control and reflection . . . (Van de Ven et al., 1989: 391)

Effective management of product innovation may be defined as 'creating and improving the capabilities needed to make new product development a competitive advantage over the long term'. The essence of effective innovation management lies in the ability continually to enhance the underlying knowledge base. This implies that all individuals involved in NPD projects be engaged in a constant process of learning, that they transmit their learning to others, and that the cumulative knowledge acquired from projects be embodied in the organization.

A delicate balance needs to be maintained between the long-term and short-term goals, to guarantee efficient and effective performance in every NPD project as well as continuous improvement through learning within and amongst projects. The focus can neither remain on short-term achievements, nor can it simply shift to the long-term accomplishments. The next section gives an overview of factors associated with success in NPD projects, based on previous research.

Innovation effectiveness

There are numerous studies which have aimed at discovering factors associated with innovation effectiveness, but most focus on short-term achievements. The existing literature is vast across many types of industries, firms and products. Brown and Eisenhardt (1995) in their review have identified three relatively coherent and distinctive streams based on pioneering works.

- The *rational* stream builds on the Myers and Marquis (1969) and SAPPHO studies (Rothwell, 1972) which focus on a broad range of determinants (for example, interaction of the various functional groups, product advantages, market attractiveness, internal organization). This stream relies heavily upon subjective judgements and retrospective inferences over complex past processes without well-defined constructs of a 'better' product or 'effective' development (Brown and Eisenhardt, 1995). Despite these shortcomings, this stream contributes to identifying factors which are essential for successful product development.
- The *communication* stream builds on the work of Allen (1971) concerned with the effects of communication on project performance (for example, technological gatekeepers as discriminators of information, personal contact as highly important communication channels, external communication for better project performance, cross-functional groups). The underlying premise in this stream is that success in innovation requires adequate information capacity in the system and such capacity is a function of the intensity of the communication patterns. Brown and Eisenhardt (1995) argue that the principal shortcoming of this stream is that other factors are neglected, and different types of new product development projects are not distinguished. None the less, the dynamics of information processing and the political dynamics underlying communication are highlighted.
- The *problem-solving* stream builds on the study by Imai et al. (1985) with an emphasis on the actual development process, and evolves with studies of Japanese product development practices (for example, Quinn, 1985; Takeuchi and Nonaka, 1986). Further contributions to product development research in this stream are: the importance of 'heavyweight' team leaders as links (capable of co-ordinating team activities while working with senior management); a clear articulated vision of products' intended image, performance and fit with the company; an experiential approach to product design through frequent iterations, testing and milestones which lead to faster product development.

Brown and Eisenhardt (1995) explain that this latter stream of research portrays product development as a 'balancing act' between product vision developed at executive level and problem-solving found at the project level.

The information processing view is extended from the organization of the information into problem-solving strategies. Given the complementary nature of past research in new product development, in their integrative model Brown and Eisenhardt (1995) summarize the key findings. They identify the key players whose actions influence project performance as the project team, project leader, senior management, suppliers and customers. They propose cross-functional teams, which are consistent and supported by empirical evidence in all streams (for example, Clark and Fujimoto, 1991; Dougherty, 1990; Zirger and Maidique, 1990). They argue that the presence of gatekeepers, team tenure at moderate level, effective internal and external communication, and problem-solving strategies for organizing work are the requirements for guaranteeing high-performing project teams. They conclude that project leaders should be the link or bridge between project team and senior management. They describe the characteristics of an effective leader as powerful (significant decision-making responsibility, organization-wide authority and high hierarchical level), with a strong product vision (creating a holistic view and communicating), and appropriate internal management skills. They argue that senior management support and their ability to provide 'subtle control' are critical to success. Finally, they emphasize the importance of extensive supplier and customer involvement to improve the effectiveness of the product concept.

The integrative model proposed by Brown and Eisenhardt (1995), which includes the key concepts and critical findings in the various streams which are complementary to one another, can be used as a basis for effective innovation management as defined here. This model, however, needs to be further refined to meet the requirements for building long-term innovative capability through organizational learning. This implies that, in addition to the principles stated above, the organizational design needs to provide a facilitating context for learning within and amongst projects. To establish the additional design criteria for learning, first the concept of organizational learning is explored; and then, the link between the organizational context, innovation and learning is discussed.

Organizational learning

There is renewed emphasis on organizational learning in the 1990s, but the concept actually appears much earlier in the literature (for example, March and Simon, 1958). Recently interest has grown, leading to different perspectives and orientations, all concerned with the fact that there is a need to adapt to changing environments, learn from the past, anticipate and respond to threats, and continuously innovate to build a desirable future. There is greater awareness of the necessity to learn, and the concept of organizational learning is becoming part of many established disciplines such as strategic management, sociology and organizational theory (Easterby-Smith, 1997).

A description of *learning* which represents a common theme in various fields of research where organizational learning has been the subject of analysis is this from Huber:

> An entity learns if, through its processing of information, the range of its potential behaviours is changed. (Huber, 1991: 89)

This description is relevant for different levels within the organizational context. It may be applicable whether the entity is the individual, a group of individuals, or the organization. When the organization is the entity, learning takes place if any of its units acquire knowledge that is recognized as potentially useful to the organization. Organizational learning from this perspective primarily involves creation of knowledge, but it also encompasses the effective use of the knowledge which results in a change in the behaviour of the individuals towards improved performance.

While many theories of organizational learning are based on individual learning, others do not explicitly deal with individual actors at all (for example, Daft and Weick, 1984; Levitt and March, 1988). Learning in its essence occurs at the individual level. Organizations ultimately learn through their members. Organizations, however, are not just a large collection of individuals; they also represent a context with a system for capturing and imparting the learning of their individual members. Unlike individual learning, organizational learning involves developing enough consensus around interpretations embedded in the content – as well as in the framing of communications and the form people use to construct a picture for organized action to result (Fiol, 1994). March and Olsen (1976) in their model of the 'organizational learning cycle' illustrate that individual actions, based on individual beliefs, lead to organizational action, which produces some environmental response that affects individual beliefs, which initiate a new set of actions.

The literature around organizational learning can be broadly divided into *learning organizations*, which is driven by the community of practitioners, and *organizational learning*, which is treated as a research topic by scholars. These two branches are often used interchangeably since they are similar and related. In this study, while organizational learning is perceived as a *process* which takes place in organizations, the learning organization is viewed as the *context* or an 'ideal type' of organization where effective learning takes place. The interdependency between the learning process and the organizational context is further explored in the next section.

The organizational context, innovation and learning

Innovation presents an opportunity for people to learn, that is, to adapt and cope with changes in a new organizational context. The paradox is that people may also effectively learn how to resist change that is enacted with innovation. It can thus be assumed that the requirement with NPD projects is that individuals learn how to cooperate and productively cope with change, rather than learning to resist change. The question to be raised is not whether learning occurs with new product development, but rather to what extent this learning contributes to effective management of innovation. This is dependent to a great extent on the organizational context, where an innovation project takes place.

As an idea moves from its inception through development and implementation, it is people within the organization who push, modify or drop the innovation (Van de Ven et al., 1989). Their behaviour, which is the outcome of an adaptive and iterative learning process, is affected by contextual factors. Salancik and Pfeffer (1978) posit that the effects of the context and the consequences of past choices, rather than individual predispositions and rational decision-making processes, explain attitudes and motivation. They explain that the social context binds people to behaviour through a process of commitment, affects the saliency of information about their past activities and provides norms and expectations that constrain their rationalization. These effects of context make behaviour in an organization different from individual behaviour and individual cognitive processes considered in isolation.

Salancik and Pfeffer (1978) further argue that the social context provides cues which individuals use to construct and interpret information. In their social information processing approach, the context has two general effects on individuals' attitudes: (1) the construction of meaning through guides to socially acceptable beliefs and attitudes embedded in the context; (2) the focusing of an individual's attention on certain information through making that information more salient within the context.

Every interaction between individuals is a transaction where knowledge is created. An individual primarily interacts with his/her immediate surrounding whether this is his/her department, task group or project team. The design of the organization sets the nature of this interaction to a certain extent. The organizational structure, for instance, determines the formal relation, communication or interaction patterns among individuals. Interaction patterns are also dependent on the individual's ties within the organization, which constitutes his/her informal communication network; and the design also sets the infrastructure or the premises of the informal organization.

It may be argued that the nature of learning and its contribution to product innovation is influenced by the *organization's structure*, the *communicative practices* and the *social context*, which all play a major role in the effectiveness of information processing. While previous research in product development emphasizes the importance of information processing, it does not take fully into account the crucial relationship between the contextual factors and information processing:

- All the factors which are identified as essential in the *rational stream* may be related to effective management of information across boundaries

of specialized functional groups. It may be assumed that they are relevant for a specific organizational context, such as the functional organization.
- The *communication stream* – which elaborates on the dynamics of information processing underlying communication – highlights the importance of the context while dealing with internal and external communication patterns, but fails to deal explicitly with contextual variables.
- The *problem-solving* stream deals to a greater extent with the context for establishing success criteria. There is an initial leap from increasing the effectiveness of information processing in a given context to changing the context in order to reduce the need for information processing. The majority of findings in this stream appear to be relevant when activities are carried out through project management in a matrix organization.
- The *integrative model* proposed by Brown and Eisenhardt (1995) further highlights the key players and their role in effective management of product development projects. Their model emphasizes the increasing necessity to manage new product development by project teams while taking into consideration the organizational context in which these projects are managed.

Reflections on design for learning and innovation

Although a distinction needs to be made between the organizational and project levels, in the case of large and complex NPD projects that are the subject of analysis, the ideas underlying organization design appear to be very relevant. Mintzberg (1979) explains that the essence of organizational design is the manipulation of a series of parameters that determine the division of labour and the achievement of co-ordination. Given the various sources of uncertainty, basic functions of organizational design may be stated as:

- creating the most appropriate configuration of work units as well as the linkages between these units (Galbraith, 1973; March and Simon, 1958); and
- facilitating the collection of information from external areas as well as permitting effective information processing within and between work units (Tushman and Nadler, 1978).

An organization's design influences to a great extent how its parts constitute the whole, to what extent knowledge and competencies are specific or shared among its parts. The design influences the effectiveness of learning in the various parts of the organization. When the organization is large and complex, it is almost inevitable that one deals with parts of the organization rather than the whole. As organizations grow, they differentiate: to realize economies of scale and benefit from specialization, subunits (which have specialized tasks and deal with specific aspects of the organization) are created (Katz and Kahn, 1966; Lawrence and Lorsch, 1967; Thompson, 1961/1967). Specialized sub-units are separated from each other by 'organizational boundaries' (Katz and Kahn, 1966). Specialization increases the efficiency of information processing within the unit, but simultaneously creates obstacles to information processing between units (Tushman and Scanlan, 1981). The challenge then is to divide the organization into parts in a way that allows managing learning, that is, knowledge creation, sharing and application, most effectively. Can this challenge be overcome? Is there a design that is best? Or should there be? These are a number of ongoing debates.

Duncan and Weiss (1979) point out the implications of organizational learning for organizational design. They argue that 'effective' organizational design does not necessarily imply organizational learning. The immediate question to be tackled then is: effective for which purpose? One cannot argue that the ultimate purpose of the organization is to learn. Viewing the organization as a system of purposeful action, Duncan and Weiss (1979: 81) define the concept of *effectiveness* as 'the degree to which firm or organizational actions lead to the outcomes intended'. Learning is a multidimensional concept and its outcome may serve varying purposes. Whether or not a distinctive style of learning is useful or productive is highly subjective and related to the specific purpose. Whether or not the organizational design is effective for learning or innovation is also related to the specific purpose to be attained.

There are numerous findings in organization theory which highlight the contingencies between innovation, strategy and structure that can be associated with organizational design (for example, Burns and Stalker, 1961; Galbraith, 1973; Lawrence and Lorsch, 1967). These findings emphasize the need for restructuring the organization for improving communication and co-ordination. The required restructuring may appear under various forms, such as changes in organizational responsibilities, use of new teams, altered control systems. This may be formal or informal, temporary or permanent.

Adopting the ideas underlying organization design presented by Galbraith (1973, 1994), project design here refers to the conscious and rational choice of the organization form to be used to accomplish the specific project objectives. It relates to large and complex projects, or a group of projects, with teams within teams. New product development projects which call for the integration of a large number of people who need to be engaged in multiple differentiated tasks thus represent a complex design problem. This design problem may appear to be even more complex with the additional requirement that learning needs to be managed along with innovation.

Galbraith, in his *Competing with Flexible Lateral Organisations* (1994), shifts the emphasis of design to building lateral organizational capability. An organizational capability is created when all the elements in his 'star' model (people, structure, rewards and processes) are aligned and support task performance, while strategy determines which tasks require this capability. He describes product development as an organizational capability and argues that lateral organizations can increase this capability. The lateral organization is a design which may take on different forms with the purpose of 'recreating the organisation in microcosm for the issue at hand' (Galbraith, 1994). Morgan's 'spider plant' metaphor (1993) creates a powerful image which demonstrates the differentiated yet integrated character of an organizational design that can be applicable for learning organizations. This implies the coexistence of different structures such as the functional, matrix and project organization. All organizational structures have their advantages and may be ideal for specific organizational/environmental contexts and contribute to learning. So one alternative approach to designing 'learning organizations' would be that parts of the organization have different structures depending on the contextual requirements for learning.

Tushman and Nadler (1978) point out that rather than asking what should be the structure of a particular organization, more appropriate questions are:

- What are the optimal structures for the different sub-units?
- What structural mechanisms will facilitate effective co-ordination among differentiated yet interdependent sub-units?

With respect to new product development, the problem that organizations are faced with is, on the one hand, to have disciplinary and functional excellence, to retain deep knowledge or capability specific to disciplines, and on the other hand, manage the interfaces among them and ensure the synergy between them. New product development requires preserving functional excellence yet inhibiting functional bias, leaving room for creative ideas to emerge yet overcoming the performance challenges to implement them. For new product development, there will always be the need to develop specific knowledge bases and technological capabilities. Leonard-Barton (1992) argues that we need to maintain a balance between a coupling so tight as not to erode specialized knowledge bases and so loose as not to overlook the interaction and system effects. The effectiveness of learning with new product development is highly dependent on the effectiveness of the design for creating a context where learning is facilitated at individual, group, project and programme levels.

Effective learning at group level implies that the total aptitude of the group is more than the sum of individuals' aptitudes. The effectiveness of learning can be amplified through interaction between diverse functional specializations, thought processes and behaviour patterns. When the know-how accumulated at the individual level is transferred to other individuals within a working group, there is an opportunity for all individuals to learn. A 'team' is a desired setting for a group of people working together to practise learning. Effective teams are multidimensional, with a variety of complementary skills with respect to technical expertise, problem-solving, decision-making and interpersonal skills (Katzenbach and Smith, 1993). Team building – the process of taking a collection of individuals with different needs, background and expertise and transforming them into an integrated effective work unit – is therefore a prerequisite for effective learning at group level. When teams reach a high maturity stage, they can become self-managing. Self-managing teams have been acclaimed for effective NPD (Imai et al., 1985; Thamhain and Wilemon, 1987). Although the concept is not new, recently the idea of self-managing teams as basic operating units of organizations is gaining wide acceptance. Imai et al. (1985) posit that to become self-managing, teams must be autonomous (have operational autonomy), self-transcendent (come up with challenging goals and keep elevating) and cross-fertilizing (with interaction between diverse thought processes and behaviour patterns).

It is argued here that a preliminary requirement for a project design effective for learning, consistent with the theory of requisite variety (Ashby, 1956), is having sufficient differences and variety with respect to knowledge, skills, values and insights within the human capital invested in projects. An additional requirement is that projects are designed in a way that establishes a communication/relation network among all project participants in which these differences are used with optimum effectiveness, and the social capital is maximized through optimizing structural holes (Burt, 1992). Cross-functional, co-located and self-managing teams where the human and social capitals are maximized may provide the context for cross-fertilization of diverse thought processes and competencies. In such teams, the frequency and intensity of communication is very high. Communication is informal and open. A project design in which such teams constitute the basic operating units may be effective for building long-term capability through learning both at the individual and group levels. This by itself, however, does not provide an integral solution for large and complex innovation projects. When the aim is effective management of innovation and learning in large and complex projects, the additional challenge is to be able to integrate teams to foster learning at project/programme level.

While the majority of effective teams have less than ten members (Katzenbach and Smith, 1993), such projects may require hundreds of people whose work must be integrated towards the successful completion of the product. Although it is obvious that more than one team may be necessary for many projects, previous research has not fully explored this issue. The project network structure presented in the following section overcomes the challenge of integration of a large number of teams. It is an alternative way of organizing project teams that can create the desired context for learning.

The project network structure

At Fokker Aircraft, through multiple case studies, initially the varying approaches and existing structures of a large number of ongoing and recently terminated projects were analysed. The majority of the ongoing projects had structures varying between functional, light-weight and heavy-weight project organization[2] using the matrix structure of the larger organization as a basis. To respond to the problems identified, the conclusions drawn from this analysis clearly indicated the necessity for a shift towards a knowledge-creating structure which would be effective not only to improve project performance but also to build long-term capability for continuous improvement with projects. The project network structure (PNS) was developed through the collaborative efforts of organizational members involved in product development, and adopted by them as the appropriate design for their development teams.

PNS ensured the required degree of integration among the various self-managing teams in every product development project. The essential characteristic of PNS was that it grew and shrunk in an organic manner in response to the changing requirements of the project (see Figure 10.1). PNS began with a cross-functional *core team*. The basic operating units in the network were the self-managing teams which split off from the core team as tasks demanded. They were dismantled once the specified tasks were completed.

In order to minimize the co-ordination needs within the project, the design of the network and its dynamics stem from the actual work breakdown structure (WBS) – the 'tree' showing the hierarchy of the required work to be performed to complete a project. Through WBS, the work packages can be defined in a way that they can be assigned to organizational units. As Globerson (1994) illustrates, different WBS patterns may be applicable for the same project, but they each demand different organizational structures and management styles. The major principle of PNS is that both the WBS and the cost breakdown structure are coupled with the organizational breakdown structure of the project.

Self-managing teams (SMT), which are the operating units, are required to manage these work packages as a 'contract' in which the work to be performed is specified together with the technical contents, cost and schedule. These teams are given full operational autonomy to perform within the specified budget and time in the work package descriptions, and to optimize their own performance. As contracts are defined by teams in layer one, new SMTs are formed. One member of the SMT from layer one becomes the leader of the SMT in layer two, without leaving the original team. The same principle is applied for transition from layer two to three. Even in a very complex project, not more than three layers are necessary and usually two may be enough to manage the integral work of hundreds of people while attending the constraints of group size for effective teamwork. Teams on the outer layer are dismantled once they finish their contract. The network at times may shrink back to the core team for some WBS items.

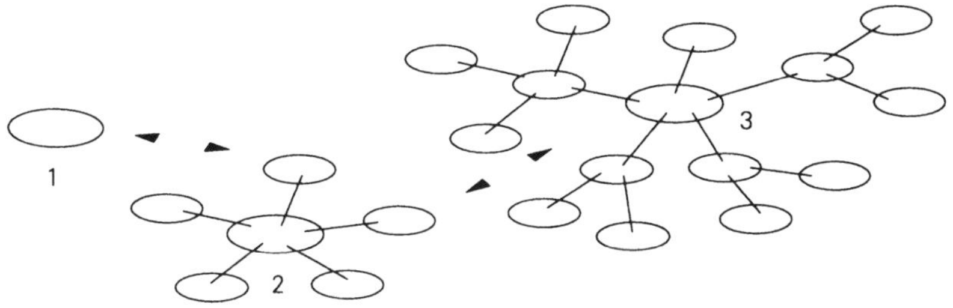

FIGURE 10.1 *The organic nature of the project network*

At Fokker Aircraft, although they operated as autonomous units, SMTs chose courses of action to solve their problems within an overall mission and set of constraints prescribed by the larger network. Co-locating the key resources and interdependent functions in SMTs minimized the need for co-ordination in the differentiated tasks. Since the teams were united by the PNS, each team also knew how its function related to other teams in the network. Furthermore, the joint staffing in the network safeguarded the effective management of the whole while dealing with its parts. Since every team leader is also a member of a team in the subsequent layer, the leaders are effective linchpins between the parts and the whole. The critical dimension of the whole is placed in an operating unit which is aware of the constraints imposed by the whole.

PNS was implemented in all ongoing product development projects at Fokker Aircraft. The product development sector was organized as an organic network of project network structures. In each project, PNS enabled integration of the work of hundreds of people while contributing to the expansion of the underlying knowledge base of the organization. The various teams in every project organized their activities autonomously, yet in an integrated way towards the desired direction and mission. They remained separate yet connected; each team was accountable for the specific results to be achieved along with a shared understanding of what ultimately was to be accomplished by the project.

The organic network for programme management, designed via the integration of separate PNS that belonged to the same programme, further encouraged transfer of learning between different projects. Following the implementation of PNS in all product development projects, the lessons learned from projects were widely shared, with the aim of improving the performance of every project undertaken.

Effectiveness of the proposed project design

It is here suggested that PNS can be an effective design for maintaining the delicate balance between short-term and long-term goals associated with new product development. Action research at Fokker Aircraft demonstrates that PNS provides an organizational context in which the project management principles of the integrative model proposed by Brown and Eisenhardt (1995) can be successfully implemented.

PNS offers a facilitating context for learning since there are no redundant connections among teams, and the nodes in the information transfer chain are significantly decreased through leaders of teams as linchpins to the subsequent layer in the network. Furthermore, due to the organic nature of PNS, when teams achieve their specific goals, they are absorbed back into the organization where individuals have the opportunity to transmit their learning to another group of individuals who were not involved in the specific project.

In order to be able to draw any conclusions with respect to the improvement attained by the change introduced by PNS, overall project performance in six new projects was compared to projects that were terminated before the transition to PNS, similar in size and scope, using the same basis for comparison (that is, the same performance indicators, based on actual performance versus planned budget and lead time). Comparing the average performance of the old projects versus new projects provided supporting evidence for the improvement in project performance with PNS. The average budget overrun had decreased from 17 to 6 per cent, while the time overrun had decreased from 11 to 1 per cent. The results further indicated the considerable scope for the organization to continuously learn and change.

These results, however, were not achieved solely by changing the structuring of the projects. As for the design of organizations, the structural changes needed to be reinforced by changes in the strategy, culture and systems within the product development sector. Furthermore, in a pilot project, work sessions referred to as 'team learning'[3] were conducted to facilitate learning at individual, group and project level. The pilot team started out as a group of individuals who succeeded in becoming a self-managing team. It took time to develop the knowledge of working as a whole, the trust and the synergy. Certainly, this was due to the deliberate attention and appropriate intervention to improve the learning process at all levels, provided within a facilitating context for learning.

Although all project teams exist for a given purpose, often the way they perform demonstrates that the related objectives are unclear, that most members do not share a clear understanding of what is expected. This was also the case in the pilot team. Even though there existed a project plan including objectives, there was no shared understanding. It took two sessions going through an extensive team exercise, whose output was a list of specific team objectives for which all members were to hold themselves accountable and feel they could contribute to meeting them. For team learning to occur, each member had to reach an understanding of his /her own reality and those of others. Team members were therefore asked to do a self-assessment exercise (Casse, 1994), to reach an understanding of their mental models and the way they communicate. This allowed them to understand the communication patterns of other team members and 'switch on' to their communication channel. Through skilful discussion or dialogue, as Isaacs (1993) defines, team members had the opportunity to expand their realities and invent new ways to see or define reality.

To measure the improvement attained through learning, before starting the sessions, a review questionnaire was used to assess present and desired performance. The initial results indicated an average of 60 per cent for the present performance, and 75 per cent for the desired performance. Assessment of the performance after team learning sessions, using the same questionnaire, indicated an average of 75 per cent for the present performance. The 15 per cent improvement in performance was reached after a total of ten (two hourly) sessions over the course of six months. Another interesting result was that the desired performance had reached 92 per cent, indicating that while the team members had reached their initial desired performance rate of 75 per cent, they no longer found this a desirable level of performance; their aspirations now were much higher. This indicated the potential for further investment in learning and considerable scope for improvement in project performance.

With the pilot project a sharp break from the past was clearly realized, new organizational capabilities were developed. The design principles embodied in the pilot project were then used as policy guidelines and decision rules for other development projects. To ensure its impact on the rest of the projects within the product development sector, some system-wide changes were initiated with respect to project learning.

Project audits as proposed by Wheelwright and Clark (1992) were coupled with the planned reviews at fixed milestones during the project as standard practice. For large projects, project audits were performed not only at project level but also at team level. These audits helped identify causes of failure and underlying sources. They were recorded as lessons learned to provide future projects with a set of recommendations to safeguard that the same mistakes were not repeated. While attempts were made to communicate these lessons learned through meetings across ongoing projects within the sector, a project history library was set up with all the documents containing these lessons. A special team was formed to complete the project history and accumulate all the reports available on former projects.

The implementation of PNS in the product development sector increased the job rotation and extended the formal and informal networks of individuals. This significantly contributed to learning from others' experiences through effective information transfer and knowledge sharing through face-to-face contact. The study suggests that replacing the more traditional, hierarchically structured project teams by organic networks of self-managing teams can lead to increased project performance. When provided with such a context, to optimize the potential learning within innovation project teams, appropriate leadership and project learning tools appear to be highly critical.

Conclusions

In an organization where every individual is a learner, the organizational context determines the extent to which organizational learning is effective for a given purpose. The underlying assumption is that individuals are willing to learn and capable of learning. This assumption is not far fetched, since every individual is born with the intrinsic motivation and potential to learn. In an innovative environment such as the case with NPD projects, this potential can be even greater. How much of this potential is used depends on the interaction of the individual with his or her environment.

The integrative model proposed by Brown and Eisenhardt (1995), derived from the findings of previous research on new product development, emphasizes the need to treat the project team as central, yet fails to link this further to the underlying organizational design. Understanding the implications of organizational design for learning and new product development can lead to a set of principles which can be used for a design that may be effective for learning and innovation. Effective management of innovation necessitates a design that enables effective learning, that is, learning which contributes to the expansion of the underlying knowledge base at individual, group, project and programme levels. At the group level, it implies transforming groups of individuals to self-managing teams and providing them with the guidance and support required. As can be observed from numerous examples provided in the literature, this is no easy task; not all working groups can become self-managing teams. Nevertheless, it is a challenge that can be overcome given the time and necessary investment. Moving to the level of projects or programmes implies further investment.

The project network structure is an organic network through which the desired interrelationships between the operating units can be defined. When self-managing teams are united through organic networks which lead to the desired interaction among teams, people in separate clusters can also share information. The organic nature implies that the constitution of the teams and networks frequently changes throughout the organization, extending individuals' informal networks of communication. As people rotate among different teams, projects or functional parts of the organization, they continually enhance the organization's knowledge base. The ability of the organization continually to improve its processes and systems with respect to innovation is directly linked to its ability to enhance its underlying knowledge base. As new innovation projects are undertaken, and new networks arise, the organization can profit from the previous experiences and lessons learned, and thus have a greater probability of success in NPD projects in the long term.

All these conclusions are derived from a fragmented part of a single organization, a natural constraint which arises when using action research methodology. Action research is preoccupied with the settings in which research is done. Participants at the research site play an important role in reaching solutions, which cannot be claimed to be universal. As Morgan

(1993) explains, this can be perceived as the process of 'seeking to generalize insights about the pattern of one situation that may have relevance for understanding a similar pattern elsewhere'. Guba and Lincoln (1989) argue that 'it is precisely because of our preoccupation with finding universal solutions that we fail to see how to devise solutions with local meaning and utility'.

But I have also tried to integrate the results with previous findings from other fields, to develop conceptual models that address different levels of integration, and to implement them in a real organizational setting. By fusing theory and practice, this study offers insights into multiple research avenues. The alternative structural arrangement for projects with teams within teams, which allows large-scale integration while keeping individual team size at optimum, is a major contribution from this research study. The results suggest that a project organization constituted through project network structures has a positive influence on project success. Potential limitations of this model include the fact that the findings are derived from a single organization and rely on a sample of product development teams. Future validation of this model would benefit from using different types of projects in multiple organizations. The focus on product development teams may also be perceived as a strength of this study rather than a limitation, since they represent one of the most demanding types of teams (Nonaka and Takeuchi, 1995). Further research can also contribute to testing the applicability of the model for programme management which integrates a large number of small projects.

Notes

1 The project management principles will not be discussed here. For an overview of the integral approach to project management, see Ayas (1996).

2 See Wheelwright and Clark's (1992) typology of organizing project teams.

3 For an overview of the sessions, questionnaires and intervention techniques, see Ayas (1997).

References

Allen, T.J. (1971) Communications, technology transfer and the role of technical gatekeeper. *R&D Management*, 1: 14–21.

Ashby, W. (1956) *An Introduction to Cybernetics*. New York: Wiley.

Ayas, K. (1996) Professional project management: a shift towards learning and a knowledge creating structure. *International Journal of Project Management*, 14 (3): 131–6.

Ayas, K. (1997) *Design for Learning for Innovation*. Delft: Eburon.

Brown, S.L. and Eisenhardt K.M. (1995) Product development: past research, present findings, and future directions. *Academy of Management Review*, 20 (2): 343–78.

Burns, T. and Stalker, G. (1961) *The Management of Innovation*. London: Tavistock.
Burt, R.S. (1992) *Structural Holes*. Cambridge, MA: Harvard University Press.
Casse, P. (1994) Revisiting communication: a 'new way' to manage it. *European Management Journal*, 12 (3): 253–8.
Clark, K.B. and Fujimoto, T. (1991) *Product Development Performance*. Boston, MA: Harvard Business School Press.
Daft, R.L. and Weick, K.E. (1984) Towards a model of organizations as interpretation systems. *Academy of Management Review*, 9: 284–95.
Dougherty, D. (1990) Understanding new markets for new products. *Strategic Management Journal*, 11: 59–78.
Duncan, R.B. and Weiss, A. (1979) Organizational learning: implications for organizational design. In: B.M. Staw (ed.), *Research in Organizational Behavior*. Greenwich, CT: JAI Press. pp. 75–123.
Easterby-Smith, M. (1997) Disciplines of organizational learning: contributions and critiques. *Human Relations*, 50 (9), 1085–113.
Fiol, C.M. (1994) Consensus, diversity, and learning in organizations. *Organization Science*, 5 (3): 403–20.
Galbraith, J. (1973) *Designing Complex Organisations*. Reading, MA: Addison-Wesley.
Galbraith, J.R. (1994) *Competing with Flexible Lateral Organisations*. Reading, MA: Addison-Wesley.
Globerson, S. (1994) Impact of various work-breakdown structures on project conceptualization. *International Journal of Project Management*, 12 (3): 165–71.
Guba, E.G. and Lincoln, Y.S. (1989) *Fourth Generation Evaluation*. Newbury Park, CA: Sage.
Huber, G.P. (1991) Organizational learning: the contributing process and the literatures. *Organization Science*, 2 (1): 88–115.
Imai, K., Nonaka, I. and Takeuchi, H. (1985) Managing the new product development process: how Japanese companies learn and unlearn. In: K. Clark, R. Hayes and C. Lorenz (eds), *The Uneasy Alliance*. Boston, MA: Harvard Business School Press.
Isaacs, W.N. (1993) Taking flight: dialogue, collective thinking and organizational learning. *Organizational Dynamics*, 22 (2): 24–39.
Katz, D. and Kahn, R. (1966) *The Social Psychology of Organizations*. New York: Wiley.
Katzenbach, J.R. and Smith, D.K. (1993) *The Wisdom of Teams: Creating the High-Performance Organisation*. Boston, MA: Harvard Business School Press.
Lawrence, P.R. and Lorsch, J.W. (1967) *Organization and Environment*. Cambridge, MA: Harvard University Press.
Leonard-Barton, D. (1992) The factory as a learning laboratory. *Sloan Management Review*, Fall, pp. 23–38.
Levitt, B. and March, J.G. (1988) Organizational learning. *Annual Review of Sociology*, Volume 14. Greenwich, CT: JAI Press.
March, J.G. and Olsen, J.P. (1976) *Ambiguity and Choice in Organizations*. Oslo: Universitetsforlaget.
March, J. and Simon, H. (1958) *Organizations*. New York: Wiley.
Mintzberg, H. (1979) *The Structuring of Organizations*. Englewood Cliffs, NJ: Prentice-Hall.
Morgan, G. (1993) *Imaginization*. Newbury Park, CA: Sage.
Myers, S. and Marquis, D.G. (1969) *Successful Industrial Innovations*. Washington, DC: National Science Foundation (NSF 69-17).
Nonaka, I. and Takeuchi, H. (1995) *The Knowledge-Creating Company: How Japanese Companies Create the Dynamics of Innovation*. Oxford: Oxford University Press.

Quinn, J.B. (1985) Managing innovation: controlled chaos. *Harvard Business Review*, 63 (3): 73–84.
Rothwell, R. (1972) Factors for success in industrial innovations from project SAPPHO-A comparative study of success and failure in industrial evolution. Brighton, UK: SPRU.
Salancik, G.R. and Pfeffer, J. (1978) A social information processing approach to job attitudes and task design. *Administrative Science Quarterly*, 23: 224–53.
Souder, W.E. (1987) *Managing New Product Innovations*. Lexington, MA: Lexington Books.
Takeuchi, H. and Nonaka, I. (1986) The new product development game. *Harvard Business Review*, 64 (1): 137–46.
Thamhain, H.J. and Wilemon, D.L. (1987) Building high performing engineering project teams. *IEEE Transactions in Engineering Management*, EM-34: 130–7.
Thompson, J. (1961/1967) *Organisation in Action*. New York: McGraw-Hill.
Tushman, M.L. and Nadler, D.A. (1978) Information processing as an integrating concept in organizational design. *Academy of Management Review*, 3: 613–24.
Tushman, M.L. and Scanlan, T.J. (1981) Boundary-spanning individuals: their role in information transfer and their antecedents. *Academy of Management Journal*, 24: 289–305.
Van de Ven, A.H., Angle, H.A. and Poole, M.S. (1989) *Research on the Management of Innovation: the Minnesota Studies*. New York: Ballinger/Harper and Row.
Wheelwright, S.C. and Clark, K.B. (1992) *Revolutionizing New Product Development*. New York: Free Press.
Zirger, B.J. and Maidique, M.A. (1990) A model of new product development: an empirical test. *Management Science*, 36 (7): 867–83.

11 Organizational Learning and Organizational Forgetting: Lessons from a High Technology Company

Frank Blackler, Norman Crump and Seonaidh McDonald

This chapter analyses the efforts of a project team in a high technology organization that set out to identify past mistakes in product design and manufacture in order to reform future practices. At the time when the project team was set up, the company was endeavouring to adjust to a range of changes in its methods of design and manufacture and its task was given high priority. Despite the urgency of the project, however, with the benefit of hindsight those involved were to conclude that organizational learning had not taken place in the way, and on the scale, that had been anticipated. The authors were asked to examine why. In the account that follows we trace the way the project team approached its task, analyse the episode as a case of organizational forgetting and explore a basic dilemma in the organization of design engineering that had developed in the company. We suggest that collective learning can be analysed in terms of the cultural and organizational infrastructure that a community uses, and in terms of the understandings of their activities that members enact. Collective forgetting occurs through silence and solitude and by disassociation and disorientation. Drawing from activity theory we suggest that a central aspect of organizational learning depends upon the ways in which communities deal with tensions and dilemmas.

Background

The company we have been studying is a small, but not insignificant player in the design and production of high-technology electro-optics products. Its main market is defence-related products. The company is based on three sites, each of which had previously been independent companies in their own right. The episode we describe took place at the longest established of the sites, here referred to as East Site.

The reputation of East Site as an innovator has been unquestioned over an extended period and until the late 1980s it had been trading profitably.

However the sudden unfreezing of East–West relations saw the company's markets contract and slump and by the early 1990s its losses were substantial. Government defence contracting had also been reorganized in the UK around this time, from a 'cost-plus' system that paid for development and production costs plus a flat 10 per cent, to a system of fixed-price contracting. Top management at East Site recognized that the quality of its products notwithstanding, the company was over-manned, it was using old-fashioned manufacturing methods and (in common with other UK organizations that had grown in the cost-plus era) it had a very bad record for meeting orders on time.

A sharp drive for cost reduction and improved delivery times was initiated and a long-term change programme was begun to create a more responsive organization. Alerted to the ways in which new approaches to manufacturing were changing the industry, management became convinced that only by working towards computer integrated manufacturing (CIM) could they bring about the productivity gains that were necessary to ensure the company's survival. The particular strategy that they developed was built upon the ideas of the Harvard academic Jaikumar, who argued that developments in manufacturing industry had moved through various stages, each of which depended on what had been achieved before. This was translated into a four phase CIM change strategy planned at East Site that envisaged: (i) a period of improved co-ordination, to be followed by (ii) a period of improved process control, then (iii) the widespread development of automation and finally (iv) the goal of systems integration. Key slogans associated with early phases of this change programme included the appeal for designers to ensure that their work was 'Right First Time' and the exhortation to all staff to make the company 'Better, Faster, and Cheaper' than its competitors.

From Jaikumar's perspective (see Jaikumar and Bohn's influential 1992 article), the aim was to move manufacturing organizations away from a static approach to the organization of manufacturing, where well-developed technological solutions are applied to organizational problems, to a system which recognizes contingencies, solves problems and learns. East Site's planned movement through phases (i) to (iv) above can be thought of as a journey away from the cost-plus era and a system based on the skills of craftworking, initially to one that would be based on tight methods of control, then to one based on advanced methods of process control such as MRPII, then to a work system heavily dependent on automation, and finally to a system built upon notions of continual improvement and learning (Blackler et al., 1999).

An integrated personnel strategy was envisaged to support these plans. A clear implication from the start was that the new business would need fewer but better trained employees and, largely through voluntary methods, in the first half of the 1990s the company reduced its payroll from approximately 3,000 to 1,000 employees. In common with practices that were widespread in manufacturing industry at this time, many specialist functions that were not part of the core of the business were outsourced. Team working was also adopted and management levels were flattened. These changes were supported by a move into a new, purpose-built and ultra-modern factory that, very clearly, symbolized the changes that the management of East Site were endeavouring to introduce.

In a short period of time early indications were that the outcomes of these changes were impressive. Stock levels and work in progress were reduced to less than a third of what they had been, lead times were reduced to less than a half and in place of a situation where only 10 per cent of orders had been delivered on schedule in the late 1980s, by the mid 1990s no less than 97 per cent were being delivered on time. None the less, at the time of our involvement with the company management had recognized that most of this efficiency was dependent on improvements in manufacturing alone associated with the early phases of Jaikumar's developmental model. Design practices were proving difficult to integrate to the approach. Top managers felt that the company had got stuck somewhere around phase (ii) of the overall change programme and that phases (iii) and (iv) were probably some three to five years away.

The 'Right First Time' Delta team and the reform of engineering design

East Site typically operates a small number of large-scale, long-term projects. In the 'cost-plus' contracting era, before the change programme sketched out above, revenue receipts had been dominated by one product. This product, referred to here as the Mark I, had been specially developed for one important customer with the need for large-scale production in mind. In the event, however, the process of turning the initial engineering design into a manufacturable product had proved extremely difficult. It had required many redesigns and the full-time attention of several engineers over an extended period to develop a product that could both be made in numbers and that would be thoroughly reliable in use.

Ultimately, however, the Mark I proved to be a highly valued product and, a number of years later the customer concerned came back to East Site to negotiate a second generation version, Mark II. Mark II was similar in functionality to Mark I, but was to have improved performance and to feature a modular design. In view of the difficulties of achieving hand-over from design to manufacture for the Mark I, and in the changing context of the business sketched out above, senior management at East Site were determined to learn from past mistakes. In particular, with the passing of 'cost-plus' contracting arrangements management was determined to keep the costs and timescale of the development of Mark II under tight control.

In order to facilitate learning, managers at East Site adopted, from Jaikumar, the idea of the 'Delta team'. We understand that Jaikumar defined a Delta team as a team of between 15 and 20 people who would be associated with a particular product development team. (Given the downsizing that was in progress around this time, resourcing the Delta teams at this level had not been considered a problem by the original architects of the approach.) Their remit would be to act as a vehicle for learning and innovation. Not only would members of the Delta team import news of new tools, procedures, approaches and materials to the product development team, but they would have a key support role in the implementation of novel endeavours, reviewing new practices and supporting their development and dissemination throughout the company.

Accordingly, the first Delta team was convened to look retrospectively at the Mark I experience initially to inform the Mark II development processes and, ultimately, to inform design and manufacturing processes within the company as a whole.

A group of senior managers were formed into a Steering Group to manage this team. In the context of the perceived needs of phase (ii) of the change programme sketched out above (that is, improved control of key processes), the team was christened the 'Right First Time' Delta team. The Steering Group informed the newly appointed team leader that they did not have the resources to allocate the 15–20 members that had originally been envisaged, but that they still wished to launch a project to look at how they could make Right First Time a reality at East Site. The team leader was asked to produce a list of those he would like within the team. He originally asked for seven to ten experienced individuals. Eventually, we were told, he was allocated three full-time engineers, all of them highly respected, and drawn from a range of design disciplines.

The Delta team was aware that ways of working on past projects in the company, even those that had proved to be very successful in their day, would be too expensive in the post cost-plus environment. The first task that the Delta team undertook therefore, was to unearth what they described as 'the cost of failure'. As its title suggests, under a regime of 'cost-plus' contracts, rework or redesign did not affect the profitability of a project. In fact, given that the company would make 10 per cent of product cost as profit, then problems which extended the timescale or costs of a project would simply make the company *more* profitable. In fact, the extent of the costs of rework and redesign had never been calculated in the company before. Analysis of the design changes and associated costs for Mark I was to show the 'cost of failure' was some 15 per cent of the (multi-million pound) project budget.

The Delta team therefore decided that an important focus for them would be to reduce the average cost per design change, and the number of changes that were made. In the spirit of Right First Time most of their efforts were concentrated on the latter. To do this they undertook a closer analysis of all the design changes that had been requested over the lifetime of Mark I. They categorized the causes of each of the changes and quickly found that a high proportion of the design changes that had been requested in every engineering discipline were due to minor human errors. Examples

TABLE 11.1 *Primary causes of design changes, by discipline*

Optical	Mechanical	Electrical
Incorrect dimensions	Incorrect dimensions	Incorrect dimensions
Incorrect tolerances	Incorrect tolerances	Missing build information
Missing build information	Missing build information	Incorrect part used
New drawing required	Missing dimension	Missing dimension
Missing dimension	Manufacturing improvement	Change of component
Manufacturing improvement	Incorrect part used	Design rule/application
Change of component	Design rule/application	
Design rule/application		
Accounted for 83% of optical design changes	Accounted for 76% of mechanical design changes	Accounted for 66% of electrical design changes

of these errors that we were given included: 10 mm screws specified for 8 mm holes; incorrect conversions from imperial to metric; specification of a plate too small to engrave the unit code on to. Occurrences of this sort of error are summarized in Table 11.1. Together, we were told, these errors accounted for 68 per cent of all changes to the design once it has been handed over to manufacture.

Once this work was completed, presentations were made to the Steering Group and recommendations made about ways to reduce these 'mundane' errors. The learning of the Delta team was to be translated into organizational learning through procedural and work technology changes. Some of the errors were to be tackled through the design of a checklist which would be signed off by the designer. Others were felt to be best approached through building standards and procedures into the Computer Aided Design (CAD) technology that was being developed by some of the engineering disciplines. A system of design reviews, held at various points in the design process and attended by senior colleagues from various disciplines, was also re-emphasized as an important safeguard against problematic designs.

The research

Our study was initiated after discussions with senior managers who felt that the Right First Time Delta team episode had not been as successful as had been anticipated. As a member of the team's Steering Group explained:

> It was seen within the company that engineers spend a great deal of time re-working and re-learning. The Delta team was to look back over the past projects. They did some very good work, identified key reasons for failure and they passed that on to the present product team, hoping they would, via 'effective engineering'

> There might have been a circular with a summary of the problems at some point, but we either already knew about them or we'd already solved them for our project or helped Mark II solve them in the first place.

> I think that the Right First Time team were concerned with a different kind of project than ours. We are more concerned with high level design. Perhaps our sub-contractors would have found the lessons useful.

A *story of forgetting*

It is, of course, normal for any event in a company to be interpreted differently by groups who will have different backgrounds, approaches and priorities. Indeed, in designing our interview programme we had deliberately sought a variety of viewpoints on this issue. It is also natural for episodes which have taken place a couple of years in the past to be recalled with varying degrees of accuracy. Following the complexity of changes in the company that had taken place in the previous years, some clouding of the memory of events surrounding the Delta team episode seemed inevitable.

None the less, in the early stages of the study we experienced unusual difficulty in assembling a chronology of events surrounding relevant episodes. For example, as noted above, when we first began to interview people who had been in the Delta team we were told that the team consisted of three members plus the leader. In the second week of the research, however, in an old set of minutes that we had located, we found reference to a *fifth* team member. When we asked about this person, we were told that he had indeed been part of the team but had subsequently left the company. His involvement in the project had apparently been edited out of peoples' memories, apparently because he was 'no longer with us'!

To deal with issues of this kind we endeavoured to go back to documentary evidence. A number of people from all levels of the organization told us that they had documents relating to this story and promised to let us have copies. However, despite sometimes numerous requests on our part and promises on theirs, very few documents were actually produced.

In the face of this frustrating turn of events we sought the 'official' story. We decided to see whether we could locate minutes for the meetings held by the CIM Steering Group which had given the Right First Time team its goal and context. Some, more recent, minutes of this important group were discovered by the secretary of one of the Steering Group members, and after heroic efforts by a number of people, a few more were discovered on the computer discs of a secretary who had left the company some years before. As no one could agree as to which engineer might have been responsible for the minutes in the intervening period, we abandoned our search for an easy check on the stories. Our efforts to trace an official statement of the objectives and time scales set for the Delta team proved just as elusive. Indeed, the only hard data that we did eventually manage to access were working notes and a large cache of presentational material that the team leader brought from home to show us.

In response to our comments about such difficulties, some people explained that the lack of documentation might be attributed to the company's 'clear desk policy' which had been introduced at the time of the opening of the new factory. The site is an impressive open-plan building. When people leave their desks at the end of the day, they must leave their desk tops clear. All that can remain is their PC, telephone and a set of in/out trays which must be no more than two high and only full to the top of the trays.

This drive for tidy working had also, we were to learn, been extended to the storage of documents. Every individual was allowed only two filing cabinet drawers for storage. The idea behind this was that people should only keep files and papers at their workplace that they were currently working on. Everything else was either thrown out or stored in the company data vaults.

It was explained to us that documents were held in storage boxes both on and off site. All of the boxes had their contents recorded on an inventory and could be recalled by a code, usually relating to a project. We duly went to the data vault and asked how we might locate information relating to one of the CIM initiatives. The operator explained that we would need to know the code of the box that we were looking for. We asked how we might find out this code and he told us that we would need to ask the person who had stored the box. His database only contained the box codes. There was no way to search by the recorded box contents because only the box owners, or their immediate predecessors or colleagues ever recalled the boxes, and they knew what was in them. We managed, however, to get a listing of all the code groups, and were surprised to learn that there was no code for the CIM change programme. Using a scatter gun approach, we asked for printouts of all the contents of boxes stored under likely codes and ordered up any boxes which seemed to hold information of the right type or period. Although we spent a considerable amount of time going through these data, ultimately we found very little.

As a result of episodes such as this, one member of our team coined the term 'organizational dementia' to describe the loss of memory of key events associated with an episode that, only a couple of years before, had been regarded as a major development for the company.

Were people's memories about technological breakthroughs likely to be as unreliable as their recollection of events associated with the story of the Right First Time Delta team, we wondered? We asked one of the current project leaders how he might access technical learning in the company. He told us about one of his more recent problems:

> The company has been kidding itself that it learns from the past, but it doesn't. A group of my engineers who worked on an early version of a sensor product 5

years ago and realized that a major problem was being caused by the wrong kind of signal, forgot this lesson. When they were working on the current version of the product, this same simple mistake took the same people ages to solve. Part of the problem is that the company has no system for finding out what other work has been done in any given area. They keep all the paper work in terms of reports and log books, but there is no way to search or access these. The memories of others is the only possible navigation system for this data and it's all a bit random. At the moment people perceive it to be easier and cheaper to reinvent the wheel than go and try to find out what others have done. Word of mouth and coffee breaks are the only form of dissemination. In the old site there was some spare time, but now the time pressure is so great that even coffee break learning is threatened.

Similarly, commenting on the problem-solving that goes on during manufacture, one production manager told us that 'due to changes from design to manufacture often the product that went out through the door did not bear much resemblance to the drawing'. He spoke of the difficulties of persuading manufacturing engineers to record the changes that they make to get units working, often under enormous pressure from the customer to begin delivery, and told us 'undoubtedly many of the problems that my people are trying to solve just now have been solved before, and will be again'.

Questioning the RFT *goal*

The third theme evident in our data was a debate about the appropriateness of Right First Time (RFT) as a goal for design engineering. As we have indicated above, RFT as an approach to design resonated with the Jaikumar-inspired change programme that the company had embarked upon. RFT has its roots in the techniques of Concurrent Engineering. This involves the formation of multidisciplinary engineering teams to support the simultaneous processing of a product by all the different disciplines involved in place of the conventional sequential process as tasks are handed from marketeer to designers to manufacturer. The objective of the approach is to smooth out problems and to speed up the time it takes for a project to pass through the company. For example, a product which has had questions of manufacturability addressed at the concept stage should move from design to manufacture with little problem. Similarly, a product developed in constant consultation with the company's representative of the customer needs, should require little configuring after trials. Concurrent engineering and the goal of RFT should make the product cheaper on at least two counts: first because it can be produced more quickly therefore incurring less engineering time, and second because design changes can be made at the concept stage, before expensive hardware or physical testing become necessary.

Objections to this general approach first came to our attention in an interview with an experienced (and, at the time when we interviewed him) exasperated manufacturing manager who had been closely involved in dealing with problems associated with the manufacture of the Mark II. He strongly felt that Right First Time was an inappropriate goal for designers; pursuit of this goal, he felt, revealed a fundamental misunderstanding of the nature of their task. This manager characterized the design process as a series of episodes of 'trial and error' where designs were built, tested and modified in an iterative way until a working product is reached. He represented this process to us using the diagram presented as Figure 11.1(a). To strive for Right First Time is, he explained, to seek to straighten out these iterative loops, as in Figure 11.1(b). Or even to straighten out the loops *and* reduce the timescale, as in Figure 11.1(c).

In this manager's experience, it is not possible to achieve a design process with no setbacks, rethinks, new ideas or mistakes. Rather, he maintained, through these processes designers gain insights into the products they are working on, learn and develop innovative ideas. He felt that it was an error of judgement to try to force mistakes out of the design process because without them there would be no learning. Concurrent Engineering in design might be relevant for mass production, he felt, but without the licence to experiment, designers would be forced to adopt low-risk, well-known design choices which would at best mean only incremental advances in the company's technological expertise. At worst this could undermine the competitiveness of the company.

He proposed instead a policy of Right On Time (ROT), which he represented as shown in Figure 11.1(d). Here the mistakes are permitted, well-resourced and analysed by a multidisciplinary team to produce creative but timely solutions.

When we questioned other engineers about the Right First Time philosophy compared with Right On Time, we found that there was much agreement with these ideas.

> Right First Time is not the main problem, you can always get RFT (because the first unit is always hand built), it's getting 2, 3, and 4 right, that's the problem.

> Right First Time is a buzzword. It means that there is a lot of pressure (on the Designers) to get the design out on time, but not to get it to work. They just give me any old thing because they know they will have plenty of time to put it right once the pressure is off.

> Some people think that Right First Time means that once something has been designed, it is practically ready to sell, but this is naive because you can never anticipate and eliminate problems altogether. Manufacturing expect to be handed a disk which they can just plug in and it will all work. Engineers know that there will always be problems. That is the essence of what we do. We deal with problems.

> I don't believe that you can ever have Right First Time when you're working with lasers. You should be aiming to get your loop times down instead. It's not

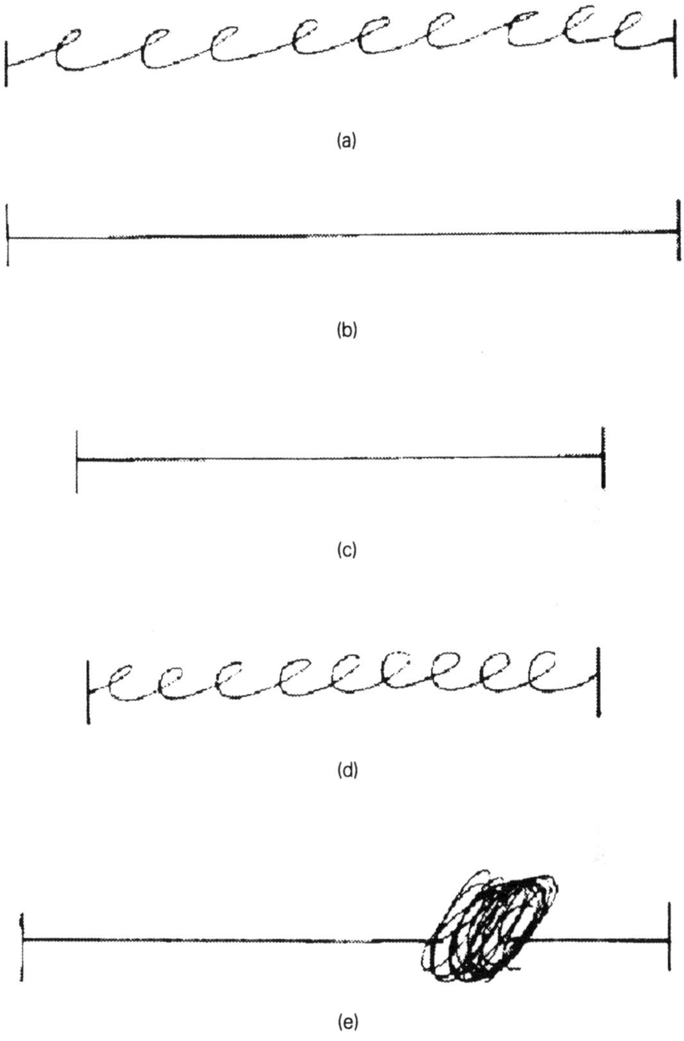

FIGURE 11.1

> like when car designers are making a new car. There is probably no axle design left unthought of, untested, unrecorded and the designers have all that experience and certainty at their fingertips. They are working with huge data pools, the only black art left in car manufacture is the swirl of petrol in the engine. Everything we do here is working with the unknown. When we start out we sometimes don't even know what we don't know.

However, since there was much pressure in the company to adopt these new ways of working, engineers told us that what was actually happening was that projects were carried out in accordance with the principles of Concurrent Engineering, but were not able to pass the reality test imposed by the handover of the designs to manufacture. One manufacturing engineer told us of a product that had been designed using Concurrent Engineering principles to ensure that a number of product modules would integrate well.

> When the project reached manufacture it went together perfectly . . . it was heralded as the best design ever, but when it was put together it did not work. It would have been better to have given us [manufacture] a box of bits that did work, and let us put them together and integrate it as we went along.

We asked him to represent what happened, and he drew the diagram reproduced in Figure 11.1(e).

He went on to question the relevance of Concurrent Engineering for high technology applications where very low numbers would ever be made.

> Sure, we knocked two hours off the manufacture of every unit, which sounds impressive. But we were only making five.

In summary, as our interviewees explained, the goal of RFT for design engineering was challenged by many of the staff we spoke to. Implied in the notion of RFT is the idea of 'zero defects': there should be no design prototypes, these need not be planned for. According to the RFT approach, the first design a design team produces *has* to be right, there is no room for mistakes. Under the ROT approach, on the other hand, the emphasis is on 'Rapid Prototyping' and on a process of iterative development through tests and modifications. Here the emphasis is not on eliminating mistakes altogether and getting the first design right, but on the production of an effective design within schedule.

Introducing the analysis

As we have already indicated, the pressure to reduce lead times, development costs and to reorganize manufacturing at East Site needs to be understood in the broader context of scientific, technological, sales, marketing and business changes that have overtaken the company in recent years. The solution of problems at the leading edge of areas such as optics, lasers and electronics are East Site's stock in trade (the company employs more holders of PhDs than any other company in its region of the UK). The development of computer aided design (CAD) systems, new approaches to simulation, the use of new materials, and importantly, the need to develop integrated systems are amongst the changes that have placed considerable emphasis on the need for new approaches to organizing. New patterns of competition in the sector the company operates within (including a recent wave of mergers that have led to the emergence of a few, very large companies), have added yet another dimension to the need for organizational learning in this company.

In the following section we offer an interpretation of how the Delta team episode can best be interpreted from an organizational learning perspective and consider what this interpretation means both for East Site and for other companies that compete through knowledge and learning. We do not think that the Delta team episode can adequately be understood in terms of the failure of individuals to follow new procedures or to remember events accurately, nor in terms of any propensity to resist changes. As we discuss below, the events of this case illustrate the difficulties of managing change in complex activity systems, the importance of an accessible infrastructure to support organizational remembering, and the potential significance of dilemma and contradiction for collective development.

Activity theory, organizational learning and organizational forgetting

Despite the current popularity of such terms as 'organizational memory' and 'organizational learning', they are poorly understood and are often inadequately defined. The idea that organizations can learn stretches conventional assumptions about learning to the limit, based as they usually are on the idea of individual learning. Individualistic approaches to learning, however, are of restricted value when the need is for a company like East Site to achieve rapid and creative organization-wide responses to changing circumstances. What is needed is an approach that explores the nature of collective, or cultural, development.

Engestrom's presentation of activity theory (Engestrom, 1987, 1991, 1993) offers an analysis of the heterogeneous nature of collective endeavour that has provided the basis of our approach to organizational learning (Blackler, 1993, 1995; Blackler et al., 1999). Basic to activity theory is an account of both *how* and *what* individuals learn.

How communities learn or forget: interaction and engagement, or silence and solitude

Activity theory suggests that knowledge should not be understood as a commodity that individuals or organizations have or may acquire. Rather, activity theory examines *knowing* as an active achievement. The term 'knowing' as we use it here is intended to avoid the imagery which is so often associated with the term 'knowledge' (often assumed to refer to a timeless, uncontroversial body of fact) and 'learning' (which can be taken to refer merely to the passive absorption of such knowledge). By using the term 'knowing' we analyse knowledge as a social construction. Activity theory explores how people do their knowing. In contrast to conventional approaches that feature personal knowledge and skill, and which treat the achievements of the individual as if they can be divorced from culture, activity theory emphasizes the culturally available resources through which knowing and doing are achieved.

The culturally available resources through which people do their knowing can be described as the *infrastructure of knowing*. It is commonly assumed, for example, that as children learn to speak they articulate thoughts that they have previously formulated; in common with contemporary theories of language, however, activity theory points out that thought is only possible because of language and that, in an important sense, language *is* thought. Similarly, activity theory points to the intimate relationship that tools and technologies have to both physical and mental acts; to the way the division of labour and the division of knowledge within a community is intimately related to the character of practices within it; and to the way in which the nature of communities of activity is defined by their distinctive rules and norms. The infrastructure of knowing can be said therefore to include the concepts, tools and technologies shared by the members of a community of activity and also its division of labour, social structure and social rules. In this connection it is interesting to note that by emphasizing not only the cognitive and technological aspects of expertise but also its social aspects, activity theory goes beyond the question 'how do people do their knowing?' It draws attention also to two further questions that are central to the study of organizational learning: 'Who do people do their knowing with?' and 'Under what circumstances can people learn to collaborate with people who have been schooled in different communities of knowing?'.

In this way activity theory reveals the process of collective knowing to be a network of processes and relationships. Distinctions between internal cognitive processes and the external infrastructure of knowledge should not be drawn too sharply. Putting this another way, the vitality of how a community knows depends upon the vigour of the interactions that take place between the cognitive processes of individual members and the infrastructure of knowing that they use. Lively interactions of this kind are necessary for learning. Organizational forgetting occurs when a community's collective infrastructure for learning disintegrates or falls into disuse, a process that Engestrom (1991) has aptly described as *forgetting by silence or solitude*.

What communities learn or forget: continuity and contextualization or disorientation and disassociation

Activity theory also emphasizes that learning is not a passive process of absorption and internalization and that the process of becoming an expert does not follow a predestined path. There is more than one way of being an expert. Engestrom's (1993) analysis of medical doctors illustrates the point. Doctors can enact: a somatic orientation towards health care and focus on the administration of medicines; a psychosomatic orientation and explore stress-related issues; an economic orientation that features the exchange value of medical practice; a community health orientation which emphasizes the importance of general education and social interventions; or they can regard themselves as a resource to help patients manage their own illnesses. The particular image that any particular doctor enacts depends on the (characteristically implicit) interpretation that she has of the appropriate role for medical activity in the contexts where she works.

In contrast to approaches that focus only on the acquisition of new skills, therefore, activity theory emphasizes also the significance of learning about how particular skills should be exercised, that is, it emphasizes the importance of learning at the level of general activity as well as at the level of individual actions. Learning at this level is learning about the overall coherency of what is done, what aspects of a role to feature, and how to enact these priorities.

We have already suggested that the distinction between cognitive processes and the externally provided infrastructure of knowing should not be drawn too sharply, for the vitality of how a community does its knowing depends upon the interactions between community members and the collective infrastructure of knowing that they share. By the same token we suggest that the distinction between particular deeds and the general activities that they constitute can be overdrawn. As people engage in new actions they develop in their understandings of their roles, and the concepts of activity that they enact leads them to conduct particular actions in particular ways. The vitality of what a community knows depends on the extent to which members appreciate how their specific deeds contribute to the collective activity, and vice versa.

Systems of activity change through time as circumstances alter and as new forms of discourse, technologies, procedures, norms and social structures develop. In times of rapid change it is possible for communities to lose touch with their intellectual and practical heritage. Engestrom (1991) refers to this as forgetting through disconnectedness. In the context of contemporary economies a loss of continuity with the past may, however, be less significant (and, perhaps, less common) than a loss of continuity with the future. Actions may become detached from their consequences. As systems of activity become more complex and interrelated they become more difficult to comprehend, disputes may develop about how communities should respond, and actions can become divorced from broader systems of activity. In such circumstances people can lose sight of the ways in which what they do relates to the changing nature of the enterprise of which they are a part. They may concentrate exclusively on the specifics of their contributions, or experience a sense of anomie. We describe this as *forgetting by disassociation or disorientation.*

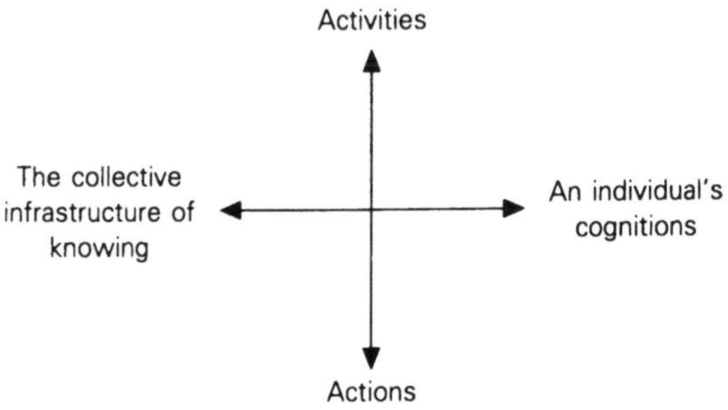

FIGURE 11.2 *Dimensions of collective knowing*

Summary: learning and forgetting in systems of activity

The points that have been introduced in this section are represented in Figure 11.2. First, the horizontal axis represents *how* knowing and doing is achieved. At one end of this continuum we feature the culturally provided infrastructure of knowing available to members of a community; at the other, the cognitive processes of individual members. Although these factors are often discussed as if they are independent from each other, as we have already suggested, in practice they are intimately related and we represent this by the arrows on the continuum. Second, the vertical axis represents *what* knowing and doing is achieved. At one end of this continuum we feature particular actions, at the other the activity of which they are a part and which renders them coherent. Again, although actions and activities can be discussed as if they are independent from each other in practice, they, too, are intimately related.

Figure 11.2 thus summarizes the general approach to organizational learning that we have described in this section. Collective knowing depends upon the intimacy of relationships along the two axes of the figure. Forgetting occurs when relationships cease or fragment through silence or solitude (along the horizontal axis) or through dissassociation or disorientation (along the vertical axis).

Analysing the Delta team episode

The framework summarized in Figure 11.2 can be used to analyse the Delta team story. As we noted earlier, people we spoke to readily acknowledged that the Delta team enquiry had a number of positive outcomes. For the lifetime of the group the Delta team acted as an internal consulting resource to the Mark II project. More generally, it alerted people to the waste of time, money and effort that was associated with mundane design errors, it produced checklists of things to do to avoid such mistakes, and it had an input to the development of CAD systems and to the conduct of design review meetings. In the terminology of Figure 11.2: (i) the Delta team introduced changes to the collective infrastructure of knowing at East Site initially by acting as an internal consulting resource to the Mark II team, later by the modifications it introduced to recommended procedures and work technologies; (ii) it had a general impact on people's understandings of the changing nature of design activity, most especially in the way it documented ways in which past practices were inappropriate in the new business context.

Organizational learning associated with the work of the Delta team undoubtedly took place, therefore. None the less, as was illustrated in our presentation of the case, the impact of the team was limited. Organizational forgetting was also a key feature of the Delta team episode.

The infrastructure of knowing and doing at East Site

Key elements of the infrastructure through which people achieve their knowing and doing are concepts and discourse, technologies and procedures, and norms and social structures. A review of each of these in turn features key weaknesses in the infrastructure of learning at East Site:

(a) Partly because of pressure of work (but, see below, not only because of this), the number of formal and informal forums for debate and information exchange between engineers was limited. In the cost-plus era young engineers were guided in their work by more experienced elders; no such system of 'mentoring' was in operation in the company at the time of our study.
(b) While the procedural changes introduced by the Delta team were of some significance they failed to address a key issue essential to reducing costs and lead times. Despite widespread acknowledgement in the company that an effective database of design solutions needed to be developed, at the time of our involvement with the company effective ways of doing this had yet to be developed.
(c) The Delta team did not address issues of norms and social structures amongst engineering groups at East Site at all. At the time of our study, competition across project groups was quite marked. The company was structured around semi-autonomous business winning groups that, to a large extent, operated independently from each other.

Weaknesses in the collective infrastructure for knowing at East Site were compounded by the way staff made only limited use of the facilities that were available to support collective knowing. Examples include: (a) the cost-conscious orientation of top management appeared not to encourage general meetings between the engineers to discuss matters of common interest; when such meetings were held we were told they were not always well attended. More experienced and highly trained engineers did not appear to make themselves especially accessible to their colleagues. (b) Formal documentation and information systems did not compensate for restricted interpersonal contact. As was vividly illustrated by the problems we had in reconstructing the history of the Delta team, the limited formal documentation available at East Site meant that individual memories could not easily be refreshed by reference to external aids. (c) Finally, the open plan environment did not appear to support a fluid network of individual and group information exchange; in the context of heavy workloads and an environment of internal competition staff who spent time in what might be misconstrued as idle chatter would have to do this in full view of others.

In summary, we concluded that collective forgetting through silence and solitude was occurring at East Site.

Changing patterns of action and activity

As we described at the beginning of this chapter, the Delta team undertook its work in the context of a long-term change programme that envisaged a stepwise progression away from a system of manufacturing based on craftworking, through stages of co-ordination, control, automation and, ultimately, of integration and learning. Although there was widespread agreement amongst the engineers that we spoke to that reform of the practices of the cost-plus era was essential, as we detailed in the case report above, there was much disquiet amongst the engineers at the implications of 'Right First Time' for design.

Although Jaikumar's image of organizational learning in advanced manufacturing organizations emphasizes flexibility as the final goal, his analysis is explicit in the suggestion that tight co-ordination and control of manufacturing systems has first to be achieved. Indeed, the image of computer integrated manufacture (CIM) that so inspired the management of East Site has its roots within a 'mechanistic image' of organization (Morgan, 1986); as Moldaschl and Weber (1998) demonstrate, its development can be traced directly to the scientific management perspective of F.W. Taylor.

Events at East Site around the time of the Delta team are fully consistent with efforts to introduce a neo-Tayloristic system. In the jargon of the day, management was turning the company into a 'lean' organization. Womack et al.'s (1990) general definition of this term neatly describes what a lean strategy meant for East Site: 'it uses less of everything compared with mass production – half the human effort in the factory, half the manufacturing space, half the investment in tools' (p. 13).

Interestingly, the way the Delta team was set up at East Site itself reflected just such an orientation. The team was composed of five members compared to the 15–20 members originally suggested; organizational learning was to be resourced no more generously than any other activity in the plant. The limited resources available to the team influenced, no doubt profoundly, the way members approached their task and it has direct implications for the results that they could be expected to achieve.

Important though the resourcing issue was, a more basic problem for the team, we think, were the objectives that had been set for it. Management was seeking to control the work of design engineers, believing that the way they used their time and resources was costly and inefficient. Engineers, on the other hand, came to feel that approaches which worked well in the organization of mass production were inappropriate for the organization of the design of high-technology products. While the engineers accepted the need to organize their work in new ways in the post 'cost-plus' era, the specific procedural changes recommended by the Delta team were seen to be a manifestation of the company's misplaced orientation to eliminate iterative approaches to design development. Staff were somewhat dismayed at this turn of events, and were uncertain what it meant for the future of their work.

In addition to organizational forgetting through solitude and silence, we concluded that collective forgetting at East Site was also occurring through disassociation and disorientation.

The future of collective learning at East Site

To conclude this discussion it is appropriate to begin to explore what might be done in companies like East Site to improve the quality of their organizational learning. Table 11.2 summarizes the approach to organizational learning that is suggested by activity theory. For clarity of presentation the approach, which emphasizes the cultural aspects of knowledge and learning, is contrasted to a cognitive, individualistic outlook.

Note that central to this approach is the idea that learning should be analysed at the collective level. Collective learning within activity systems may involve more than incremental developments. The notion of 'paradigm shift' is used in Table 11.2 to capture what this means. Transformations in the paradigms of practice that members of an organization enact involve significant developments both in the character of collective activity and in the infrastructure of knowing and doing that they use.

The changes being attempted through the four-stage CIM programme at East Site were of this kind, aiming, as we have described, to steer a route through approaches to manufacturing as diverse as Fordism and flexible manufacturing. But paradigmatic change is not easily introduced. In particular, as the Delta team episode reveals, a concentration on new procedures and techniques alone is unlikely to be successful. This is not to say that the design engineers were insensitive to the broader implications of procedural changes recommended by the Delta team. Indeed, perhaps the main learning outcome of the work of the team was to focus the attention of the design engineers at East Site on what was *wrong* with the orientation

TABLE 11.2 *An activity theoretical approach to organizational learning*

Traditional orientation	Activity theory orientation
Knowledge depends on cognitive processes	Knowing depends also on linguistic, material and social resources
New learning is manifest in new skills and actions	Learning is also understood in terms of overall meaning and coherency
Learning involves the passive assimilation of established ideas	Knowing is an active, creative process
Knowledge is personal	Knowing is culturally situated, artifact mediated and socially distributed
Learning is a cumulative process	The development of new activities results from shifts in the practice paradigms that distinguish particular communities
Learning is a function of individual ability	Paradigm shifts can develop from 'normal accidents' that are a feature of activity systems. Such learning depends on the ways in which communities deal with tensions, incoherencies, conflict and paradox

behind the Delta team's approach and, as a result, to awaken their interest in considering what else might reasonably be attempted.

When learning processes are examined at the level of the collective rather than at the level of the individual, it becomes clear that, correctly managed, tensions and paradoxes in the heart of activity provide major opportunities for collective learning. The fact that the 'Right First Time' approach to design engineering was proving inappropriate was not the real problem. In our view, the basic problem for organizational learning at East Site was that there was no collective search for alternatives at the time of our study. Management's apparent assumptions about the appropriate 'division of learning' (a terminology first used by Zuboff, 1988) at East Site, that is, that they alone should steer significant developments was, we think, inappropriate given the growing complexity of activity systems at East Site. Discussions between designers and the senior management team that was steering the change programme were not a feature of life at East Site.

In fact, although most of the engineers we spoke to were unaware of it at the time, senior managers too had begun to recognize the problems of the 'Right First Time' approach. Not only, they acknowledged to us, had the approach provoked some incredulity amongst their engineers, but they recognized that it had probably suppressed innovation in the company: the easiest way for an engineer to be right first time is to use an approach that he has used before. In the competitive environment in which the company operates such an approach would, quite quickly, cause serious problems.

Aware of a growing use in other companies of multidisciplinary design teams to promote innovation, at the time of the study reported here managers at East Site were taking a renewed interest in creativity, and insisting on the formation of multidisciplinary project teams to bring together different engineering disciplines in a united approach. Management was also beginning to look for ways to encourage closer relationships between engineers and specialist sales and marketing staff, specialisms that until recently had not commanded a high profile in the company. This shift in emphasis was significant. In place of the need to promote *accelerated learning* during design and manufacturing that had preoccupied the Delta team, management was beginning to want their design and manufacturing staff to develop broader conceptions of their priorities and allegiances. (Expressed in the terminology of activity theory, management was beginning to recognize the need for *expansive learning* at East Site.) At the time of our study of the Delta team it was not clear how successfully this emerging priority would be managed but our analysis of the Delta team episode offered some strong pointers to what the difficulties would be. Moves towards multidisciplinary team working place a heavy emphasis on social skills. This was an aspect of the infrastructure of knowing and doing that had attracted little priority in the organization in the past. Ways would be needed also to involve different specialists in a widespread dialogue and debate about problems in the organization of work and how they might be solved. In this respect too it was our feeling that significant developments would be needed and that a new division of learning was required.

Such problems were not unique to East Site; indeed East Site was probably doing no worse, and in many respects it was probably doing a lot better, than similar organizations that had grown in the 'cost-plus' era. Situations where the nature of activity is changing in unfamiliar ways place a heavy premium on the ability of organizations to achieve collective learning. The general points to emerge from our study are that success in organizational learning depends upon vigorous developments both in individual knowing and in the collective infrastructure for knowing, and upon a lively awareness of relationships between actions and activities. Most especially, solitude, silence, disassociation and disorientation must be replaced by an emphasis on community, dialogue, (re)engagement and (re)orientation.

Acknowledgements

The research reported here was funded by the UK Economic and Social Research Council under their Innovation Research Programme. Also involved in the research were Colin Brown, Brian Kingsman and Alan Mercer.

References

Blackler, F. (1993) Knowledge and the theory of organizations: organizations as activity systems and the reframing of management. *Journal of Management Studies*, 30: 863–84.

Blackler, F. (1995) Knowledge, knowledge work and organizations, an overview and interpretation. *Organization Studies*, 16: 1021–46.
Blackler, F., Crump, N. and McDonald, S. (1999) Managing experts and competing through innovation: an activity theoretical analysis. *Organization*, 6 (1): 5–31.
Engestrom, Y. (1987) *Learning by Expanding: an Activity Theoretical Approach to Developmental Research*. Helsinki: Orientat Consultit.
Engestrom, Y. (1991) Organisational forgetting: an activity theoretical perspective. In: D. Middleton and D. Edwards (eds), *Collective Remembering*. London: Sage.
Engestrom, Y. (1993) Developmental studies of work as a test bench for activity theory. The case of primary care in medical practice. In: S. Chaiklin and J. Lave (eds), *Understanding Practice: Perspectives on Activity and Context*. Cambridge: Cambridge University Press.
Jaikumar, R. and Bohn, R. (1992) A dynamic approach to operations management: an alternative to static optimisation. *International Journal of Production Economics*, 27: 265–82.
Moldaschl, M. and Weber, W. (1998) The 'three waves' of industrial group work. *Human Relations*, 51 (3): 347–88.
Morgan, G. (1986) *Images of Organization*. London: Sage.
Womack. J., Jones, D. and Roos, D. (1990) *The Machine that Changed the World*. New York: Rawson.
Zuboff, S. (1988) *In the Age of the Smart Machine*. New York: Basic Books.

12 Developing Learning Managers within Learning Organizations: the Case of Three Major Retail Banks

Elena Antonacopoulou

The image of organizations as learning systems has emerged in recent years with the popularization of the concept of the 'learning organization' (Garvin, 1993; Jones and Hendry, 1992; Nevis et al., 1995; Pedler et al., 1991; Senge, 1990). Despite the appeal of this image there is little agreement about the nature of learning within organizations and indeed whether it is possible to claim that organizations learn. For example, how learning develops within organizations, how it is to be conceptualized and demonstrated and what factors facilitate or inhibit learning within organizations although addressed in the literature (Argyris, 1993; Argyris and Schön, 1978; Carley, 1992; Fiol and Lyles, 1985; Hedberg, 1981) remain unresolved. One of the basic concerns is whether learning at the organizational level is the sum total of individual and group learning or an integral part of organizational functioning regardless of whether people learn (Argyris and Schön, 1978; Cyert and March, 1963; Fiol and Lyles, 1985; Hedberg, 1981; Kim, 1993; March and Olsen, 1976; Pedler et al., 1991).

The diverse perspectives provided in the existing literature regarding the nature of learning at the level of the organization confirm that there is a long way to go before agreement can be reached about what is learning within organizations and how it may (or may not) differ from individual learning. It certainly raises the question whether 'learning organizations' can be developed and sustained without 'learning people'.

It appears that the preoccupation of existing research with learning at the organizational level is losing sight of the significance of people as the key to unlocking much of the mystery around learning. After all, learning is one of the most prominent human activities. It could well be argued that an understanding of the nature of learning within organizations from the individual's perspective may provide valuable insights into the factors which facilitate or inhibit individual learning within organizations, as well as the consequences of individual learning (or lack of it) for the organization. This point emphasizes the importance of understanding the interaction between the individual and the organization in relation to learning.

This chapter focuses on the significance of the interaction between individual/personal and organizational/contextual factors and the impact on individuals' receptivity to learning. Using the individual manager as the unit of analysis, this chapter seeks to raise awareness of the nature of learning within changing organizations from the individual's perspective, highlighting the factors which facilitate or inhibit managerial learning within organizations. Attention will be drawn to the phenomenon of *mathophobia* and *philomathia* (Antonacopoulou, 1995) which reflect more clearly how the interactions of personal and organizational factors create conditions that affect individuals' receptivity to learning. Mathophobia and philomathia are the products of a complex set of interactions between personal and organizational factors and reflect respectively the negative or positive attitudes of individuals towards learning. This analysis will form the basis for discussing the concept of the *learning manager*. The perspective in this chapter questions the presumed compatibility of individual and organizational learning goals and seeks to establish how the learning needs of the individual are negotiated in relation to those of the organization, particularly in the context of change.

The first part of this chapter reviews the existing literature in relation to the factors which facilitate or inhibit individual learning within organizations. The focus of the analysis is the concept of the learning manager which is defined and analysed by examining the main characteristics of mathophobia and philomathia.

The second part of the chapter discusses recent findings from a longitudinal study of managers in the financial services sector in the UK. Selected findings are presented and analysed across three retail banks to show comparatively how the interaction between personal and contextual factors influences individuals' receptivity to learning. Evidence of mathophobia and philomathia is presented as reflected in managers' perceptions of the interrelationship between learning, self-development and career development during periods of change.

The chapter concludes by considering the implications of the positive and negative attitudes of managers, for theory and practice, in the development of learning managers within learning organizations.

Learning within organizations

> There is something paradoxical here. Organizations are not merely collections of individuals, yet there are no organizations without such collections. Similarly, organizational learning is not merely individual learning, but organizations learn only through the experience and actions of individuals. What, then are we to make of organizational learning? What is an organization that it may learn? (Argyris and Schön, 1978: 9)

The dilemma voiced by Argyris and Schön is as vivid today as it was nearly 20 years ago. Despite the continuous efforts of many researchers to understand the nature of learning within organizations there is still limited understanding of the relationship between individual and organizational learning. Theoretical contributions in the field argue that individual learning in the context of organizations is influenced by the organization and has consequences for the organization (Simon, 1991). Moreover, it is argued that it is very important to draw a distinction between organizational and individual learning so that we avoid the trap of either obscuring the actual learning process, by ignoring the roles of the individual while anthropomorphizing organizations, or simplifying organizational complexities by representing organizational learning as an extension of individual learning (Kim, 1993).

Interestingly, the way organizations acquire knowledge has so far been understood primarily through the metaphor of individual learning. Hence, theories of individual learning (for example, Piaget; 1981; Skinner, 1953; Thorndike, 1932) may seem crucial for our understanding of organizational learning, an issue which is reflected in some of the existing theoretical accounts (for example, Kim, 1993; Schein, 1993a). However, these theories are outdated and it seems clear that although we are still far from fully clear on the workings of individual learning in relation to organizational learning, we must move on. Perhaps one way of addressing the outstanding issues surrounding learning within organizations is to explore the way individuals construct reality within their organizations and in particular the role of learning in informing their understanding, perceptions and attitudes towards events. Key questions to be examined are when, why and how individuals are willing, or not, to learn. Perhaps a critical issue in our efforts to understand the relationship between individual and organizational learning is less to question 'how' and 'what' individuals learn, but rather as Illich (1971: 80) puts it: 'What kinds of things and people might learners want to do or be in contact with in order to learn.' Awareness of the factors that facilitate or inhibit individual learning within organizations is imperative.

The factors facilitating and inhibiting individuals' learning within organizations

The interest in what facilitates or inhibits individual (managers') learning has attracted the attention of many researchers over the years (Humble, 1973; Jones and Hendry, 1992; Mumford, 1989; Salaman and Butler, 1990; Stewart and Stewart, 1981; Stuart, 1984; Temporal, 1978). These studies demonstrate the impact of both personal and organizational factors on managers' learning. Existing research has established that individuals cannot be forced to learn against their will. The learning process will be most effective when managers themselves recognize a learning need and decide to engage in this process (Humble, 1973; Lloyd, 1990). According to Stewart and Stewart (1981), there are four conditions that facilitate

TABLE 12.1 *The factors facilitating learning*

- Encouraging managers to identify their own learning needs
- Reviewing regularly performance and learning
- Encouraging managers to set learning goals for themselves
- Providing feedback both on performance and learning
- Reviewing managers' performance in developing others
- Assisting managers to see learning opportunities on the job
- Providing new experiences from which managers can learn
- Providing or facilitating the use of training on the job
- Tolerating some mistakes
- Encouraging the review and planning of learning activities
- Challenging the traditional ways of doing things

learning: first, the learner must see a connection between what (s)he takes as the learning task and the potential consequences. Secondly, there must be feedback on performance if it is to improve. Thirdly, opportunity to practise is very important, especially when learning a new skill, and fourthly, help with a poor vocabulary can be useful in those areas where people's analytical capabilities are impoverished – interpersonal skills, the language of unfamiliar specialities, etc. Gagné (1983) points out that the capabilities that already exist in the individual before learning begins are also significant in facilitating learning.

Although it is generally perceived that every individual would have some capacity to learn, the significance of the context in which learning takes place has been receiving prominence. Researchers (Lyons, 1985; Roberts, 1974) have argued that a basic requirement if learning is to take place is a climate which encourages, facilitates and rewards learning. The context in which learning takes place could determine what and why the individual chooses to learn (that is, the underlying motive behind learning), as well as how the individual is likely to go about learning. In the context of organizations in particular, a constructive organizational climate would encourage individuals to have positive attitudes towards learning and recognize the need to develop learning, to overcome their own resistance to change, to understand their own shortcomings as learners and to be more open to experiences and ready to learn from them. Mumford (1989) emphasizes the 'learning culture' of an organization and provides a list of factors which, in his view, should be present in any organization that is said to encourage learning (Table 12.1).

Personal and organizational factors do not only facilitate management learning, they also inhibit it. Previous research shows that mental defences, emotional, cultural and motivational factors inhibit managers' receptivity to learn (Argyris, 1990, 1991; British Institute of Management, 1984; Hague, 1973; Stuart, 1984). Many researchers have observed that some of the barriers to learning are self-imposed by the individual (Brookfield, 1986; Knowles, 1973; Rogers, 1992; Smith, 1988). The individual's personality and self-esteem/self-worth, the nature of the individual's expectations in pursuing a learning goal, the physical condition at the time of learning (for example, level of stress), the immediate affect (mood), as well as their perceptions of their ability to learn (for example, whether the learning ability is innate vs. developed) are all some of the self-imposed restrictions on learning (Antonacopoulou, 1995, 1996a). Moreover, an individual's perception of their learning style (Honey and Mumford, 1982; Lessem, 1991) may affect their receptivity to different learning resources. Individual perceptions on these issues may determine their receptivity and openness to learning.

Stewart and Stewart (1981) propose further that managers' learning would be inhibited, first, if managers are out of practice, that is, have forgotten or never have acquired learning skills, and secondly, if they reject anything that is likely to change their ways or more significantly, expose or threaten them. A third factor identified by the same authors is if managers are 'overmotivated' to perform well, which as a result may inhibit their actual learning (both in terms of quantity and quality), because they aim to achieve too many things at once. The sub-conscious and implicit nature of some of these barriers identified creates defences embedded in the individual's emotional reaction to events and forms part of an individual's unspecified inner self.

Social, cultural and political factors, have long been seen as the critical organizational factors affecting learning (Jones and Hendry, 1992; Lyons, 1985; Roberts, 1974; Salaman and Butler, 1990; Stuart, 1984; Temporal, 1978). More recently, the organizational structure, culture and communication are found to have a major significance in the learning process and to act as organizational barriers to managers' learning. Salaman and Butler (1990), for example, argue that the organization's structure and culture may be a block to learning if they contradict the message provided during formal training sessions. Moreover, with reference to the hierarchical structure they emphasize the political dimension of learning within organizations. Similarly, communication and dialogue may inhibit the learning process if the message is inconsistent and there is little trust in the information available (Argyris, 1994; Schein, 1993b). The main obstacles to managers' learning identified in the existing literature are summarized in Table 12.2.

The discussion of how managers learn and the factors which facilitate or inhibit learning, show that the existing body of knowledge in this field is dominated by the psychological perspective. In other words, what motivates individuals to learn and how this shapes the various stages of the learning process has been a central theme in theory and research in this field. However, many of the contradictions experienced by managers result from the social dynamics in the context of their employing organization. In order to be able to explore fully the complexity of learning as a human activity, one would have to appreciate how social and psychological factors interact such that they create often competing priorities as the individual attempts to reconcile them. This proposition is reflected in the interaction

TABLE 12.2 *The obstacles to managers' learning*

Personal factors	Organizational factors
• Perception of the need to learn	• Internal organization of work
• Perception of ability to learn	• Organization systems, e.g. training
• Cultural values and beliefs	• Culture and climate
• Emotions-feelings/reactions	• Decision-making processes
• Attitude towards updating	• Communication and feedback
• Intellectual-mental capability	• Politics and aversion to risk
• Age	• Instability and change
• Memory	• Economic position, competition
• Ability to communicate	• Power and control

between personal and contextual factors which underpin the positive or negative attitudes of individuals towards learning. The next section concentrates on this interaction by discussing the main characteristics of mathophobia and philomathia[1] (Antonacopoulou, 1995).

Mathophobia, philomathia and the learning manager

Mathophobia and philomathia describe respectively the negative and positive attitudes of managers towards the need to learn. Their identification is not restricted to manifestations of individuals' learning behaviour alone, but rather they illustrate the complex set of psychological, mental and emotional aspects underlying individuals' reactions in relation to learning. It is beyond the scope of this chapter to provide an extensive analysis of these phenomena (a more detailed discussion is offered elsewhere, see Antonacopoulou, 1995). Instead, the discussion focuses on how these phenomena may provide valuable insights into the development of 'learning managers'.

For the purpose of clarity it is important to note that mathophobia and philomathia are *situation-specific*, therefore, they may be demonstrated in different ways among individuals in the same context and any one individual is likely to become mathophobic or philomathic in relation to the same issue at different points of time. Mathophobia and philomathia illustrate the individual's attitude towards a given learning situation. This implies that a positive or negative attitude towards learning is created under certain situational circumstances and in relation to the personal characteristics of the individual. Positive or negative attitudes towards learning are not permanent. These attitudes are subject to change depending on the resulting information from the interaction of personal and organizational factors. This point suggests that mathophobia and philomathia are constituted by personal (internal to the individual) factors which are developed and shaped in the light of contextual (organizational) factors. Therefore, mathophobia and philomathia do not distinguish between individuals in relation to their personal competencies or their learning ability. Mathophobia and philomathia represent the mental and emotional reasoning supporting individuals' attitude towards learning. Finally, mathophobia and philomathia provide a clearer illustration of the interdependency between the individual and the organization in learning and are useful for differentiating more clearly between 'learned' and 'learning' managers (Argyris, 1982).

Mathophobic managers are those who are aware of the need to learn, yet they are reluctant to learn (that is, would deny taking the responsibility). Mathophobic managers tend to be risk-averse in their learning approach. They tend to go by the book, to wait passively for the organization to provide them with the necessary resources to learn and on the whole lack personal initiative and are apathetic about their self-improvement. On this basis, an individual would be described as being mathophobic if they lack confidence in their ability to learn, if they lack ambition to progress, if they refuse to take personal responsibility in developing themselves or have no determination or clear sense of direction and are unwilling to explore different learning avenues.

On the other hand, **philomathic managers** are the individuals who are appreciative of the need to learn and engage in a conscious and active learning process to improve themselves, beyond the boundaries of the context in which they operate. They may demonstrate this attitude by seeking exposure within their job, aiming to make the most out of the learning resources and opportunities they have available and taking personal initiative. For example, within a changing organization, philomathic managers actively seek to improve themselves by being resourceful in their approach to learning. Philomathic managers have a close resemblance to self-developing managers (Binsted et al., 1980; Pedler, 1984), in that they are self-motivated, enthusiastic and energetic, active in seeking and creating learning opportunities etc. The concept of philomathia, however, is different from the concept of self-development. Self-development explains how personal abilities and a willingness to learn may act as enabling objectives in the continued development of the individual (Mumford, 1979; Pedler, 1988; Pedler et al., 1978). Philomathia, describes the richness of individuals' cognitive maps, the psychological and emotional factors which underlie their positive response to an identified learning need. Philomathia is the passion for self-development. This distinction, however, is not to suggest that there is no association between philomathia and self-development. On the contrary, philomathia is reinforced through self-development and self-development is part and parcel of philomathia. It is within this strong interconnection between philomathia and self-development that one finds the 'learning manager'.

Learning managers are not only those who continuously seek to develop and improve themselves by being resourceful, self-directed, inquisitive and creative in their approach to learning. A learning manager is also one who is emotionally competent in understanding and addressing the 'internal conflict' between the personal need of self-actualization and self-fulfilment (psychological needs) against the need for belonging, security and acceptability as a member of a social group (social needs) (Antonacopoulou, 1996b). Learning managers depoliticize learning for themselves and those around them. They would be less concerned to portray an image or manage impressions in order to be consistent with the organizational ethos or culture (Foucault, 1977; Giacalone and Rosenfioeld, 1991; Goffman, 1959; Hochschild, 1983; Mangham and Overington, 1987; Wayne and Liden, 1995) and more likely to see unlearning (that is, changing their attitudes towards learning) as a function of knowing who they are and what they are capable of becoming.

This is not to suggest that the emotional response of the individual in relation to learning and development (that is, their attitudes, motivation and willingness to learn) are free from the political forces they are experiencing. Instead, learning managers recognize the tension between the drive to 'fit in' or creating the impression of 'fitting in' (normative conformity) (Ralston and Elsass, 1991), and instead of managing impressions which do not reflect who they are, they are more likely to stand up for who and what they believe they are. Learning managers are more likely to be honest with themselves and others and would, therefore, be more inclined to openly recognize what they do not know as this would present them with possibilities they may have not considered. Learning managers would accept their weaknesses and inadequacies and would consciously try to improve upon them by drawing on the resources within themselves and around them.

Therefore, learning managers are more likely to be continuously seeking to identify or create opportunities to learn and improve themselves while exercising critical self-reflection to enable themselves to be closer to their thoughts and feelings, recognizing the factors which underpin their attitudes. Although from the above description learning managers appear to thrive on their philomathic attitude, they are not freed from negative attitudes which may inhibit their receptivity. Learning managers would be equally prone to a mathophobic attitude if they were complacent enough to assume that they are always receptive to learning. Learning managers would be more likely to question their assumptions about the learning process and their learning goals and are more likely to seek actively to understand the factors which influence their attitudes towards learning.

In summary, mathophobia and philomathia are individual characteristics which consist of idiosyncratic elements of each person and which may be influenced by situational factors of the environment in which they operate. Mathophobia and philomathia are generative processes, which result from the orchestration of different factors in the light of different situations and circumstances. An understanding of the forces which determine the positive and negative attitudes of managers towards learning may shed some light on the implications of learning (or lack of) for organizations, and highlight key issues which organizations aspiring to become 'learning organizations' would need to consider.

Methods

The notion of the learning manager is based on recent empirical evidence which illustrates mathophobia and philomathia among managers, particularly during periods of change. The key focus of the study is the way individual managers in the financial services sector in the UK learn and adapt during periods of change, and the contribution of organizational systems (such as training and development) to these processes. The study examines how the internal conflict due to the dilemmas experienced by individuals affects their perceptions of the relationships between phenomena. The approach adopted in this study to examine these issues is by exploring the impact of the interaction between personal and organizational factors on managers' perceptions of the interrelationship between change/adaptability, training, learning, self-development and career development. The study sought among other things to explore how managers perceive organizational processes and their interrelationship in the context of change and to track, review and analyse the conditions which facilitate or inhibit the interrelationships between processes.

The study compared three retail banks (the top three in the UK in size and financial strength) and has adopted a case study approach for contextualizing the analysis of the findings. The data have been collected using a longitudinal approach which unfolded in five main phases and took three years to complete. The main strand of the field research was the qualitative interview (semi-structured), while observation, questionnaires and the critical incident technique were the supplementary data collection methods employed. The managerial sample (78) in the three retail banks was randomly selected, incorporating managers across a broad spread of age, seniority, specialization, gender and background. Managers classed as fast-track (who experienced different educational opportunities) were included in the sample and compared with non fast-track managers. Although the individual manager was the unit of analysis, it was imperative that the main processes and their interconnection were examined from both the perspective of the individual and that of the organization. In order to obtain the organization's perspective apart from using organizational records, and archive research material, a series of interviews were conducted with senior HRM/Training figures. A total of six to eight HR managers were interviewed within each bank to obtain data from the perspective of the organization. The analysis focuses on three levels. The first level is that of the individual manager and the second that of the organizational systems (particularly training and development). The third level aims to establish an understanding of the interaction between personal and organizational factors in the context of change. The interaction between individual and organizational factors is intended to explain why relationships between processes exist, what is the value and significance attached by the individual manager to these relationships and what are the conditions which influence the nature of their interconnection. Choosing from the emerging findings of the study, the following section presents evidence of mathophobia and philomathia in the way managers associate learning, self and career development.

Results and analysis

In order to preserve the richness of the findings, it is imperative that the analysis highlights the main characteristics of the industry and the organizations in question. A sensitivity to the contextual characteristics is intended to form the backdrop for presenting the main similarities and differences across the three banks.

Retail banking in the UK and the three banks: a profile and overview of recent changes

The retail banking sector provides an interesting example of an industry which has undergone a process of reconstruction, which demanded fast responsiveness to change and a high need for learning. In recent years, the seemingly stable income source of personal customers has placed many of the banks' services in the UK and elsewhere under scrutiny (as exemplified by reports such as Folly, 1990). No longer are 'new' customers and sales the most important determinant of business success. Instead, the emphasis has switched to the virtues of customer retention (Carroll, 1992; Gwin and Lindgren, 1986). Therefore, as banks are increasingly faced with a new set of requirements, some commentators have argued the need to rethink the basics of (retail) banking (Cappon, 1994; McCormick and Rose, 1994).

Unlike any other period in the history of banking in the UK, the past 15 years (1980–95) have probably witnessed one of the most turbulent eras. The rate of change has been unprecedented and the recent changes have threatened to redefine the business of banking. The main changes over the past 15 years have been triggered both by external and internal forces. The external forces arise from the trends in the world economy, whereas internal forces within the sector arise from changes in the market, the intensification of competition and the continuous developments in information technology (IT) which have forced a new era of efficiency in the sector and have triggered a new orientation towards the basic principles of banking. The changing market has contributed to new marketing and management techniques and a renewed attention to the way organizations in the industry are structured.

As a result of the changes in the financial services sector in the UK the three banks (Bank A, Bank B and Bank C) examined in this study have been undergoing numerous operational and strategic changes over the past few years. One of the most significant changes, however, has been the cultural shift from being operational to becoming more sales-orientated. This shift has been reflected in the redesign of the banks' premises and in particular the branch network, the technology for delivering services etc. These changes have caused a reconsideration of the training and development policies and practices of the three banks and a greater emphasis on self-development. Each bank has addressed this issue in a different way which consequently has produced a different result in terms of the adaptability of their staff to the new culture/image of retail banking. For example, Bank A has remained highly centralized in its human resources philosophy and the approach to management training and development continues to be focused primarily to the needs of the organization. In Bank B a great deal of emphasis has been placed on learning and self-development and the ultimate effort of this bank is to become a 'learning organization' (Garvin, 1993; Senge, 1990; Stata, 1989). However, despite the effort of the organization to encourage individuals to engage in learning more actively and to take responsibility for their development, a very large proportion of the managers interviewed perceive the organization's approach as an 'expectation' which provides little freedom and reflects again primarily the needs of the organization. Finally, in Bank C recent changes have provided a clearer focus for management training and development (in relation to the identified 'competences' of the organization) and a wider set of learning resources with an emphasis on individual differences in learning needs and styles. Unlike the other two banks, Bank C demonstrates its continuous commitment towards facilitating individual learning by introducing mechanisms which encourage individuals to take responsibility for their development. For example, this bank has been operating an internal library of training and development resources since 1988. The aim of this library has been to facilitate a positive attitude towards self-development by providing additional learning sources 'to be used either voluntarily by individuals for their own personal interest, studies or development, or as part of training/development objectives agreed with their manager'. The bank sees the aim of this scheme as 'to benefit the individual personally by enhancing their knowledge, self-awareness, self-confidence, skills and competence levels', while the benefit to the organization will be 'as a result of its employees having access to resources which have relevance to their work, and which improve their motivation, performance and contribution to the effectiveness of business operations' (Bank C internal publication).

The sections which follow present and analyse results from the study which illustrate mathophobia and philomathia in managers' perceptions of the interrelationship between learning, self and career development.

The interaction of personal and organizational factors: the interrelationship between learning, self and career development

The perceived interrelationship between learning, self and career development sheds light on managers' expectations from the learning process, their perceptions of the purpose of learning and their orientation (short- versus long-term) towards development. Moreover, this interrelationship shows what is the impact of the organization and how its policies and practices shape individuals' attitudes towards learning. Placed in the context of change, the interrelationship between learning, self and career development shows more clearly the dilemma experienced by the individual when trying to balance their personal needs with those of the organization (Bolton and Gold, 1994; Hampden-Turner, 1990). The findings in relation to this dilemma reflect more clearly the internal conflict experienced by individuals in relation to learning in the context of change. The evidence from this study suggests that the difficulties of balancing self and career priorities do not only represent the tension in balancing work and family responsibility (Schein, 1978). They also reflect the conflict within the individual when evaluating opportunities which may be beneficial for personal development yet are not in line with the organization's expectations and priorities. The tension in balancing self and career development presents the manager with another set of competing psychological and social needs.

Managers' perceptions of the interrelationship between learning, self and career development vary across the three organizations. For example, in Bank C the interrelationship between learning, self and career development is very strong, because managers draw clear connections between the role of their learning in developing themselves and directing their career and vice versa. In Bank B, where the emphasis on learning and self-development has recently become part of the bank's philosophy for staff development, the interrelationship between these processes is beginning to emerge, but is not as strong as in Bank C. Finally, in Bank A the interrelationship between learning, self and career development is unexplored, because even though the bank has recently encouraged more attention to self-development as an opportunity for learning, managers do not feel confident taking responsibility for their learning and personal development, because they have never taken this responsibility in the past. These variations indicate some of the unique cultural characteristics of each bank and can be explained with reference to managers' perceptions of the organization's encouragement to learn and to take responsibility for self-development, their perceptions of the impact of the organization's policy on learning and their perceptions of the controllability and variability of personal and organizational factors affecting the learning process.

The organization's encouragement for learning and self-development

The different way in which each bank has introduced self-development has evidently affected managers' perceptions of what constitutes self-development and how it may be associated with learning. In Bank A the emphasis on self-development has only been a feature of recent years, whereas in Banks B and C the emphasis on self-development has been maintained for much longer. In Bank C in particular self-development has been part of the organization's management education philosophy since the late 1980s and has been gradually enhanced by new initiatives and by this

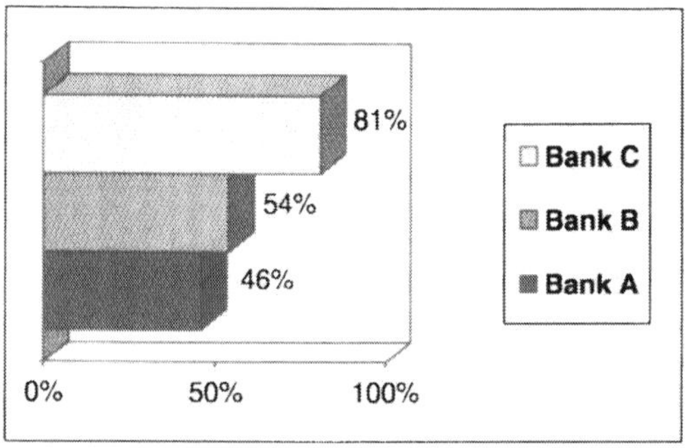

FIGURE 12.1 *The proportion of managers across the three banks who perceive that the organization encourages them to learn*

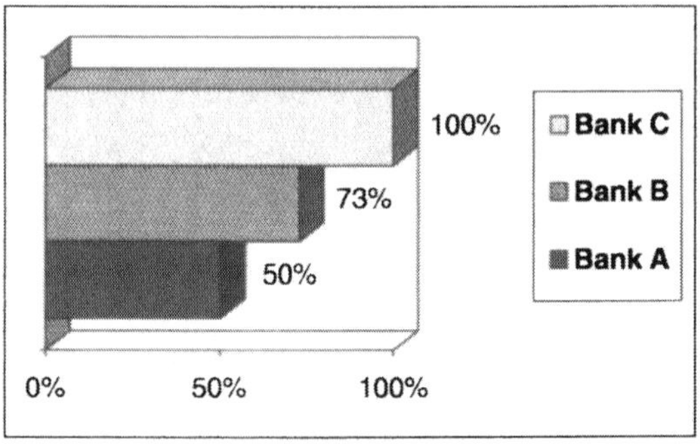

FIGURE 12.2 *The proportion of managers across the three banks who perceive that the organization encourages them to develop themselves*

bank's practical indications of the importance attached to self-development.

Comparing managers' perceptions in each bank regarding the organization's encouragement for learning and self-development it is evident that managers in Bank A, by comparison to managers in the other two banks perceive themselves to be the least encouraged to learn and to develop themselves. Figure 12.1 shows that by comparison to Bank B and Bank C, 46 per cent of managers interviewed in Bank A perceive that they are encouraged to learn. Moreover, as evident in Figure 12.2, 50 per cent of the same sample of managers in Bank A consider that their organization encourages them to take responsibility for their self-development. It is interesting to note that a large proportion of managers who feel that the organization encourages them to learn, tend to be senior and fast-track managers. In some instances, these managers acknowledge that their position and status influence positively their perceptions of learning and self-development, and even consider themselves as being 'lucky', because they have been given more opportunities to participate actively in each of these activities. These findings are in sharp contrast to the responses of managers in Bank C on the same issues. Figure 12.1 shows that a comparatively larger proportion (81 per cent) of the managers interviewed in Bank C perceive that their organization encourages them to learn, while Figure 12.2 shows that within this bank managers unanimously (100 per cent) perceive that the organization encourages them to take responsibility for their self-development.

In Bank B the encouragement of the organization to learn and take responsibility for self-development is acknowledged by some managers (54 per cent perceive they are encouraged to learn and 73 per cent perceive they are being encouraged to take responsibility for self-development, see Figure 12.1 and Figure 12.2, respectively). However, the organization's encouragement is often interpreted as an expectation. Despite the emphasis of this organization on learning and self-development and the introduction of systems to support this, managers do not interpret these initiatives as providing a wider personal choice. It is evident from the findings in this bank that the annual appraisal process assesses managers on their personal development activities and the learning they claim they have undertaken. A manager within this bank explained that: 'in the performance management system, individuals are asked to identify personal development initiatives. In some respects it forces you to think of something.' A senior manager added: 'you're not encouraged, you're expected to. You're expected to know things . . . you do it for your own protection.' Therefore, managers in this bank engage in learning and self-development because the organization expects them to do so, rather than because they personally understand the significance of this relationship. It is evident that because the message of the bank is inconsistent (as is largely the case in Bank A), managers in Bank B explore the interrelationship between learning, self and career development superficially. In other words, they do not make clear connections between their learning and self-development in relation to their career progression. By comparison to Bank A, however, managers in Bank B are beginning to draw some connection between learning, self and career development, recognizing that unless they take responsibility for their learning and self-development they will have little future in the organization. The fact that managers in this bank translate organizational encouragement as an expectation explains why some managers may be 'forced' to perceive a connection between learning, self and career development.

Managers in Bank C present a more unified understanding of the interrelationship between learning, self and career development, because they demonstrate more clearly that in pursuing a learning goal they take into account their personal development and their career growth. Moreover, managers in Bank C appear to explore this relationship because they have come to recognize the existence of this interconnection rather than because they are expected to do it, which is the case in Bank B. The strong interconnection between learning, self and career development perceived by managers in Bank C may also be explained with reference to the emphasis on ownership which has been a central feature of the bank's education strategy. This message, by the bank, has been consistent and has been gradually enhanced by additional measures such as the introduction of competencies. Moreover, the recent emphasis on developing more coherent career paths for individuals has been carefully placed in the context of personal development, thus making managers feel 'empowered'.

The differences observed in the three banks show how the implicit or explicit message of the organization as reflected in the policies and practices in place affect whether individuals feel encouraged to learn and to develop themselves. The perceived encouragement by the organization affects the importance attached by individuals to learning and the extent to which they might be willing to develop and improve themselves. More importantly, the findings suggest that individuals' positive or negative attitudes towards learning and their willingness to take responsibility for their self-development are influenced by the organization's position towards these issues. It appears that the organization may set the example that individuals follow. The extent to which the organization's position towards these issues is consistent and clear appears to influence whether individuals are likely to follow this example and, more importantly, genuinely believe in its significance. For example, the findings of the present study show that in Bank C, where the message about the importance of learning and self-development has been clear and consistent, this has encouraged managers to develop a stronger connection between their learning, personal development and career growth. On the other hand, in Banks A and B, where there has been confusion about the organization's expectations and position towards the importance of learning and self-development, managers have been more disorientated about the significance of learning and developing themselves. This issue is further evident in the significance attached by individuals to the policy of their organization in relation to further education.

The significance of the organization's policy on individual's learning

As part of the longitudinal analysis, managers were asked to briefly describe an identified learning goal and the factors which influence their decision to pursue that goal. Managers' descriptions of their identified learning goals show that managers who are more reliant on the organization's resources and direction are more likely to pursue learning goals that are perceived by the organization to be important. For example, managers in Bank A are more likely to pursue a qualification which is valued by the bank and acquire skills which are likely to enhance their career prospects within the organization. On the other hand, managers who are encouraged by the organization to take responsibility for their learning and self-development and to be more self-reliant are more likely to pursue

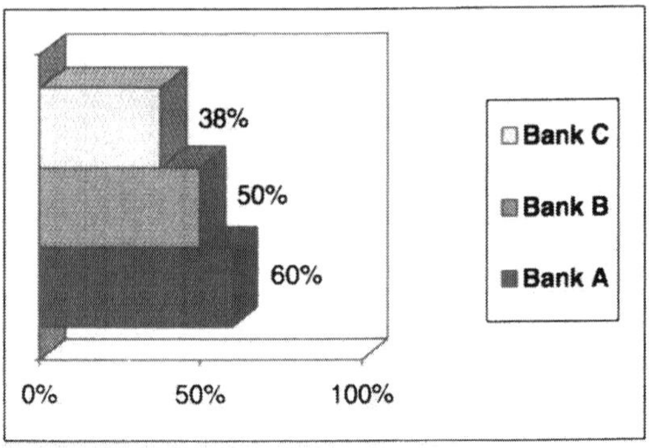

FIGURE 12.3 *The proportion of managers across the three banks which believe that the organization policy influences their learning*

learning regardless of the organization's requirements. Managers in these organizations (e.g. Bank C) would tend to pursue learning goals which are personally developmental and which widen their employability. Put differently, self-reliant managers are more likely to seek to broaden their perspective through a dynamic interconnection between their learning needs for personal development and their needs for career growth.

Further findings from the study suggest that the significance attached by the individual to the organization's education policy is a factor influencing whether managers may be passive or active in relation to learning and self-development as well as the nature of the learning goals they set for themselves. Figure 12.3. illustrates diagrammatically the findings on this issue as evident from managers' responses across the three banks. It is evident from the diagram that a comparatively larger proportion (60 per cent) of managers in Bank A feel that the organization's policy influences their decision to engage in further education and learning, whereas a much smaller proportion (38 per cent) of managers in Bank C feel that the organization's policy has an impact on their decision to learn. The differences observed across the three banks suggest that the more individuals conform to the bank's way of doing things the more this restricts the choices they make for themselves as their preoccupation is to try to align their learning goals to those of the organization. However, the lack of clarity and the inconsistency which often characterizes the organization's message leaves some managers disorientated and feeling helpless.

A representative example here is the ACIBD (Association of Chartered Institute of Bankers Diploma), a professional qualification in the financial services sector. Managers across the three banks admit that they qualified for the ACIBD, because it was one of the qualifications their organizations valued in the past. They also admit that they would not be equally keen to pursue a qualification as long as the organization did not value it. The words of a manager in Bank B explain this notion most aptly. He said: 'when I first joined, the emphasis was on examinations [ACIBD], not so much now . . . I am not pushed, I am not motivated to do it.' A fast-track manager in the same bank explained further that the ACIBD qualification was one of the conditions of joining the organization. He also explained that he would not go ahead to do a postgraduate degree, because this is not encouraged by the organization. Another manager illustrated the effect of the organizational policy by saying that he did not complete the ACIBD qualification once it became clear to him that it was no longer considered important by the organization. He went on to say that: 'I would be more keen to pursue marketing qualifications rather than complete and qualify for the banking exams, because this is now the focus of the bank and they are more relevant.'

Unlike managers in Banks A and B, some managers in Bank C when revising their learning goals, do not rush to embark on another learning task which appears to be more valuable in the eyes of the bank. Instead, they critically assess their development needs and are 'more keen to develop general skills which increase [their] employability' (Branch manager). As one manager pointed out: 'I would do it regardless of the organization policy, for myself, for personal satisfaction.' Another manager added: 'Personal development is instigated by the personal need to have something to strive for.'

These examples illustrate how the shifting emphasis brought about by recent organizational changes affected what the organization perceived to be relevant, and consequently the way individuals responded to this change by revising their learning goals. It is evident from managers' responses across the three banks that the organization's policies and practices do not only affect what learning goals managers set, they also affect the meaningfulness and value of the learning task for the individual. The latter point highlights some of the expectations of managers from pursuing a learning goal and shows that contextual factors not only affect the learning goals identified, but whether individuals will seek to address them.

The section which follows discusses why some managers may be less receptive to learning than others and the impact of the perceived controllability and variability of contributing factors.

The impact of the perceived controllability and variability of personal and organizational factors

The longitudinal findings from the study show that in identifying a learning goal managers across the three banks are guided both by personal factors (such as the perceived learning need, recognition of weaknesses), and organizational factors (such as the bank's expectations and perceived criteria of success, the requirements of the job etc.). It appears from the findings, however, that the perceived level of controllability and the variability of personal and organizational factors influences whether managers are likely to pursue and fulfil the identified learning goal or abandon it altogether. Moreover, it is evident from the present study that managers

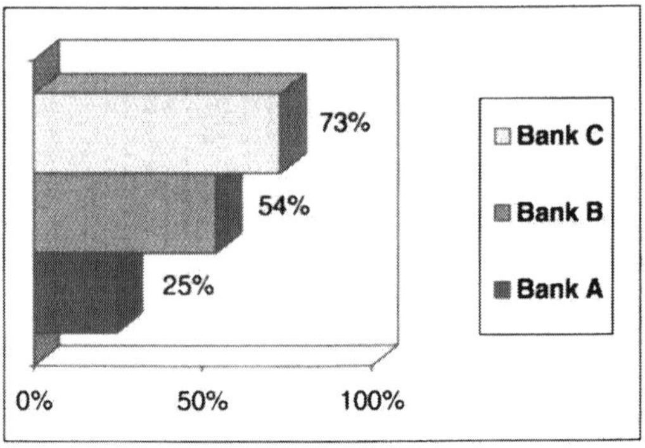

FIGURE 12.4 *Managers' perceived locus of control over career development across the three banks*

feel they have more control over personal factors than organizational factors which forces a greater dependency on organizational resources to learn. For example, it is evident that there is great variation across the three banks in managers' perceptions of their locus of control in relation to their career development which consequently affects their decision to engage in further education and to pursue the fulfilment of their identified learning goal. Figure 12.4 illustrates diagrammaticallly the proportion of managers in each bank who perceive they can control their career development. It is evident from the diagram that managers in Bank A perceive they have the least control over their career development, whereas a much larger proportion of managers in Bank C perceive themselves able to affect their career development in directions which are desirable to them. Managers in Bank B appear to be rather divided on this issue, because 54 per cent of the managers interviewed believe that they can exercise control. The importance of these findings is that they are consistent with the picture developed on previous issues in relation to the impact of the organization's encouragement to learn and to take responsibility for self-development, as well as, the impact of the organization's policy on the extent to which individuals will engage in meaningful learning.

The findings in relation to the perceived locus of control over career development across the three banks show that the more managers have a clear view of their future development and feel in control of their career development, the more likely they are to relate to learning and self-development. Failing that, managers seem to pursue learning and self-development in a more unstructured and opportunistic manner. The perceived ownership of self- and career development affects the value attached by managers to learning and their commitment in pursuing the learning goals identified.

This observation is reflected in the approach Banks A and B have adopted in introducing self-development. These banks may encourage personal responsibility and self-reliance in development and learning, however, as evident from the findings, Banks A and B have sought to control how self-development activities are undertaken and how the organization will benefit from this process. In these two banks it appears that the introduction of self-development did not offer managers more autonomy in their learning. In fact, self-development reflects a more sophisticated means of indoctrination. This finding supports the observations of Pedler and Boydell (1980), Temporal (1984), Williams (1987), Mumford (1989), Salaman and Butler (1990) and others, namely that the organizational culture and the attitude of top management towards learning and self-development are significant obstacles determining whether learning and self-development take place. The perceived lack of control and variability in organizational practices in relation to learning and development show more clearly the interaction of personal and organizational factors and its impact on managers' perceptions of the purpose of learning. The findings from the present study provide clearer insights into the reasons *why* managers 'don't' or 'won't' learn (Al-Maskati and Thomas, 1994; Salaman and Butler, 1990).

Discussion

The analysis of the findings from the present study illustrates the complexity of learning within organizations, the politics underlying the learning process and shows the richness of learning as a process which entails both psychological and sociological dimensions (Argyris, 1982; Bandura, 1977; Frier, 1972; Gagné, 1983; Vygotsky, 1962; etc.). The findings of this study support the personal and organizational obstacles to learning identified by previous researchers (Jones and Hendry, 1992; Salaman and Butler, 1990; Stewart and Stewart, 1981). However, these findings show more clearly how the product of the interaction of personal and organizational factors affects managers' attitudes towards learning. The findings discussed in this chapter demonstrate mathophobia and philomathia among managers and highlight some of the potential determinants of such attitudes.

As evident from the findings of the present study within an organizational context, attitudes towards learning may derive from the individual, from the nature of work and from others in the work environment. Mathophobia and philomathia may also develop as a result of previous learning experiences and the factors which the individual believes to have contributed to its success or failure. The findings of the present study suggest that managers are more likely to perceive they are successful if the organizational cues, on which they rely, suggest that they have followed the direction desired by the organization. On the other hand, managers who are reliant on the organization for guidance in order to develop may believe they have failed if the learning experience has not led to the expected rewards. Having said this, the findings of the present study also suggest that in organizations where managers are encouraged to be self-reliant and to take responsibility for their development and growth (for example, Bank C) are more likely to define success in ways that extend beyond their present context. For example, a manager who interprets the success of previous learning experiences to hard work is more likely to approach a new learning opportunity with this preconception in mind. The extent to which the manager is willing or not to work hard in succeeding in another learning goal will determine the way he or she will react.

An assessment of the self and of the context, the contributing factors and their relative importance or effect on the learning process, is also likely to affect an individual's receptivity to an identified learning gap. The perceived expectations of the organization reflected implicitly or explicitly on the criteria of success, even though rarely communicated clearly, would affect individuals' judgements of what is perceived as acceptable or unacceptable behaviour. The extent to which personal and organizational learning needs can be reconciled could present individuals with a significant dilemma which may affect their attitude towards learning. For example, reluctance to learn may be the result of the difficulty in prioritizing personal learning goals in relation to the learning goals of the organization. Individuals may become mathophobic if their personal goals are constantly abandoned for the sake of organizational expectations. This may lead to disorientation regarding the level of perceived difficulty in a learning task before pursuing it and the number of stages involved in completing the learning goal. Therefore, one of the factors which determines individuals' attitudes towards learning is the way individuals assess the interaction of personal and contextual factors. The assessment of the relationship between personal and contextual factors is reflected in the level of importance attached to contextual factors in relation to personal, the perceived relative controllability and variability of personal and contextual factors.

In the light of the continuously changing priorities of the organization, managers feel more disorientated about what the organization expects and what they need to do in order to be successful. The confusion created by the frequently contradictory messages of the organization are a source of conflict within the individual in relation to striking a balance between personal and organizational priorities. The superiority of the organization in terms of power and information create an imbalance in the relationship with the individual, often resulting in managers becoming more dependent on the organization as they feel vulnerable and unable to exercise any control over the resources that they value and perceive necessary for their personal development and learning.

Therefore, managers' attitudes towards learning emerge as they negotiate personal priorities with those of the organization, and are shaped by contextual factors to which individuals attach greater importance in relation to personal factors. The relative importance attached by individuals to organizational factors is also related to the perceived element of risk involved in neglecting organizational factors, which varies across domains of functioning and situational circumstances. Mathophobic managers, as is evident across the three banks (primarily in Bank A and B), are concerned with how to be politically correct in relation to development and learning. As is evident from the findings of the present study, the perceived lack of control over organizational factors affecting learning makes a large proportion of managers across the three banks reluctant to learn more liberally, thus feeling helpless and frustrated. The negative attitude towards learning is reflected in the level of dependence and reliance of managers on the organization's resources, often limiting the prospect to explore learning through a variety of sources.

It appears from this study that the limited number of examples of philomathic managers within the three banks is partly due to the highly political nature of learning which generates various negative perceptions and feelings. The internal conflict within the individual is evident in the way managers try to maintain their self-image against admitting ignorance which is exacerbated as they try to play by the rules of the political game. The perceived implications of accepting ignorance and the need to learn, when by virtue of being a manager the organization expects that they should possess the necessary knowledge, illustrate the point. This observation is reflected in managers' comments which suggest that there is an element of fear which inhibits individuals from being open about their true feelings. For example a manager in Bank A said: 'One must be careful how much one discloses [during the appraisal process], because career progression may be affected negatively.' A senior manager in the same bank added: 'Often I am afraid to ask my line manager for a refresher course, because I am expected to know it by now.'

The limited evidence of philomathia among managers (primarily within Bank C), as reflected in their less intense reliance on the organization's resources to learn, their personal appreciation of the need to learn and their willingness to see learning as a continuous process of self-improvement, shows further the impact of contextual factors. The variations in the perceived interrelationship between learning, self- and career development across the three banks show the different context of each bank and the unique approach adopted in encouraging managers to learn and take responsibility in developing themselves. The key issue arising from this study is that it is not so much the existence of human resource development policies which makes the difference in individuals' expectations, beliefs and intentions in relation to learning, but *how* such policies are operated in practice.

Moreover, the underlying motives of each bank in encouraging individuals to pursue self-directed approaches to personal growth show that although each of the three banks introduced several mechanisms in support of self-development – some more structured than others – all are characterized by an element of control to different degrees. In encouraging managers to become responsible for their self-development, these organizations indirectly expect managers to develop themselves mainly in relation to areas which are relevant to the context of their organization and the industry at large. There is little indication that these banks (possibly with the exception of Bank C) are encouraging learning and self-development with a view to broadening individuals' perspective and consequently their wider employability. This point has significant implications about further efforts to understand learning at the level of the individual and the organization.

Individual and organizational learning: developing learning managers within learning organizations

The issues discussed in the preceding paragraphs highlight the significant impact of the interaction between personal and organizational factors on the learning process. The analysis of this interaction illustrates more clearly the factors facilitating and inhibiting individual learning within organizations and indicates how these act as conditions leading to positive or negative attitudes towards learning.

A key theme emerging from the analysis is the dialectic relationship between the individual and the organization which makes more prominent their interdependence in creating a learning environment. The findings presented in this chapter, on the one hand, highlight the inequality characterizing the relationship between the individual and the organization and the tension between their often competing priorities and learning goals. On the other hand, the findings show how individual learning is both influenced by the organization and is represented in the organization in the form of action patterns, standard operating procedures and the dominant culture. In essence, individual learning within organizations is influenced by organizations and produces reactions/phenomena (such as mathophobia and philomathia) which could affect the organization beyond processes or activities which could be inferred to as 'learning'.

The multiple realities of individuals prompt them to perceive different things and to interpret the same issues in different ways. One of the characteristics of individual learning within organizations, as evident from the findings reported in this chapter, is the focus on what leads to success. In other words, what individuals do right, instead of what they might be doing wrong. Therefore, the learning strategies of the majority of managers across the three banks are characterized by the emphasis on avoiding failure rather than broadening horizons and questioning existing knowledge. The banks' norms in relation to failure and avoiding mistakes affects individuals' learning. The majority of managers in this study tend to choose to follow a 'safe' course of action in relation to their learning. This strategy is prescribed by the organization, therefore, it is expected to be less risky and more in line with the image the organization wishes to portray. The findings across the three banks examined in this study show that in attempting to maintain control of the development and learning of individuals, organizations limit individuals' freedom to explore the variety of interconnections between processes. By doing so they shape individuals' attitudes toward processes (for example, learning, self- and career development) and their perceptions of the interconnection between these processes.

Clearly, a more in-depth understanding of the nature and conditions leading to mathophobia and philomathia can provide further insights into the multiple and often competing 'realities' of organizational members, the way these are negotiated and the impact of implicit and explicit messages embodied in policies and artifacts. Moreover, the analysis in this chapter indicates that we need to find out more about the consequences of individual learning (or lack of it) for the organization. In particular, how individual learning is diffused and shared and how it affects organizational practices in response to environmental pressures would be equally valuable in our efforts to understand learning at the organizational level. The importance of finding out more about how the interaction between personal and contextual factors contributes to the development of 'learning managers' is potentially one of the first steps in this direction. The concepts of mathophobia and philomathia may provide researchers and practitioners with a more integrative framework for articulating and representing the unclear and unpredictable nature of learning within organizations.

At the individual level there is clearly a need for more research into the emotional and cognitive aspects which form the internal conflict experienced by individuals in the context of change. If we are to explore fully the complexity of learning as a human activity, we need to appreciate learning as a social as well as a psychological process.

Conclusions

This chapter has sought to examine how the nature of learning within organizations from the individual's perspective may provide further insights into the factors that facilitate or inhibit individual learning within organizations. The analysis has illustrated the interaction between the individual and the organization in relation to learning by presenting recent empirical evidence of mathophobia and philomathia among managers in three retail banks in the UK. By identifying the main characteristics and determinants of the negative or positive attitudes of managers towards learning, this chapter has shown the interdependence of the individual and the organization in relation to learning. The analysis suggests that there is a need to find out more about the interactions between organizational and individual learning. In the context of changing organizations in particular, it does highlight the need for a clearer understanding of the nature and role of the *learning manager* in developing and sustaining the learning organization.

Note

1 The concepts of mathophobia and philomathia have their roots in Greek words. Both concepts derive from the word *mathisis* which means learning. Mathophobia derives from a combination of the words *mathisis* and *phobia* (dislike,

fear) while philomathia derives from the words *mathisis* and *philos* (friend, supporter). Mathophobia describes the reluctance or otherwise negative attitude of individuals towards learning, whereas philomathia describes the positive attitude towards learning and a readiness to explore and improve through learning (Antonacopoulou, 1995).

References

Al-Maskati, H. and Thomas, A.B. (1994) Why Managers don't Learn. Paper presented at the British Academy of Management Conference, Lancaster.

Antonacopoulou, E.P. (1995) Mathophobia and Philomathia: a New Perspective and its Implications for Management Education. Paper presented at the Annual Meeting of the American Academy of Management, Vancouver, Canada.

Antonacopoulou, E.P. (1996a) Understanding Individuals' Receptivity to Learning: the Interdependence Between Emotion and Learning. Paper presented at the Annual Meeting of the American Academy of Management, Cincinnati, USA.

Antonacopoulou, E.P. (1996b) A Study of Interrelationships: the Way Individual Managers Learn and Adapt and the Contribution of Training Towards This Process. PhD Thesis, Warwick Business School, University of Warwick.

Argyris, C. (1982) *Reasoning, Learning and Action*. San Francisco: Jossey-Bass.

Argyris, C. (1990) *Overcoming Organizational Defenses: Facilitating Organizational Learning*. Boston, MA: Allyn and Bacon.

Argyris, C. (1991) Teaching smart people how to learn. *Harvard Business Review*, 69 (3): 327–37.

Argyris, C. (1993) *On Organisational Learning*. Cambridge, MA: Blackwell.

Argyris, C. (1994) Good communication that blocks learning. *Harvard Business Review*, 72 (4): 77–85.

Argyris, C. and Schön, D.A. (1978) *Organizational Learning: a Theory in Action Perspective*. Reading, MA: Addison-Wesley.

Bandura, A. (1977) *Social Learning Theory*. Englewood Cliffs, NJ: Prentice-Hall.

Binsted, M.P., Stuart, R. and Long, G. (1980) Promoting useful managerial learning: problems of translation and transfer. In: J. Beck and C. Cox (eds), *Advances in Management Education*. Chichester: John Wiley.

Bolton, R. and Gold, J. (1994) Career management: matching the needs of individuals with the needs of organisations. *Personnel Review*, 23 (1): 6–24.

British Institute of Management (BIM) (1984) *Action on Education: the New Initiative*. Education Policy Panel Report, UK.

Brookfield, S. (1986) *Understanding and Facilitating Adult Learning: a Comprehensive Analysis of Principles and Effective Practices*. Milton Keynes: Open University Press.

Cappon, A. (1994) A life-cycle view of banking. *Journal of Retail Banking*, 16 (1): 33–7.

Carley, K. (1992) Organizational learning and personnel turnover. *Organization Science*, 3 (1): 20–46.

Carroll, P. (1992) The fallacy of customer retention – the truth of customer retention. *Journal of Retail Banking*, 13 (4): 15–25.

Cyert, R.M. and March, J.G. (1963) *A Behavioural Theory of the Firm*. Englewood Cliffs, NJ: Prentice-Hall.

Fiol, C.M. and Lyles, M.A. (1985) Organizational learning. *Academy of Management Review*, 10 (4): 803–13.

Folly, M.J. (1990) Retaining customer loyalty in an increasing competitive market. *The International Journal of Bank Marketing*, 8 (4): 17–24.

Foucault, M. (1977) *Discipline and Punish*. London: Allen and Unwin.

Frier, P. (1972) *Pedagogy of the Oppressed*. Harmondsworth: Penguin.
Gagné, R.M. (1983) *The Conditions of Learning* (3rd edn). New York: Holt, Reinhart and Winston.
Garvin, D.A. (1993) Building a learning organization. *Harvard Business Review*, 71 (4): 78–91.
Giacalone, R. and Rosenfioeld, P. (eds) (1991) *Applied Impression Management: How Image Making Affects Managerial Decisions*. London: Sage.
Goffman, E. (1959) *The Presentation of Self in Everyday Life*. Harmondsworth: Penguin.
Gwin, E. and Lindgren, A. (1986) Reaching the services sensitive retail consumers. *Journal of Retail Banking*, 11 (1): 11–17.
Hague, H. (1973) *Management Learning for Real*. London: IPM.
Hampden-Turner, C. (1990) *Charting the Corporate Mind: From Dilemma to Strategy*. Oxford: Blackwell.
Hedberg, B. (1981) How organizations learn and unlearn. In: P. Nyström and W. Starbuck (eds), *Handbook Of Organizational Design*. Oxford: Oxford University Press.
Hochschild, A.R. (1983) *The Managed Heart*. Berkeley, CA: University of California Press.
Honey, P. and Mumford, A. (1982) *The Manual of Learning Styles*. Maidenhead: Peter Honey.
Humble, J. (1973) *Improving the Performance of the Experienced Manager*. London: McGraw-Hill.
Illich, I.D. (1971) *Deschooling Society*. UK: Galder & Boyars.
Jones, A.M. and Hendry, C. (1992) *The Learning Organisation: a Review of Literature and Practice*. London: HRD Partnership.
Kim, D.H. (1993) The link between individual and organizational learning. *Sloan Management Review*, Autumn, pp. 37–49.
Knowles, M.S. (1973) *The Adult Learner: a Neglected Species*. Houston: Gulf Publishing.
Lessem, R. (1991) *Total Quality: Building a Learning Organisation*. Oxford: Basil Blackwell.
Lloyd, B. (1990) A learning society. *Modern Management*, 4 (2): 32–4.
Lyons, T.P. (1985) *Personnel Function in a Changing Environment*. London: Pitman.
Mangham, I. and Overington, M.A. (1987) *Organisation as Theatre*. London: John Wiley.
March, J.G. and Olsen, J.P. (1976) Organizational learning and the ambiguity of the past. In: J.G. March and J.P. Olsen (eds), *Ambiguity and Choice in Organizations*. Norway: Unversitetsforlaget. pp. 54–65.
McCormick, J.M. and Rose, S. (1994) Restoring relevance to retail banking. *Journal of Retail Banking*, 16 (1): 5–10.
Mumford, A. (1979) Self-development: flavour of the month. *Journal of European Industrial Training*, 3 (3): 13–15.
Mumford, A. (1989) *Management Development – Strategies for Action*. London: IPM.
Nevis, E.C., DiBella, A.J. and Gould, J.M. (1995) Understanding organisations as learning systems. *Sloan Management Review*, Winter, pp. 73–85.
Pedler, M. (1984) Management self-development. In: B. Taylor and H. Lippitt (eds), *Handbook of Management Development*. London: McGraw-Hill.
Pedler, M. (1988) Self-development and work organisations. In: M. Pedler et al. (eds), *Applying Self-Development in Organisations*, London: Prentice-Hall. pp. 1–19.
Pedler, M. and Boydell, T. (1980) Is all management development self-development? In: J. Beck and C. Cox (eds), *Advances in Management Education*. Chichester: Wiley. pp. 165–96.

Pedler, M., Burgoyne, J. and Boydell, T. (1978) *A Manager's Guide to Self-Development*. London: McGraw-Hill.
Pedler, M., Burgoyne, J. and Boydell, T. (1991) *The Learning Company*. London: McGraw-Hill.
Piaget, J. (1981) *Intelligence and Affectivity*. California: Annual Reviews.
Ralston, D.A. and Elsass, P.M. (1991) Conformity: a subtle means of impression management? In: R. Giacalone and P. Rosenfeld (eds), *Applied Impression Management: How Image Making Affects Managerial Decisions*. London: Sage. pp. 243–53.
Roberts, T. (1974) *Developing Effective Managers*. London: IPM.
Rogers, A. (1992) *Adult Learning for Development*. London: Cassell.
Salaman, G. and Butler, J. (1990) Why managers won't learn. *Management Education and Development Journal*, 21 (3): 183–91.
Schein, E.H. (1978) *Career Dynamics: Matching Individual and Organizational Needs*. Reading, MA: Addison-Wesley.
Schein, E.H. (1993a) How can organizations learn faster? The challenge of entering the Green Room. *Sloan Management Review*, Winter, pp. 85–92.
Schein, E.H. (1993b) On dialogue, culture and organisational learning. *Organizational Dynamics*, 22 (2): 40–51.
Senge, P.M. (1990) The leaders' new work: building learning organizations. *Sloan Management Review*, Autumn, pp. 7–23.
Simon, H.A. (1991) Bounded rationality and organizational learning. *Organization Science*, 2 (1): 125–34.
Skinner, B.F. (1953) *Science and Human Behaviour*. New York: Macmillan.
Smith, R.M. (1988) *Learning How to Learn: Applied Theory for Adults*. Milton Keynes: Open University Press.
Stata, R. (1989) Organizational learning – the key to management innovation. *Sloan Management Review*, Spring, pp. 63–74.
Stewart, V. and Stewart, A. (1981) *Tomorrow's Managers Today* (2nd edn). London: IPM.
Stuart, R. (1984) Frameworks for the practice of learning interventions. In: C. Cox and J. Beck (eds), *Management Development: Advances in Practice and Theory*. Chichester: John Wiley UMIST. pp. 187–206.
Temporal, P. (1978) The nature of non-contrived learning and its implications for management development. *Management Education and Development Journal*, 9: 93–9.
Temporal, P. (1984) Helping self-development to happen. In: C. Cox and J. Beck (eds), *Management Development: Advances in Practice and Theory*. Chichester: Wiley. pp. 165–75.
Thorndike, E.L. (1932) *The Fundamentals of Learning*. New York: AMS Press.
Vygotsky, L.S. (1962) *Thought and Language*. Cambridge, MA: MIT Press.
Wayne, S.J. and Liden, R.C. (1995) Effects of impression management on performance ratings: a longitudinal study. *Academy of Management Journal*, 38 (1): 232–40.
Williams, M. (1987) Management self-development. In: D.M. Steward (ed.), *Handbook Of Management Skills*. Aldershot: Gower. pp. 5–28.

Index